Public Financial Management in the European Union

This book reveals how to create efficient institutions and coordinate policy on a transnational scale to ensure that European Union integration can best meet social needs. It offers a combined technocratic and humanist perspective on the discussion of public financial management.

The state, as part of its public policy, should seek to preserve our social and environmental values, yet there are mounting imbalances in society which point to the growing role of the state in minimising them. Under such circumstances, it is worth reflecting on how new challenges could require updated, more complex formulas, to deal with crises in current times and for social and economic policy making by states and the European Union generally, which would ensure their compatibility with the world financial markets.

The work offers an in-depth and unique performance analysis of European Union institutions compared to the national entities of EU Member States. It contributes to the ongoing debate on global public goods and the processes involved in managing their provision. Further, it discusses public finance management instruments, indicating their historical evolution in practice and their effectiveness measured with the Human Development Index. The author presents a proposal of how to manage global, European and national public goods across three areas: environmental protection, transnational infrastructure projects and social policy. The book analyses public financial management instruments used during the recent pandemic, making a distinction between "regular" and "emergency" instruments and assessing their effectiveness in specific economic situations.

This will be of interest to researchers and students of economics and finance, as well as decision makers and practitioners from governments, international organisations and specific non-governmental organisations concerned with issues of public finance management.

Marta Postuła is Head of the Finance and Accounting Department at the Faculty of Management, University of Warsaw, Poland.

Routledge Studies in Public Economics and Finance

The Challenges of Public Procurement Reforms
Edited by Annalisa Castelli, Gustavo Piga, Stéphane Saussier and Tünde Tátrai

Public Financial Management in the European Union
Public Finance and Global Crises
Marta Postuła

For more information about this series, please visit: *www.routledge.com/Routledge-Studies-in-Public-Economics-and-Finance/book-series/LICPUBECONFIN*

Public Financial Management in the European Union

Public Finance and Global Crises

Marta Postuła

Routledge
Taylor & Francis Group
LONDON AND NEW YORK

First published 2022
by Routledge
4 Park Square, Milton Park, Abingdon, Oxon OX14 4RN

and by Routledge
605 Third Avenue, New York, NY 10158

Routledge is an imprint of the Taylor & Francis Group, an informa business

I would like to thank my translator Joanna Łuczak for helping me reach out to an English-speaking public.

British Library Cataloguing-in-Publication Data
A catalogue record for this book is available from the British Library

Library of Congress Cataloging-in-Publication Data
Names: Postuła, Marta, author.
Title: Public financial management in the European Union : public finance and global crises / Marta Postuła.
Description: Abingdon, Oxon ; New York, NY : Routledge, 2022. | Series: Routledge studies in public economics and finance | Includes bibliographical references and index.
Identifiers: LCCN 2021054198 (print) | LCCN 2021054199 (ebook) | ISBN 9781032118901 (hbk) | ISBN 9781032118918 (pbk) | ISBN 9781003222033 (ebk)
Subjects: LCSH: Finance, Public—Europe. | Government financial institutions—Europe. | European Union. | Europe—Economic conditions. | Europe—Economic policy.
Classification: LCC HJ1000 .P67 2022 (print) | LCC HJ1000 (ebook) | DDC 336.4—dc23/eng/20220113
LC record available at https://lccn.loc.gov/2021054198
LC ebook record available at https://lccn.loc.gov/2021054199

ISBN: 978-1-032-11890-1 (hbk)
ISBN: 978-1-032-11891-8 (pbk)
ISBN: 978-1-003-22203-3 (ebk)

DOI: 10.4324/9781003222033

Typeset in Bembo
by Apex CoVantage, LLC

Dedicated to Professor Grzegorz W. Kolodko

Contents

Figures

Tables

Introduction

The financial crisis and pandemic experience have proven that most EU Member States' economies have relatively low resilience to the consequences of external shocks. The last decade of the 20th century saw a significant shift in the way market economy operates, called financialisation. This phenomenon changed and complicated the research on how to ensure durable social and economic development and take effective action amid crisis. The discussions to date have been based on two main participants of economic phenomena, i.e. the market and the state. It is hard to disagree with researchers who believe that financialisation has changed the principles reflected by the economic policy, making them ineffective. It must be observed that a third, high-impact partner has interposed itself between market and state, the two entities that are well known and quite thoroughly researched. This partner is financial markets, which weaken the other two. This is what caused the detrimental deformation of the existing divisions, income polarisation and the high level of poverty in the globalised world. Financial markets, uncertain by nature, by being a major participant of the processes taking place have brought impermanence and instability to the real sphere, too. This was illustrated by the financial crisis, which manifested itself with full force in 2007–2008 and quickly turned into an uncontrollable phenomenon, showing how off-the-mark the mechanisms of state influence were and how much irrationality there is to market processes. The crisis was caused not only by a sharp economic downturn; researchers (Kołodko, 2013; Galbraith, 2016) presume that this downturn was not one-off in nature and that the world must tackle its root causes, otherwise they will have an increasing influence on the ongoing economic processes.

Under such circumstances, it would be worth reflecting on whether the challenges of the new, more complex reality do not require new, more complex formulas for dealing with the surrounding reality and for social and economic policy making by states and the European Union, which would ensure their compatibility with the world, financial markets and, obviously, the market.

Public policies at the Community level and in respective countries emerge from a confluence of politicians' initiative and creative ideas, the administration's rational expertise-based actions and limited room for manoeuvre. Public policy aims do not follow directly from diagnoses conducted by strict and

DOI: 10.4324/9781003222033-1

objective analysts. Instead, they result from political visions, development ideologies, interplay of interests and political competition, and a response to the occasional crises, which we have witnessed during the Covid-19 pandemic. An expert social diagnosis and public policy analysis should verify the correctness of situational diagnoses and definitions adopted by politicians, identify the causality links, balance the resources necessary for relevant activities and outline scenarios arising from the measures proposed. However, they always only serve as support for politicians' initiative.

There being so many objective elements at play, it is necessary to analyse the in-depth causes of ineffectiveness of the state impact, by depicting "things as they are" and prompting "about the way things should be" (Kołodko, 2016), as well as figure out which of the elements affecting the implementation of public policies are a weak link and how to eliminate them. Such research is a focus of the economists who appreciate the role of material processes, institutions and pragmatic approach to economic matters, increasingly taking into account humanistic aspects in their analyses. The economics of the future, coming into existence before our eyes, points that it should be an increasingly applied science, where the state plays a significant role.

Nobody needs convincing that the European Union or the state – its structure and functioning – is of great significance to the economy. A question arises, though: when can it be determined that these entities are "expeditious", effective and rational in the actions they undertake. Every citizen and company engaging in any economic activity will experience the state's impact nearly on a daily basis. There are rare occasions where we are fully satisfied and can say our state is efficient and operates according to rational motivations. And yet such state of affairs should be the supreme goal of the medium-term social and economic policy in place, which should also take account of crises being part and parcel of the contemporary world.

Meanwhile, the economists reluctant to look into the state and its sphere of operations give definitely more attention to what is going on in the market. The ongoing discussions and proposals within contemporary economics also largely focus on the issues related to market functioning, and are concerned to a much less extent with how the state or the Community functions. This happens even though in highly developed countries the state distributes nearly half of the gross domestic product among the economic players and has a major impact on how the other half is generated and distributed. It is also mostly the state that determines the economic and social (not to mention personal) security of its citizens and the economic balance. There is a shortage of research in the literature which evaluates the structure of fiscal expansion and its impact on economic growth amid the financial (Jansen et al., 2008; Baldacci et al., 2009) or pandemic crisis in the short term and post-crisis in the medium term. Even though much time has passed since the first signs of the financial crisis, scientists are still not unanimous about the actions the state should take to ensure long-term social and developmental effects for its citizens. Should we follow the path of new nationalism, new pragmatism, new causalism or another "new" variety of the existing paradigm? Should states incur debts to implement public policies or is that a measure for which future generations will pay too high a price? Despite those dilemmas, scientists have proved, however, that fiscal policy is more effective than monetary policy during financial crises, meaning that fiscal expansion may reduce the loss of output, and consumption impulses may provide the foundation on which to rebuild economic growth (Gali et al., 2005; Ghosh et al., 2009; Rogoff and Reinhart, 2009). This is why action undertaken at peaceful and crisis time alike should rely on two pillars: financial stability and stable development (Buti et al., 2005).

The crisis of 2007–2008 demonstrated that the tools used in the past in the economic policy making and their scale of impact did not make it possible to predict or prevent this phenomenon. One of the books most often quoted post-crisis, dealing with the determinants and the course of the global economic crisis, begins with the following words: "The only surprise about the economic crisis of 2008 was that it came as a surprise to so many" (Stiglitz, 2010a). In this context, the economic slowdown and financial turbulence have contributed to the strengthening of the role of governments and supranational organisations in driving the social and economic policy (Tomaskovic-Devey et al., 2015; Dembinski, 2012). This trend reflects the awareness of the costs brought on by insufficiently regulated market forces whose effectiveness was so often emphasised by neoliberal economists. An active but clearly defined role of the government in the economy is desirable: that of being an involved participant of the interdependencies arising and of the money flows between economic players. However, when considering the proposed government action as part of the social and economic policy, one should bear in mind the civilisational changes and those additionally spurred by the globalisation process (Persson and Tabellini, 2002).

The growing income inequalities and the widening areas of social exclusion were the reason why a quest for different economic policy making styles started. Neoliberal theories were replaced with new economic concepts, for example by new nationalism, new economics and a theory with Polish roots – new pragmatism. Each of these economic trends – or one could even hazard the term "economic and political systems" and economic policy pursued as part of them – suggests new ideas, but unfortunately they are quite rarely progressive and socially appealing. Especially considering objective factors such as the current phase of technological revolution or the globalisation process, which, even in the opinion of its greatest critics, can no longer be stopped. Moreover, the ongoing transformation of the global process of adapting to and mitigating the climate change enforces a number of measures and modifications to the social and economic policies in place. The transition to a low-carbon economy is an inherent part of the integrated sustainable corporate strategies and despite the crisis caused by the current pandemic, it will remain a long-term priority for companies. In the European context, the narrative is based on the EU actions and its ambitious plans to become climate-neutral continent by 2050. These assumptions translate into measures required from

Member States, which have been reflected in the 10-year national energy and climate plans. Coupled with the planned changes resulting from the adoption of the European Green Deal and Fair Transition Fund assumptions, this means that Member States must face certain challenges and expectations of profound changes in different spheres of economic life, without which it will be simply impossible to meet the climate goals.

Irrespective of the proposed direction of change, these approaches include issues related to the redistributive role of the state and to the scale and scope of its intervention in the economy. This aspect is also one of the main distinguishing characteristics of respective economic concepts, which informs the discussion of their evolution. From the point of view of citizens of all countries of the world, theoretical disputes are of little significance. What mostly matters to them is striving to achieve two goals: to ensure socially sustainable income distribution enabling, in turn, the achievement of the other goal that is economic growth. Such an approach is a characteristic of new pragmatism propagated by G.W. Kolodko (see Kolodko, 2017). A different perspective on these two issues is proposed by the neoliberal school and by the economic policy based on this trend, which led to the recent financial crisis (see Roubini and Mihm, 2010). It advocated an economy based on free market with a minimised role of the state, which resulted in social stratification – the so-called income polarisation. Yet another approach is represented by state capitalism, where means of production are mostly privately owned, but the state controls the allocation of credit and investment; this trend does not have a bright future ahead, either (see Halper, 2010). Meanwhile, nationalism emphasises its pursuit of the goal of serving the interests of a nation as a whole, while overlooking the fact that this cannot be squared with low economic growth, which a policy founded solely on national interests may cause.

Adding to the European discussion about the directions of economic policy making in Member States is the debate on the future of the European Union and the directions of its further development, though it would be better to talk of "reforms" that need to be undertaken by the Union to enable it to achieve the goals set already in its early days. The growing public debt in the aftermath of the pandemic crisis, a decision by the majority of British voters to leave the EU, the ever-increasing support for anti-European parties in other EU countries – these are the determinants of the ongoing discussions of the need for change in the Community.

In the context of the aforementioned shifts that brought forth the nascent schools of economic thought, the successive crises and the ongoing discussion of the future and shape of the European Union, it is worth reflecting on the role that can be played in this process by public finance and by the challenges faced by it. In the Monograph, the Author attempts not only to identify some of the imperfections of the existing system at national and EU level but also to indicate directions of change in public finance management which best address the challenges at hand. In her earlier publications, the Author has pointed to the high importance of the rational management of public resources used to implement public service tasks. In most cases, however, these analyses related to the national level of public finance management and drew on earlier economic trends and concepts. This time the Author focuses on the issues related to the rationality of public allocations at different levels, especially national and European, where expenditure increased in response to the consecutive crises. Hence, these analyses closely align with the current discussion of the future of the EU, acceptable public debt level and nationalist trends increasingly influencing the economic policy in place, which may be seen as a source of future crises.

Rational management of resources should be among the key determinants of allocative decisions taken by authorities at each management level to ensure optimum benefits to be reaped from them. When taking decisions on managing public resources, one should follow the principles of correct reasoning and effective action to achieve the goal pursued. National and Community authorities should be guided in their decisions by attempts either to maximise the outcomes with predefined expenditure or to minimise expenditure with predefined outcomes. Such an approach appears to be the fundamental and supreme criterion that should guide the decision-making process. Unfortunately, the reality around us suggests that those in power not always follow such principles, especially at crisis times. The key purpose of the measures taken not only by the EU authorities but also by respective countries is to provide an environment that allows people to enjoy a long, healthy and creative life. This may seem self-evident but is often forgotten in the immediate concern with accumulating goods and wealth (Gopalakrishna and Leelavathi, 2011). Hence, economic growth is a necessary but insufficient condition for promoting social development. When it comes to growth, quality, in addition to quantity, is of key importance to the welfare of human beings. Rather than with just economic growth indicators, it should be measured with metrics reflecting the level of poverty and the quality of natural environment, such as Human Development Index published by UNDP (Jahan, 1998). In this respect, economic growth is a means to development rather than its purpose.

Higher income largely contributes to an improved standard of life, but an increase in income level is not an end in itself. A balanced social and economic development should focus on people, and economic growth must be fair to ensure that its benefits have an impact on the lives of all citizens. It should be therefore assumed that the outcome of public allocation is not only a GDP growth (Stiglitz et al., 2018) but also an increase in HDI. Moreover, when striving to improve the citizens' quality of life, one needs to ensure this improvement does not come at the cost of unstable public finance, which, in the medium run, could cause development trends to be reversed. To that end, it is necessary to design supranational mechanisms and regulations to help curb the pre-election measures by politicians which are often aligned with the electoral rather than the economic cycle.

When preparing this book, the Author set two groups of goals for herself: cognitive and methodological goals regarding an assessment of the public policy implementation process at EU and national level as well as that of the EU level economic coordination process, both of which strengthen an even social and economic development of Member States. Hence, the book presents and evaluates the practical tools to determine the efficiency of public policy implementation both at the EU level (management based on strategy documents, definition of the scope of economic policy coordination for respective countries, use of EU budget expenditure evaluation method) and at the national one (aligning the expenditure structure with the Community's strategic goals, leveraging EU membership to increase the quality and sometimes also the scale of implementation of public service tasks) (Manoharan et al., 2015). A full assessment of both national and EU budget allocations and of their impact on the social and economic development requires adopting a comprehensive approach, taking account of all national and European expenditures jointly and identifying their effect with quality indicators.

The book is composed of five chapters. The first one discusses theoretical aspects related to the varied approaches to the scope of public policy implementation in contemporary economic trends and concepts. The following three chapters are analytical in nature, indicating the directions of impact of the implemented public policy tasks financed from national and European funds as well as the outcomes obtained. Meanwhile, Chapter 5 contains the Author's proposed classification of public service tasks indicating how to manage them at respective stages, starting from ideas through implementation to evaluation.

Chapter 1 presents the challenges reflected in the currently emerging economic trends and various policy making styles they underlie. The last crisis clearly revealed that gone are the times of neoliberalism and of the pure form of Keynesianism. The ever-growing scope of global processes attracts much criticism, and researchers can increasingly see the impact of behavioural elements on the ongoing social and economic processes, as demonstrated, among others, by the work of R. Thaler and C.R. Sunstein (Thaler et al., 2012). All of these elements have a significant impact on the economic policy and on decisions taken as part of it to counter the effects of crises and prevent new ones from happening. It is against this background that the relatively new economic trends and concepts are discussed such as: new nationalism, the emerging new pragmatism, new economics, liberalism trying to rebuild itself or other schools of economic thought which are the topic of scientists' and practitioners' debates on the best outcomes these can help achieve in the social and economic development. This chapter focuses on the role of the state and its involvement in line with new economic trends and concepts, especially when it comes to public service tasks at national and supranational levels. New economic trends gaining popularity in Member States following the difficult recovery from the last crisis also left a mark on the functioning of the European Union as a whole. This is why this subchapter also presents the current discussion of the directions of the EU reform in the context of its impact on Member States. Irrespective of which scenario is eventually chosen, the proposed changes to the EU functioning are strictly linked to the public policy implementations solutions adopted at national and EU levels alike. Relevant decisions should be taken in a manner to ensure that they contribute to the global allocation of not only financial but also human capital and address the challenges of the contemporary world, among which migration, security, environmental protection and building national and supranational cultures.

Chapter 2 provides an analysis of the instruments of EU macroeconomic policy coordination introduced into the Community legislation in the aftermath of the crisis of 2007–2008 and of the pandemic crisis. The solutions implemented following the financial crisis were to prevent future fragility of public finance in EU countries and help those in power adopt anti-cyclical measures. The chapter presents the impact of fiscal rules defined as part of Maastricht criteria, i.e. the impact of the debt- and public deficit-to-GDP ratios on the national fiscal policy making. However, regardless of whether such a correlation indeed exists, these tools, designed at supranational level, do include a mobilising aspect but do not fully meet the challenges of the contemporary world as they fail to broadly define the tasks of the state, limiting them merely to balanced public finance. The Monograph restricts its focus only to those two elements, i.e. the level of debt and of the public finance deficit as these are very concrete, measurable and comparable. EU regulations (European Commission, 2005c), admittedly, contain quite a number of instruments Member States are obliged to apply (Wagner, 2013; Osiatyński, 2014), but it is usually difficult to compare them and assess their efficiency and effectiveness objectively, while both debt and deficit are more reliable, equally perceived and have the same scope of definition and impact (Abdel-Maksoud et al., 2015). Another coordination instrument evaluated here is medium-term documents, i.e. updates of convergence or stability programmes submitted each spring to the European Commission by Member States. The assessment looks at the compliance with and the presentation of the programmes as well as their credibility, also outside of Europe.

Chapter 3 also contains findings of the analyses of the degree to which selected European fiscal rules and the functioning of independent fiscal institutions impact the scope of policy making (especially for fiscal and socio-economic policy) in Member States. These are among elements of impact and of assessment of the effectiveness of measures implemented by the European Union. Their evaluation provides input into the reflections on the issue of greatest significance from the perspective of policy making and of the effectiveness of measures taken by the European organisation, namely the approach to budget issues, allocation of public resources, possible instruments used in their redistribution and areas for which they are earmarked.

Chapter 4 clearly identifies changes introduced in the social and economic policy making in post-crisis times in response to new contemporary challenges and evaluates the effectiveness and efficiency of that policy at both supranational and national levels. It also presents the weaknesses of the evaluation system currently in place and the new challenges it is facing. The evolution of this system is also described, from 1995 through respective developments related to new countries joining the European Union. On the one hand, new members confronted international organisations with new challenges, for example as regards evening out of the social and economic differences in the development of respective EU Member States. At the same time, though, they contributed to the Community their own solutions and problems which had to be taken into account at the level of international organisations. The chapter also shows how the European Union and other European organisations identify issues related to the effectiveness and efficiency of their own operations, and then introduce changes to improve the outcomes achieved. First and foremost, the effectiveness of the European Union's social and economic policy making is presented. In addition, an assessment of the effectiveness of strategy documents has been conducted from the perspective of fiscal policy making and control at the level of Member States. This part of the Monograph also presents an analysis of effectiveness of EU budget expenditure conducted by the European Court of Auditors (ECA), emphasising the shortcomings identified in this process.

Chapter 5 contains the Author's proposed division of public service tasks into three categories: national, European and global tasks, the classification criterion in this case being the responsibility for managing these tasks. The division is backed with an analysis of the efficiency of its application as exemplified by three specific areas of public intervention, i.e. environmental protection, supranational infrastructure projects and social policy. The results obtained clearly demonstrate the benefits of implementing some tasks at supranational level, yielding measurable outcomes in the form of indicators of impact on the citizens' social and economic life (West and Blackman, 2015).

Heterogeneous methods of gathering empirical knowledge have been used in the Monograph, i.e. literary review and documentary method (indirect observation). The Monograph is an input into the discussion of the future economic policy coordination at EU level and an attempt at assessing the tools used in the EU to prevent economic crises in the future, which were developed on the basis of the past experiences. The ongoing economic and political processes require an in-depth theoretical discussion and reasonable practical solutions to meet the upcoming changes at national, European and global levels. The Author hopes the book will inspire the readers to further explore this interesting field.

1 Contemporary challenges to the European social and economic policy

Introduction

The crisis of 2007–2008 revealed a tremendous weakness of the economic policies implemented by those in power, as a result of which tackling its effects and building new solutions to mitigate the consequences of crisis phenomena in future proved to be a huge challenge to the Community as a whole. Though only 11 years have passed since the beginning of the then crisis, with its economic effects still being felt, the world has become engulfed in another crisis, one related to the Covid-19 pandemic and having significant long-term implications in the health sphere, obviously, in the socio-economic one. Two crises of such magnitude happening in quick succession have made it necessary to apply non-standard measures in the realm of social and economic policy and fiscal instruments used by the European Union and national governments.

An analysis of the situation in the European Union a decade after the financial crisis, as reflected in the European Commission's report (European Commission, 2018a), pointed to major differences in the methods respective Member States adopted to counteract the results of the crisis. Some of them had to carry out consolidation measures as part of their fiscal policy, aimed to reduce the budgetary imbalance, while others had a certain room for implementing an active fiscal policy contributing to an improved life quality of their citizens. Such state of affairs required a varied approach to domestic fiscal policies, also taking account of the change in the respective roles played by the European Union, national authorities and administration.

The lessons learned from those experiences show that the economic policy coordination undertaken by Member States and the European Union alike may have direct or indirect implications for the fiscal policy and income distribution globally. The pandemic crisis, following which the role of the EU and national authorities in the economic life has increased beyond the established standards, has demonstrated that the aforementioned elements have intensified. In the first quarter of 2020, the European Union, in response to the Covid-19 pandemic, proposed a comprehensive package of measures including those aimed at coordinated medical action and alleviating the impact of economic consequences on individuals' livelihoods and on the functioning of economic

DOI: 10.4324/9781003222033-2

operators. Moreover, as a next step, a long-term EU budget was proposed to Member States, i.e. the Multiannual Financial Framework (MFF) coupled with Next Generation EU (NGEU). The resources included in those proposals can be seen as the largest stimulation package to have ever been financed in Europe. A total of EUR 1.8 trillion is expected to boost economic development post-Covid-19 in EU countries. The new EU MFF also marks a change in the approach to the way Community funds are managed, i.e. more flexible solutions are proposed in this respect to guarantee that it will be able to meet the needs that could not have been foreseen at the time of its creation.

The questions of whether and what kind of solutions for redistribution by the EU and national authorities will be optimal in a given country and what the role is of the EU in this process are hard to answer unambiguously. There is a variety of views on which tools are the most effective in policy making and implementation, and on the role of supranational organisations and associations in this respect.

The academic and public discourse, in which states are considered as economic operators in international relations, seemed to be losing relevance, but the pandemic crisis has unequivocally showed that this was a misunderstanding. A new discourse is also emerging, stressing a domestic approach to having an economic policy based on country-specific goals and interests defined within a country itself. Adding to this is a very strong post-Brexit discourse on the future of the EU and the growing need for its reform. These discussions have calmed down due to the Covid-19 outbreak, but they cannot be considered gone as they have already returned at different political, decision-making levels, the Eurosceptic community being still very active in many Member States (e.g. Poland, Hungary). Today, i.e. in 2021, the European Union is facing unprecedented geopolitical challenges as regards the direction of further changes (Hubner, 2021; van Middelaar, 2019). This is confirmed by the Conference on the Future of Europe. The platform was opened on 19 April 2021 and officially inaugurated on 9 May 2021. Moreover, it is planned that debates and civic conferences will be held as part of this initiative until mid-2022 to identify priorities expected by the Community citizens. This is an important project to the current European Commission, intended to engage societies and citizens in European affairs. In this situation, a question presents itself: Would the challenges of the new, more complex reality not require new, more complex remedies, better adapted to the circumstances at hand and to the public policy needs? Europeans will hopefully choose EU priorities for action as part of the Conference on the Future of Europe; it would be worthwhile creating efficient fiscal and redistributive tools to implement them well.

1.1 Determinants and causes of the crisis of 2007–2008

The crisis (2007–2008) of economic theories, including the one of financial tools used in the implementation of economic policy and market measures, is linked to the barriers accompanying the processes taking place, with special focus on costs of resources, the discipline imposed by climate change and fallibility of institutions, identified with the uncontrollable, happy-go-lucky and often deceitful financial system (Galbraith, 2016). This is a relatively unoriginal statement as the history of contemporary economics has recorded a number of unsurmountable crises which have occurred over the last couple of centuries. There is no capitalism without cyclicality of the macroeconomic reproduction process. Neither is there market economy without periodic crises. There is none and there will be none. This phenomenon was proved already a century and a half ago by K. Marks (Mazlish, 1972), and afterwards confirmed again by J.M. Keynes (Cutler et al., 2003). Contemporarily, the inevitability of this phenomenon is discussed, among others, by N. Roubini and S. Mihm in their publication *Crisis Economics* (2010).

One of the first crises pointed out by J.K. Galbraith (2016) was a crisis over the correlations between factors such as demand, employment and ownership. It was crisis that consequently led to taking measures reflected in the Keynesian revolution, and, as a next step, to those ushering in the neoclassical counter-revolution. It is worth noting that the causes of respective crises are different. The crisis of 1929–1933 was a crisis of overproduction, while the crisis which occurred in 2007–2008 was a crisis of excessive crediting. Nevertheless, both recessions proved that independent market players (whether companies or financial institutions) are not viable without adequate regulation and market coordination by national government or by a community. Its absence may be the source of asymmetry of information and of the lack of security mechanisms developed to control individual market game players.

The crisis of 2007–2008 triggered an unprecedentedly heated debate over the state of economics as a science and its actual role in decision-making and shaping economic processes. Scientists and practitioners dealing with this domain attempted in the post-crisis years to identify the causes of the situation (Bremmer, 2010; King, 2010; Legrain, 2010; Rajan, 2010; Stiglitz, 2010b; Thaler, 2008; Zakaria, 2009). In their analyses, economists tried to answer the question of whether the crisis we were dealing with back then is a sign of dysfunction of economy alone or also that of some trends of economic thought applied in practice? Some researchers put forward quite a bold hypothesis that the contemporary economics failed as, on the one hand, it did not use the correlations that could have helped predict the crisis and, on the other hand, it was unable to offer effective remedies to prevent such phenomena in future (Lin, 2012). The observably divided views among the economists following the crisis of 2007–2008 were perfectly captured by the 2008 Nobel Prize winner P. Krugman (2009) saying that the economic crisis that had claimed about 6.7 jobs in the United States demonstrated the inadequacy of the fundamental tenets of the neoclassical economics, which is based on the idea of rational investor and consumer behaviour, as well as that of the theory of finance, which relies on efficient market hypothesis. Assuming the validity of such a diagnosis of the cause of the crisis, one can conclude that the market mechanism is effective when the prices of the products offered are a very precise reflection of all publicly available information having an effect on stock valuation, and the rates of return depend on the level of risk taken by investors. When it comes to the state's role in this process, he can see a need for government action in the economy.

Many economists (e.g. Harvey, 2007; Kołodko, 2010) believe that the source of the crisis lies in the neoliberal capitalism. They argue that the crisis could not have possibly emerged in countries with a social market economy, which functions, for example in Scandinavia; it was only possible within a neoliberal Anglo-American model. According to researchers, a crisis bringing about such a sharp shock could have only resulted from a concurrent mix of many political, social, technological and economic circumstances (Eyraud et al., 2017). A moment in which all of those factors started to interpenetrate each other, showing themselves at their worst, caused an accumulation of phenomena and processes with a crisis-generating potential. As pointed out by researchers, the confluence of those factors proved dangerous for the combination of values, institutions and economic policy typical of neoliberalism.

From the perspective of discussions presented in this Monograph, of special significance is the then ongoing debate over the limits of government intervention and the effectiveness of market mechanisms. Fiscal policy implemented by authorities can have a direct impact on the net income by designing an adequate tax and pension system. Moreover, fiscal policy can also indirectly influence income distribution via two main channels, which the EU and national authorities have tried to make use of during the Covid-19 pandemic crisis. Firstly, it can elicit behavioural responses in companies, employees and consumers, which will have an effect on economic results and market income (i.e. before tax and social insurance). For example, higher social transfers or taxes may distort incentives to work, drive up the unemployment rate and increase market imbalance (in gross income) (Wilkin, 2012; Caselli and Reynaud, 2020). Secondly, indirect effects also depend on the public finance stability as high public debt encumbers economic growth and exposes the economy to a risk of a deeper recession in the event of a financial crisis. Generally speaking, indirect results of some policies may partly compensate for the direct impact on unequal treatment. In the context of such elements of impact of state policy, it is worth reflecting on the validity of the hypothesis that neoliberal economic policy was among the main causes of the financial crisis in 2008; on what use this economic trend made of government, and whether it did at all. Such diagnosis will be useful in the next subchapter's deliberations on the optimisation of instruments of the state, especially that following the crisis of 2007–2008 and during the Covid-19 pandemic its scope of intervention has manifestly increased in many fields.

Going back to historic times, neoliberalism as a trend in the history of economic thought and a political and economic doctrine calling into question the Keynesian theories that had been predominant since the Great Crisis of the 1930s, developed in the second half of the 20th century, reigning supreme in the global economy since the beginning of the 1980s. It urged a return to free market principles and limiting state's interference with the ongoing economic processes to the bare minimum. The history of neoliberalism itself, however, dates back to earlier times. What should be seen as the roots of neoliberalism is the association established in Switzerland by F.A. von Hayek in 1947 under the name of Mont Pelerin Society (Hampe, 2010). The association was financially supported by the wealthiest citizens and their foundations. At its core was a group of more than 20 liberals hailing from Germany, Austria, France and the United States (its members included L. von Mises, M. Friedman and K.R. Popper). With their help, F.A. von Hayek started building a sort of neoliberal international trans-Atlantic network of scientists, business people, journalists and activists (Jones, 2012). Rich proponents of the movement financed the creation of a network of think tanks, which perfected and promoted the new ideology. These included American Enterprise Institute, Heritage Foundation, Cato Institute, Institute of Economic Affairs, Centre for Policy Studies and Adam Smith Institute. These institutions actively built the position of the neoliberal school of thought in the academic community, especially at the universities in Chicago and Virginia (Monbiot, 2016). The first meeting of the Society was attended by eminent personalities such as W. Eucken, W. Röpke, A. Rüstow, F. Knight and M. Friedman, as well as the founder himself – F.A. von Hayek. Eucken soon became the leader of ordoliberalism, which had been developing in Germany since the 1940s, while Knight, Friedman and F.A. von Hayek are key figures of the Chicago school of economics. It is this school of economics that, following years of combating socialism, statism and Keynesianism, would determine, from the early 1970s, the prevailing way of thinking of economists and economic policymakers, making it subordinate to the neoliberal doctrine. It is generally accepted that neoliberalism solidified itself in the 1970s and ultimately emerged as the consequence of criticism of the Keynesian policy resulting from the growing inflation and monetarist propositions by the founder of the Chicago school of economics – M. Friedman (Dumenil and Levy, 2009). Experts on the subject point to the sharp drop in the income of the wealthiest section of the American society as the origin of neoliberalism. This fact is of significance to our further discussions because the polarisation of a society is one of the causes of the crisis and the breeding ground for the nascent new economic trends. The changes taking place in the structure of income distribution in the United States may be regarded as the impulse for the popularity of neoliberal theories. In the period before the 1970s, the share of 1% of the wealthiest US households represented about 35% of total national wealth, although the downward trend was already visible for that ratio. In the following decade, this share went down to little above 20% and this was undoubtedly an unfavourable situation and trend for the group of Americans who consequently decided to give their support to the process of change and actions taken as part of the neoliberal school. As a result, the trend was reversed – in the 1980s, 1% of the wealthiest Americans owned as much as 30%, and in 1990s as much as 40% of the national wealth (Alvaredo et al., 2018). Bearing that in mind, neoliberalism can be interpreted as an endeavour by the richest section of the humanity aimed to stop this downward trend. This is another argument in favour of the proposition that neoliberalism was the cause of the phenomena that took place in 2007–2008 (Dumenil and Levy, 2009; Torbat, 2008). Neoliberalism is defined as the revival of the foundations of liberalism, such as unbridled free market, private ownership and no government interference. If we were to capture the liberal programme with one word, this word would be "ownership" – private ownership is a concept understandable to and not questioned even by communists. All other principles of liberalism stem from that fundamental demand (Mises, 1989). A. MacEwan wrote in *Neo – Liberalism or Democracy* (1999) that neoliberalism is the renaissance of the 19th-century classical economic liberalism. Neoliberalism is ethics unto itself, capable of serving as guideline for all human actions – which after 1970 began to prevail in both economic theory and practice (Harvey, 2007). It was concluded worldwide that neoliberalism was the natural order of things and a remedy to the prevalent evil (*there is no alternative* – TINA), representing the cornerstone of the economic policy and economic programmes in developed countries (Dembiński, 2012).

Quite an exhaustive description of neoliberalism as a scientific doctrine can be found in the oeuvre of D. Harvey, who said (2008a, p. 16) that "neoliberalism is a theory of political and economic practices proposing that human well-being can be best advanced by the maximization of entrepreneurial freedoms within an institutional framework characterized by private property rights, individual liberty, unencumbered markets, and free trade". In a theory defined this way, the state's one and only responsibility is to strive to create and then maintain an adequate institutional framework (Ratajczak, 2017). As regards the scope of public services which government should supply, according to neoliberals, these are only limited to creating military, defence, police and legal structures and functions to safeguard private ownership rights (Sadowski, 2011a). In this school of thought, the role of the state is so restricted that while in some areas in the countries swearing by Keynesian paradigm only the state supplied services (in areas such as land, water, schooling, healthcare, social security and environment protection), here, opportunities should be created to have these services successively replaced by those provided on a free market basis.

Neoliberalism perceives competition as the defining characteristic of human relations. It redefines citizens as consumers whose democratic choices are best exercised by unbridled consumerism (Stockhammer et al., 2011). It posits that "free market" ensures benefits which can never be achieved by a centrally planned system. Any attempts to limit competition – whether by government or by other entities or organisations – are treated as actions against freedom. A model neoliberal is of the opinion that taxes and regulation must be minimised and public services should be privatised (Palley, 2018; Dembiński, 1992). Labour market organisation by trade unions is presented as a disturbance which impedes the creation of a natural hierarchy. The earlier examples make it perfectly clear that neoliberalism sees both the state apparatus and its regulations as the enemy of a free economy. It imposes a concept of minimum state interference in the social, economic and market life (Streeck, 2013). Indeed, it is believed that the state's actions can reduce the effectiveness of market mechanisms "because, according to the theory, the state cannot possibly possess enough information to second-guess market signals (prices) and because powerful interest groups will inevitably distort and bias state interventions" (Harvey, 2008a).

In practice, neoliberalism means greater influence of financial institutions, limiting state intervention not only in the social sphere but also in all sorts of workplace performance and quality improvement plans. In addition, literature and the not-so-distant past prove that neoliberal countries do not fully implement the main tenets of neoliberalism and do not abandon state intervention in economic processes, nevertheless, the same takes on a different dimension, aimed to help those branches of economy which, following their own decisions, have come to the brink of bankruptcy (the US financial sector). Helping the *blue collars* is no longer what state intervention is about – neoliberalism changed it in a tool to safeguard the interests of the *white collars* (Brown, 2018). In addition, it can be said that the level of the financial development and the incidence of crises play the key role in the society's income stratification in response to the capital market liberalisation reforms (Ferucci et al., 2004; von Mises, (1927) 2005).

The financial crisis of 2007–2008, the mounting risk of ecological disaster, the slowly widening inequalities in the access to good healthcare and good education, causing further health and educational disadvantage of the poorer social strata (e.g. inheriting poor or good education, caused by inheriting poverty or the elites' resources) – neoliberalism has sadly played a major role in all those phenomena.

Critics of neoliberalism take the position that it is government and its actions, along with a developing market, that are key to economic success. Institutional interventionism is a necessity of the contemporary capitalism, which neoliberalism fails to accept due to its cherished values, and, most of all, due to its concern for specific group interests (Kołodko, 2010).

Neoliberalism does not approve of institutional interventionism in the social and economic life because it believes that, without the state's "helping hand", the market will develop better on its own (Dodson, 2006). However, the problem is that neoliberalism does not view long-term sustainable development, benefiting all social strata, as the objective of the economic policy (Ferge, 2000). It should be observed that neoliberalism has become an apparatus to support a narrow section of the society at the expense of its remaining part. At the same time, it refers to and leans on values such as freedom, democracy, entrepreneurship, competition and economic liberty – which most people subscribe to without thinking twice. Nevertheless, how to implement these values remains an open question – is there, in a democratic, transparent society, a consent to any ideas being used for the benefit of a minority at the expense of the majority?

Perhaps the most dangerous result of neoliberalism is not the economic crises it has caused, but the political ones. It is worth noting that as the state's role decreases, our civic capability to influence the directions of change and action through voting undergoes change, too. Instead, the neoliberal theory posits that people can exercise choice through spending. The problem is some have more to spend than others: in great consumerism or shareholder democracy, votes are not evenly distributed (Greenwood, 2011). The outcome strips the poor and middle classes of any power.

In spite of all, there is something awe-inspiring about the neoliberal project, at least at its early stage. This was a clearly defined, innovative philosophy promoted by a cohesive network of thinkers and activists who had a clear action plan. The success of neoliberalism also reflects the failure of the left wing. When the *laissez-faire* economics brought about a disaster in 1929, Keynes developed a comprehensive economic theory to replace the latter. When Keynesian demand management fell apart, an alternative solution emerged in the 1970s. However, when the fundamental paradigms of neoliberalism collapsed in 2008, it was difficult to find one clearly marked direction – a paradigm for further action (Thorsen and Lie, 2006).

Proposing Keynesian solutions during the crisis of 2007–2008 and the pandemic crisis shows an utter disregard for the obvious problems that have manifested themselves, and for the changes taking place in the global environment. It is hard to mobilise people around old ideas; their already revealed shortcomings have not disappeared and, more importantly, they have nothing to say about our most difficult situation, which is crisis (Venugopal, 2015; Codogno and Nucci, 2007; Codogno, 2012).

It can be generally said that "neoliberalism" is neither the name of a pro-market policy, nor that of compromise with financial capitalism. It is the name of a premise, which, like the "invisible hand of the market", regulates all we practice and believe in: that competition is the only legitimate principle on which to organise human activity (Metcalf, 2017).

Neoliberalism became a hegemonic discourse with such an all-powerful influence on ways of thinking and on political and economic practices that it was integrated in our common-sense interpretation and understanding of the world we lived in. How did neoliberalism achieve such a high status and what does it mean? Neoliberalism was most of all a project of restoring the domination of upper classes in sectors where their fate was under threat due to the strengthening of social democratic efforts after World War 2 (Glendinnin, 2016; Guzek, 2015). Although neoliberalism had a limited effect as an engine of economic growth, it managed to redirect wealth from subordinate classes to the dominant ones and from poorer to richer countries. This process entailed dismantling the institutions and narratives which promoted more egalitarian means of distribution in the previous era (Harvey, 2007).

F. Modigliani (Klein et al., 2013) claimed that monetarists were wrong to believe that economy was already well protected from shocks and that, consequently, there was no longer any need to apply stability policy. Their argument that stability policy did not eliminate problems and, in fact, caused trouble, fails to be corroborated, among others, by data from the United States and other industrial countries. In addition to Modigliani's experiments in 1988, also the results of fiscal and central bank interventions after 2007–2008 demonstrate that stability policies have led to consolidation of the economy.

1.2 EU political and institutional problems heightening as a result of the crises

Adding to the discussion over the directions and instruments of state intervention – one that does not deal with the question of whether to exert it but rather to what extent and in what public services – is the 2010–2021 discussion of the future of the European Union as a community and of its role in the process of creating even development of Member States. The latter have at their disposal both domestic instruments used as part of the available economic concepts and those established at the EU level. The crisis of 2007–2008 not only laid bare the aforementioned weaknesses of economic doctrines but also magnified the crisis of the EU itself. As a matter of fact, the European Union had been facing, for over a decade, questions about the further direction of development and the scope of integration. The existing plans for major deepening of integration received a cold welcome of societies in respective countries, even before the crisis. Despite the data obtained in the second half of 2005 in the *Eurobarometer* survey, indicating support for the idea of establishing a Constitution for Europe (63% across the EU as a whole), in Denmark and in France most voters were in favour of dropping the idea (*Standard Eurobarometer 64* . . ., 2005). This made it necessary to verify the assumptions again and led to abandoning a constitution in favour of an evolution by adopting the Treaty of Lisbon. The treaty included measures related to further integration, but they did not go so far as the original assumptions of the constitution.

The above events showed how complicated a process it is to define the directions and terms of further integration (or of abandoning it). While 70% of respondents in the standard *Eurobarometer* survey consider themselves EU citizens and 54% of those polled believe the greatest benefit of the EU membership is the free movement of persons, goods and services – main pillars of the EU – surveys regarding issues of deepening the integration are not so unambiguous, especially when there are mounting economic problems within a given country. In 2017, when asked about issues of importance to the future of the EU, only 18% of those surveyed pointed to common decisions on the economy, 13% to common army and 12% to introducing euro in all Member States. By way of comparison, most people (52%) pointed to comparable standard of living in respective countries. These results may suggest the need to take measures to streamline EU policy without directly increasing the integration in the strict sense in respective sectors or tasks (*Standard Eurobarometer 89*, 2018). The direction of measures in place was shown by the data of autumn 2019, i.e. the last survey not to be affected by the pandemic circumstances. According to

Eurobarometer 92, four out of ten Europeans responded that they had trust in the European Union and, importantly, the results showed trust in the EU is 9% points higher than trust in national governments and national parliaments (both at 34%) (*Standard Eurobarometer 92*, 2019).

The oscillation of sorts of social trends – for example the percentage of people who are optimistic about the future of the EU fluctuated from 69% in 2007 to 48% in 2011, 58% in 2015, 50% in 2016 and again to 58% in 2018 – directly translates into political oscillation between the proposed directions of the EU structure evolution. The social reception depends on many factors, for example on the current state of the economy, any economic and social problems (Kleer, 2017). This translates into the electoral results in respective countries, as evidenced, for example in 2009 when parties referred to as Eurosceptic obtained high electoral results in the United Kingdom, Greece and the Netherlands. In the following years, the ranks of countries where Eurosceptic parties were gaining an increasing support were joined by Denmark and Ireland – especially surprising in the latter case as Ireland is characterised by the EU's highest ratio of citizens with an "optimistic" view of the future of the EU (*Standard Eurobarometer 89 . . .*, 2018). In the recent years, a Eurosceptic party also obtained majority in Italy. At the same time, in Hungary and Poland, the ruling parties try to implement their "soft" Euroscepticism by taking measures to minimise the impact of EU authorities on the internal affairs, while retaining the ability to benefit from EU funds, which represent a major stimulus for the economic development of those countries.

The changing reality, the increasing number of countries where new nationalism was gaining traction and Brexit forced the EU institutions to be more active and mark out the Community's further directions for action. On 1 March 2017, the European Commission presented the *White Paper on the Future of Europe*, 2017. In that document, the European Commission presented the key challenges facing the EU and proposed five scenarios of reforms to be implemented (see Table 1.1).

1. **Carrying on scenario –** provides for continuing the existing direction of reforms, gradually updating and adjusting priorities as needed. The choice of this alternative will mean the EU focusing its efforts on the same areas as before, i.e. employment, growth and investment projects to strengthen the single market, and the improvement of transport, energy and communication infrastructure. The suggested case for choosing this scenario is the ability to define concrete measurable results. Another thing that is emphasised is the need for all the countries to commit jointly to the measures identified, to enable the achievement of relevant goals. With this scenario, the European Commission suggests it is worth taking community-based opportunities to implement an active development policy, while making it possible to measure its impact with specific metrics. A discussion of the extent to which these promises can be trusted is presented in Chapters 2 and 3 of this Monograph.

Table 1.1 EU policy in different reform scenarios.

Areas	*Scenarios*				
	Carrying on	*Nothing but the single market*	*Those who want more do more*	*Doing less more efficiently*	*Doing much more together*
Single market and trade	Single market is strengthened including the energy and digital sectors; the EU pursues progressive trade agreements	Single market for goods and capital strengthened; standards continue to differ; free movement of people and services not fully guaranteed	As in "Carrying on", single market is strengthened and the EU pursues progressive trade agreements	Common standards set to a minimum but enforcement is strengthened in areas regulated at EU level; trade exclusively dealt with at EU level	Single market strengthened through harmonisation of standards and stronger enforcement; trade exclusively dealt with at EU level
Economic and monetary union	Incremental progress on improving the functioning of the euro area	Cooperation in the euro area is limited	As in "Carrying on" except for a group of countries who deepen cooperation in areas such as taxation and social standards	Steps are taken to consolidate the euro area and ensure its stability; the EU does less in some parts of employment and social policy	Economic, financial and fiscal union is achieved as envisioned in the report of the Five Presidents of June 2015
Schengen, migration and security	Cooperation in the management of external borders stepped up gradually; progress towards a common asylum system; improved coordination on security matters	No single migration or asylum policy; further coordination on security dealt with bilaterally; internal border controls are more systematic	As in "Carrying on" except for a group of countries who deepen cooperation on security and justice matters	Cooperation on border management, asylum policies and counterterrorism matters	As in "Doing less more efficiently", cooperation on border management, asylum policies and counterterrorism matters are systematic

(*Continued*)

Table 1.1 (Continued)

Areas	*Scenarios*				
	Carrying on	*Nothing but the single market*	*Those who want more do more*	*Doing less more efficiently*	*Doing much more together*
Foreign policy and defence	Progress is made on greater coordination of foreign affairs; closer defence cooperation	Some foreign policy issues are increasingly dealt with bilaterally; defence cooperation remains as it is today	As in "Carrying on" except for a group of countries who deepen cooperation on defence, focusing on military coordination and joint equipment	The EU speaks with one voice on all foreign policy issues; a European Defence Union is created	As in "Doing less more efficiently", the EU speaks with one voice on all foreign policy issues; a European Defence Union is created
EU budget	Partly reformed in line with the provisions of the Bratislava Declaration	Refocused to finance essential functions needed for the single market	As in "Carrying on"; additional budgets are made available by some Member States for the areas where they decide to deepen the integration in additional aspects	Significantly redesigned to fit the new priorities agreed at the level of the EU	Significantly modernised and increased, backed up by own resources; a euro area fiscal stabilisation function is operational
Capacity to deliver	Positive agenda for action yields concrete results; decision-making remains complex to grasp; capacity to deliver does not always match expectations	Decision-making may be easier to understand but capacity to act collectively is limited; issues of common concern often need to be solved bilaterally	As in "Carrying on"– some countries achieve better results in certain domains; decision-making becomes more complex	Initial agreement on tasks to prioritise or give up is challenging; once in place, decision-making may be easier to understand; the EU acts quicker and more decisively where it has a greater role	Decision-making is faster and enforcement is stronger across the board; questions of accountability arise for some who feel that too much power has been transferred from domestic level to the Community level

Source: based on European Commission's data.

2. **Nothing but the single market scenario** – there being no consensus as to the EU political goals, this scenario provides for focusing only on the issues related to the single market, refraining from dealing with migration, security and defence. These tasks would be then limited to domestic level. Should this change scenario be adopted, by 2025, the EU will be based mainly on the single market, possibly extending its activity to include issues where political agreement has been reached as to the need for joint action. Implementing this scenario may result in difficulties in solving newly emerging problems which oftentimes require the involvement of many countries. Admittedly, the decision-making process will be more transparent, but the possibility of joint action will be greatly reduced.
3. **Those who want more do more scenario** – respective Member States may express a desire for broader cooperation and decide in favour of a deeper, voluntary integration in relevant areas, for example defence, security, taxation or social affairs. Implementing this scenario will help preserve the EU unity while enabling those wishing to broaden the scope of integration to do so. Nevertheless, society's rights in respective areas may vary as a result, depending on the place of residence – between a country opting for further integration and one that remains at the minimum level thereof. This can undo the benefits of taking joint action in public policy spheres and the European society may be consequently divided into countries with better (higher standard) public services and the rest.
4. **Doing less more efficiently scenario** – the EU focuses on specific sectors in which specific goals and solutions are planned to be achieved while reducing involvement in other areas. Such a scenario would enable a better presentation of the EU responsibilities and goals and a more efficient delivery of outcomes in specific areas.
5. **Doing much more together scenario** – Member States decide to share a greater number of tasks, resources and decisions as part of the EU. Cooperation between states is deepened, significantly increasing the decision-making powers at EU level. As a result, more rights will be shared by the society in all Member States. However, the question is how compatible and attractive to national authorities this scenario is. If this scenario is pursued, they would become merely signatories of decisions taken at a supranational level.

In the light of the discussion on the directions of impact of economic policy, as presented in the previous subchapter, admittedly, the proposals of the European Commission are quite radical and the response to them could have been equally extreme. Consequently, a decision has been made to include the position of the countries which have been net payers for quite some time now and, at the same time, are affected by the impact of crisis, which they cannot prevent to a greater extent, because their financial balance as part of the EU Community is negative. No response from EU bodies and no offer extended to those countries could cause their natural opposition to a deeper integration or to adopting a stability scenario. Indeed, societies in those countries may have increasing doubts about the integration, knowing that their public levies which currently flow to the European budget could instead, after the crisis, contribute to a larger scale implementation of some public policies to improve their standard of living or reduce fiscal burden. As a follow-up to the debate held after the *White Paper* was published, the President of the European Commission Jean-Claude Juncker, during his speech at the European Parliament on 13 September 2017, presented an additional sixth scenario based on the fundamentals of freedom, equality and the rule of law. As he pointed out, of greatest importance is the EU focus on the euro area, Banking Union and Schengen Area as the main policy directions and aspects which can positively influence the European integration (McCarthy, 2018). Moreover, as a response to the growing significance of populist parties which reproach the EU for not taking the will of the voters sufficiently into account, he proposed institutional reforms.

It cannot be overlooked that the discussion on the direction of economic integration was held with the migration crisis in the background, which, at its very onset, exposed all of the EU's weaknesses and showed the national approach prevails over the all-EU approach. The European process of building a common refugee reception system collapsed as a result of a mass-scale, uncontrollable influx of migrants from the Middle East and North Africa in 2015. The south of Europe, mainly Italy and Greece – countries on the EU external border – were hit the hardest by the lack of cohesive asylum system. The result was an uncontrollable migration to the north of Europe, mainly to Germany. Over there, those who arrived from Greece could no longer be deported back to that country, as a 2011 ruling of the European Court of Human Rights held that the conditions in Greek camps were "inhuman" (Kaplanoglou and Rapanos, 2011) and, consequently, the German Constitutional Tribunal, in its ruling of 2013, made such deportation impossible. Hence, the waves of migration into the EU and within it were practically out of control at that time. In this crisis situation, the EU countries opted for a measure that violated the existing legal procedures but introduced new ones, which make a reference to the EU legal system founded on EU Member States' values and solidarity. In the face of the humanitarian disaster, in September 2015, the Council of the European Union adopted a decision to relocate 160 thousand refugees. The solution was contested by many Member States and was amended on many occasions and its interpretation became respective countries' political manifesto rather than a law in force. This was a very tough lesson for the European Community, mirroring the differences manifesting themselves between the EU and national interests. This problem was successfully handled by offering a financial compensation to Turkey for receiving migrants.

In the course of a parallel debate, many Member State leaders voiced an opinion on the proposed direction and scope of further integration and the future of the EU. First of all, let us take a closer look at the representatives of the six net payers described earlier. President of France Emmanuel Macron called, already back in mid-2017, for a broader and faster integration, pointing to the need to include additional aspects in the common policy, for example defence. He also urged a deeper euro area integration by establishing the position of a common minister of finance and common budget (Rankin, 2017). In addition, he advocated a deepening of the integration within the existing common policies. The European Commission prepared proposals to deepen the euro area integration and to establish a European monetary fund to replace the current European Stability Mechanism. The proposal was presented in late 2017, but due to the problems with the appointment of a new government in Germany, it has not yet been adopted.

Moreover, it should be noted that France proposed to the European Union measures to strengthen strategic autonomy. EU strategic autonomy, understood as the capacity for independent response to crises and threats, was mentioned in the European Council's conclusions of December 2013 and then in the European Union Global Strategy of 2016. Ever since the beginning of Macron's term in office, France has used this concept to loosen trans-Atlantic cooperation and promote the idea of the EU as a superpower. The US–EU misunderstandings during Donald Trump's presidency favoured the French aspirations. The change of US president did not make French authorities give up on the idea of strategic autonomy but enforced the quest for new arguments in its favour. Most probably France will continue to promote strategic autonomy as part of the EU, during its presidency of the Council of the European Union it wants to cause the Strategic Compass to be adopted. This document is to set EU military ambitions and define a common view of threats and challenges around the EU. France, along with Cyprus, Greece, Spain and Italy, will aim for focusing the EU attention on its southern neighbours and on the Mediterranean Sea. The key to redefining the trans-Atlantic cooperation will be to recognise – as urged by France – the threat posed by the US–Chinese rivalry to the EU and the lack of explicit support from the United States (Maślanka, 2021).

With the difficulties with forming a new German government and the focus on migration issues, the debate on the future of Europe – with respect to the further integration model – was placed on the back burner. Nevertheless, on 3 June 2018, Angela Merkel addressed the French proposal presented in 2017, expressing her support for establishing the euro area investment budget and a European monetary fund (Schulz, 2018). This means that two largest net payers whose joint contribution exceeds the sum total of all other eight net payers are in favour of following a scenario combining a deeper integration and voluntary integration. This scenario is consistent, in its main assumptions, with the new, sixth scenario presented by the President of the European Commission in 2017.

The new Italian government has not taken so far a clear stance as to the future of Europe. However, there is a concern that the Five Star Movement – an Italian party which sees itself as populist and anti-establishment – will not be inclined to deepen the integration, especially considering a significant percentage of the Italian society has a negative perception of the future of the EU.

The United Kingdom, for obvious reasons, did not address the proposed reforms related to the future of the EU. Nevertheless, it is worth closely monitoring further Brexit-related action as some doubts can be already observed among those in power, as well as measures aimed to exit the EU in a more compromise-seeking and moderate manner than the one demanded by the hard-line Brexit proponents.

In 2017, the Prime Minister of Sweden pointed out the need to approach the challenges facing the EU in a more harmonised and cohesive way (Government Offices of Sweden, 2017). At the same time, consultations were held in the Swedish parliament to deepen the debate on the directions of integration proposed by the European Commission (Government Offices of Sweden, 2018). The outcome of the debates reveals that the Swedish parliament has a more reserved approach to the proposal to deepen the European integration. Rather than repudiating the very direction of such action, it indicates the potential problems, risks and weaknesses of the solutions proposed. It is worth emphasising here that the way the debate is held in Sweden should be treated as a model example. It both enables gathering detailed information on the position of democratic institutions in Sweden and enlivens the debate in other countries – or so it should – thanks to the clearly and precisely worded position. Another fact of relevance is that the government's position was posted in public domain in English, making it significantly more accessible to people outside of Sweden.

The Prime Minister of the Netherlands, during a debate at the European Parliament in June 2017, spoke in favour of focusing on fulfilling the EU's current goals, while stressing that "more and more Europe is not the answer to the many problems that people face in their daily lives" (*Parliament Sets Out . . .*, 2017).

As revealed by the data presented, even among the six net payers analysed in this subchapter there is no unanimity as to which course the EU should set. The debate is still on and – so far – no specific, prevailing course of action has been outlined. One should bear in mind that the politicians in respective countries must reckon with the current needs, sentiments and the way their societies perceive the world around them. Hence, it is hard to wonder at the Netherlands' reluctance towards further integration, considering the significant increase in the support for extreme parties. Major role is also played in this context by the information policy adopted by respective governments and by the EU. It is only by precisely highlighting the benefits of integration to be reaped by individual citizens and social groups that a good image of the EU can be gradually built, consequently reducing the reluctance for further integration.

The position of the Visegrad Group (V4) should also be mentioned here. According to their declaration, V4 countries can see the need for further integration in more areas, but what they consider a priority is to sustain what has been achieved to date in respective areas – especially as regards single market and free movement of persons. Moreover, the need to maintain the states' autonomy has been emphasised, pointing out that there is no strong

EU without strong Member States. The V4 declaration is quite imprecise and largely reflects the quite selfish attitude of Poland and Hungary to the EU, manifesting itself, for example, in denying the right to discuss domestic solutions at the level of EU institutions, while making a lavish use of European funds. Poland's and Hungary's attitude to the EU is slightly "softened" by a greater pro-Europe approach of the other V4 members – Czechia and Slovakia.

The discussion presented earlier has clearly demonstrated the diversity of individual countries' attitude to the EU. The debate on the future of the EU is still on, though it becomes often dominated by more urgent topics that require fast decision-making, such as migration, for example. Even though, most countries have identified their negotiation positions in this respect, which will make it possible to start a debate on actual solutions. It must be borne in mind, however, that the results of the 2019 European Parliament election greatly changed the balance of power, and may, consequently, shift the fate and direction of this debate.

As philosopher Lévy claims (2021), we should write off as fiction the belief that Europe, as if by an absolute law of nature, will always unify at the time of crisis. Why do we assume that Europe, in its great wisdom, will counter each authoritarian or populist attack with an equally strong call for the progress of democracy? His words were confirmed by the results of the parliamentary election held in 2019, where Euro-sceptics such as the PM of Hungary, Viktor Orban and PM of Czechia, Andrej Babis were given political legitimacy to continue on their path.

Europe has not given up, though, and is fighting for its unity. The European Parliament, elected in a democratic election, and the newly constituted European Commission have continued discussions on the future of the European Union, listening attentively to the ideas submitted and exploring the arguments. These debates have not been in the forefront as joint measures to combat the Covid-19 pandemic, described in more detail in the next subchapter, were the issue of greatest importance in 2020.

The large number of proposals put forward by the European Commission in response to the Covid-19 pandemic strengthened in Member States' citizens the belief that the European Union is the right place to look for practical solutions as part of the ongoing social and economic processes. However, it should be remembered that nothing should be taken for granted. We could see how fragile this increased support was when deliveries of AstraZeneca vaccines were stopped at the time of the European Commission's internal disagreement and disagreement with the vaccine manufacturer. There was an immediate response to these events, i.e. EU citizens started to doubt again the efficiency of the EU.

On average, more respondents polled in the Eurobarometer 94.1 survey believe that the situation is on the right path at EU level compared to actions taken domestically, 66% are optimistic about the future of the European Union and nearly three-fourths respondents (72%) are of the opinion that the EU recovery plan will help boost the economy of their country faster than the negative outcomes of the Covid-19 epidemic. EU measures in 2020 during the pandemic contributed to the positive opinions of the Community's public, as evidenced by Eurobarometer surveys indicating a visible growth in support for the EU, i.e. at the end 2020 compared to autumn 2020, the number of citizens having a positive opinion of the EU increased by 10% points (a 50% increase).

In 2021, the most important aspect of discussions related to the future of the European Union is the initiative called Conference on the Future of Europe, which offers a unique opportunity to EU citizens to engage in the debate on Europe's challenges and priorities. The Conference is governed by three institutions represented by the President of the European Parliament, the President of the Council and the President of the European Commission, who act as joint leadership. The initiative opens a brand new phase in the discussion on the future of the Community, which is not to be an institution functioning merely within the framework of technocratic decisions but also taking account of Member States' citizens' expectations. This is not the first EU-level initiative aimed to engage Member States' citizens in discussions on future actions, but efforts in this area have never before been so wide-reaching. A similar role was to be played by meetings organised in 2014–2019 by the European Commission as part of the so-called "European dialogue" of which ca. 1300 were held in that period. In addition, "good deliberative practices" have multiplied over recent years in various forms – of civic assemblies, conventions – for example in countries such as France, Ireland, Finland and Lithuania. (Truszczyński, 2021). In the context of those experiences, a conclusion has been reached that it is worth strengthening the role of social dialogue, mobilising citizens as part of democratic procedures to indicate the direction of the European Commission's action. The Conference on the Future of Europe is also a clear message sent by the EU institutions and Member State governments that citizens' aggregated preferences and proposals find their way to the substance of European policies and law (Truszczyński, 2021). It is also worth noting the parallel debate on the EU strategic autonomy launched by France and now eagerly continued especially as regards security policy and the role of NATO in this process.

1.3 Pandemic crisis as an impulse to strengthen European integration and joint action in the economic field

As the pandemic was casting its shadow over Europe in its subsequent waves, governments had to take tough decisions. Closing down restaurants, cafés, museums and theatres, limiting social contacts – these were always measures necessary to flatten the curve of Covid-19 cases, even if they were known to greatly slow down the economy in 2020 and the first half of 2021. National authorities, in response to the emerging social and economic results, put in place, already in the first half of 2020, measures focusing on a number of areas:

- ensuring, based on the redistributive role of public finance, a positive fiscal impulse to prevent a decline in demand. To that end, national authorities changed the scale and structure of public spending (such as medical resources, keeping people employed, subsidising SMEs, public investment) and reducing tax collection (e.g. cancelling some taxes and social security contributions). This kind of measures immediately lead to a deterioration of the budget balance, without any direct compensation afterwards.

- suspending the collection of public charges and levies, i.e. a couple of countries decided to defer some payments, including taxes and social security contributions, which, as a rule, should be repaid later. These measures improve financial liquidity of individuals and businesses but do not cancel their obligations. In this case they had no impact on the general budget balance in 2020, only on some monthly budget balances. Deferments expiring in 2021 or later cause a deterioration of the budget balance in 2020 but later improve it. Some countries also deferred loan servicing or the payment of utility bills, which are also important tools to improve the liquidity position of those involved, which is why they are included here. These measures also have an impact on the budget.
- other liquidity regulations and guarantees: these measures include export guarantees, liquidity assistance, lines of credit granted by national development banks. Some of those measures improve the liquidity of private sector, but, contrary to deferments, which are automatic and generally only apply to target groups, lines of credit require action from the entrepreneurs involved.

Events related to the spread of the pandemic entailed a number of fast measures also at EU level, such as: NGEU recovery instrument, MFF for 2021–2027, pandemic emergency purchase programme (PEPP), the temporary increase of public deficit goals for Member States, as well as the State-aid framework to assist companies and businesses heavily impacted by the Covid-19 crisis (Heimberger et al., 2020).

Despite such a quick response, according to the data presented by the European Commission, EU's GDP significantly decreased in 2020 to be slightly rebuilt in 2021 (see Figure 1.1).

The first solution adopted at EU level was the decision to work on establishing the EU recovery fund aimed to alleviate the effects of the crisis. On 23 April 2020, EU leaders requested the European Commission to urgently present a concrete proposal of supranational action to include long-range measures related to the EU long-term budget. In response, the economic recovery plan for Europe was proposed by the European Commission on 27 May 2020.

In addition to the recovery package, EU leaders have agreed on the MFF of the European Union in the amount of EUR 1,074.3 billion for 2021–2027. This EU multiannual budget is intended to support investment in the green and digital transition, and resilience. The European Parliament and Council have reached a preliminary agreement as to the package on 10 November 2020. The European Council, on 10–11 December 2020, addressed the concerns voiced in the agreement and paved the way for the adoption of the recovery package.

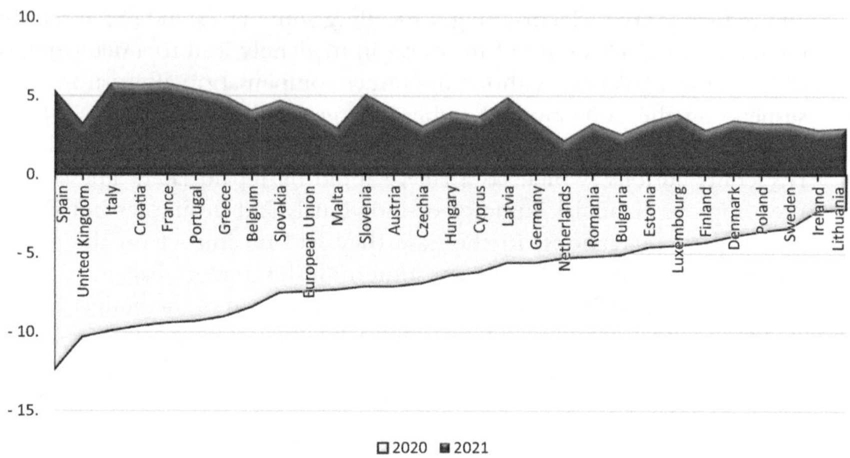

Figure 1.1 Real gross domestic product growth rate forecasts in selected European countries from 2020 to 2021 in per cent

Source: https://ec.europa.eu/info/sites/default/files/economy-finance/ip136_en.pdf.

The regulation establishing a Recovery and Resilience Facility (RRF) was adopted by the Council on 11 February 2021. This instrument, being at the heart of the NGEU, will provide Member States with a support of EUR 672.5 billion to help them solve economic and social consequences of the Covid-19 pandemic (European Commission, 2021a).

Of the first package of three measures adopted by Eurogroup in April 2021, the first one to be implemented is "Support to mitigate Unemployment Risks in an Emergency" (SURE). Over the last couple of weeks, the Commission has undertaken two very successful issuances of SURE social bonds in the total amount of EUR 31 billion, and SURE funds have already been disbursed to a number of Member States. These bonds have been oversubscribed ca. 13 times, which represents a strong vote of confidence to the overall EU recovery plan – NGEU.

At the centre of the agreement reached at the European Council session in February 2021 is the RRF, which will provide up to EUR 672 billion in the form of subsidies and loans. These funds will be available to Member States based on the implementation of National Recovery Plans. Preparation of these documents of strategic importance to the development of Europe is the responsibility of respective Member States, which will be accountable for implementing the reform and for investments as part of the proposals submitted. The role of the Commission will be to thoroughly evaluate each plan submitted to make sure it corresponds to the goals of the facility, such as support for economic growth and creation of new jobs, and contributes to green and digital transition of economies. The latter point is of significance as some observers fear that the Covid-19 outbreak will cause Europe to retreat from its ambitious climate and sustainable development commitments. When analysing such an approach of the European Commission to the development of national recovery plans, a certain element of disintegration can be observed across the EU as the most strategic decisions will be made at domestic level. Two key supranational elements, which have been strongly outlined in these solutions, are the adherence to the European Green Deal and Digital Europe as growth strategies and taking the opportunity offered by the recovery plan to place sustainable development at the heart of the European economic policy.

To begin with, the European Commission proposed to increase the EU 2030 emissions reduction target to 55%. Next, it identified financing to be made available to each Member State through the RRF, of which 37% should contribute to green transition, and further 20% to digital transition. Moreover, a commitment was made that 30% of the issuance to finance the EU Next Generation will be in green bonds. This comes on top of EUR 100 billion planned to be raised via social bonds under SURE. The NGEU may be one of the largest stimulus packages worldwide, triggering investment and reform in many key areas, from renewable energy sources and network infrastructure to energy-efficient buildings and sustainable transport; from 5G and AI to public and private sector digitalisation. Nevertheless, continuous learning, training and re-skilling programmes will be of equal importance. Moving on to the New Generation EU implementation phase in the coming months, the key challenge to Member States will be to fully and efficiently absorb the immense amounts earmarked from the EU funds for those purposes. To each Member State, it will be of paramount importance to establish a governance structure to ensure strong central steering and coordination between national and local levels. The European Commission will work in close partnership with Member States in that respect as this will be a test case for the EU as a whole.

Another sphere of economic support was also proposed by the European Investment Bank. On 26 May 2020, EIB Board of Directors agreed on the structure and business model of the new Pan-European Guarantee Fund to tackle the economic consequences of the Covid-19 pandemic. The Fund was approved by the European Council on 23 April 2021 as part of the overall EU Covid-19 response package. All 27 EU Member States have been invited to contribute to the Pan-European Guarantee Fund (EGF), with a share of EUR 25 billion equal to their share of EIB capital. The Fund will become operational as soon as Member States with at least 60% of EBI's capital have signed their contribution agreements and a Contributors Committee has been set up. The Contributors Committee will decide on how the guarantee will be used.

Member States' contributions to EGF will have the form of guarantees and may include an upfront payment. Such guarantees will cover losses sustained in operations supported by EGF. All losses will be covered pro rata by the participating Member States. The Fund will initially approve operations by the end of 2021, but this period may be extended by Member States. This will enable the EIB Group to increase support mainly for small- and medium-sized

European companies, mobilising up to EUR 200 billion in additional funding. EGF will provide financing to companies which are profitable in the long term but are struggling to survive in the present crisis. At least 65% of the financing is intended for SMEs. No more than 23% will go to companies with 250 or more employees, with limitations applying to larger companies with a staff of over 3,000. A maximum of 5% of subsidy can go to public sector companies and entities operating in healthcare or health research or providing core services related to the health crisis. Further 7% of the financing supported by EGF can be earmarked for venture and growth capital and venture debt to support SMEs and midcaps.

The aforementioned events and problems described in the next chapters of this Monograph call for taking a closer look at the possible directions of EU integration once the period of mitigating the economic and social consequences of Covid-19 is over. As a matter of fact, countries more sceptical about further and especially deeper integration within the EU will naturally not be interested (or will be interested to a limited extent) in implementing the solutions proposed in this Monograph. Nevertheless, despite a great difference in opinions and the mounting problems, a discussion thereon is necessary and is still going on, and a greater integration of the euro area, as urged and contemplated by France and Germany, among others, should encourage relevant analyses in this respect in other Member States, especially those which do not currently belong to that group. A number of interesting ideas have already been put forward, for example by the European Fiscal Board, such as creating a permanent fiscal capacity, mechanisms to facilitate investment, especially for the climate transition.

Bearing in mind all those circumstances – irrespective of the final direction of EU development – adopting the solution proposed in this Monograph, which defines relevant policy aspects as European, domestic or global tasks, should contribute to the achievement of goals pursued by all parties involved. Hence, the decision should only be about the extent to which to implement such a solution – based on Member States' choices regarding the future of the EU – rather than about the legitimacy of its implementation.

1.4 Government as an active participant of the free play of the market? Which path is the European Union following in response to the emerging crises?

Looking from a historical perspective, one can observe that as soon as the economic boom arrived, economic entities (banks, companies) immediately tried to reduce the regulatory and controlling role of the state, but once crisis symptoms were detected, they required that the state should take measures to counteract its consequences and stimulate the economic growth, exert an influence and support the economy. The crisis caused by the Covid-19 outbreak fully confirmed such an approach, in the sense of growing expectations as to the state's fast and significant financial involvement in the sphere of real economy. A similar thing happened at the onset of the crisis of the neoliberal system in 2007–2008.

In the context of the currently growing role of the state, it is particularly important in this process to use public finance which is based on sound and transparent terms and readily available to a strong and active state that pursues an economic policy based on a paradigm to match the contemporary challenges. Research on the efficiency of measures taken by the authorities in respective countries and communities (e.g. EU) has an ever-widening scope, especially as a result of the crisis. The first stage of the last crisis manifested itself in the area of financial mechanisms and institutions as well as that of their regulatory and supervisory structures. Categories related to the banking sector, which had until recently been associated with the classic doctrine governed by market laws, now are increasingly contemplated not only in the context of the state's regulatory policy but also that of financial impact. Measures put in place at the time of crisis demonstrated that on both the international and national levels, private banks are unable to support continuous economic activity without the participation of the state, international cross-border regulations, effective supervisory control as well as sporadic budgetary subsidies and state intervention. This is perfectly reflected by data presented by the European Commission (Eurostat for 2017), which reveals that general government assets in financial institutions rose as a whole in EU Member States (UE-28) from EUR 150 million in 2008 to EUR 359,946 million in 2016. This means that banks fare much better when they operate in compliance with regulations and make a proper use of the opportunities offered by the regulatory framework and the state's capital support alike, rather than when they achieve "their" success in a free market space.

Political and social requirements focusing on sustainable development, financial stability and alleviation of economic and social vulnerabilities call for new economic paradigms and efficient national and international institutions (Erhard, 2012;). In the 40 pre-crisis years, the economy came closer to business science and business approach, which – as demonstrated in the previous subchapter – is inadequate to the current challenges (Rodrik, 2011). Preventive legislation, which sets an effective course for government action and prevents crises, as well as modified economic content and social expectations on how government and public services should function, have become the main substance of political sciences, and one of the main challenges of the modern time is to find the way to reflect in science the processes occurring in practice.

In recession, the attempts to enforce the economic policy criteria have proven that neither a classical instrument of economic policy, i.e. the government's fiscal policy, nor the use of other instruments which are much more abundant than at the times of previous crises, is sufficient to alleviate the consequences of recession. The crisis experienced by us showed that its burden cannot be overcome without the involvement of at least some of the central banks, which – independently of governmental institutions – undertook measures having implications for the social and economic development. This way the public finance system became bipolar and the government fiscal policy was extended to include the central bank's institutional system, which is aligned with that policy, on the one hand, and on the other, remains independent.

Government and central bank interventions undertaken as part of post-2008 crisis management – as pointed out before – were definitely stronger and had a much wider scope, which resulted in a reorganisation of social sciences (Lewin, (1851) 1964). As part of crisis management, government was given a stronger mandate to regulate and supervise markets. This is why the authorities focusing on preventing the crisis from deepening and on achieving consolidation also started to use, in its efforts to ensure even social development, budgetary tools and instruments used in financial markets. The measures adopted: coordination, intervention and supervision over activities of economic organisations can be only effective as part of a well-organised and effective economic management which aims to use the best instruments of market intervention.

In other words, state intervention can be successful only with a transparent and efficient support for respective sectors within public finance, and with disciplined and controlled money market. Thanks to effective tools, national and European authorities may develop institutional and legal means not only to impact only economic growth but also to alleviate income disparity within the society, which WAS so badly aggravated during the reign of the neoliberal economics.

As mentioned before, after the crisis of 2007–2008, there was no ready-made paradigm, school of thought that could be implemented in the area of state intervention. Hence, it became essential to look for a new economic paradigm providing new insights from practical knowledge on the processes taking place in the economy. It turned out that it would no longer suffice to rely on the existing instruments of active state involvement developed by respective scientific disciplines, such as descriptive law and "business approach" economics (Lin, 2017). As it happens, neither is it enough to apply the Keynesian approach based solely on intervention through public services and monetary flows injected into the economy, which also became outdated categories. The incompatibility of these theories stems from a number of factors. One of them is undoubtedly the reinterpretation of the scale and scope of state ownership, which, after several decades of pro-privatisation trend – especially in the Central Eastern Europe – was not only discontinued but also reversed as emphasis was again placed on strengthening state ownership by buying back some assets or by a clear message being sent by those in power that such is the official course of national policy. Actions such as these attest to the crisis of globalisation whose goal is to liberalise the integration of national markets, which previously functioned largely separately, into one interconnected global market. Academic discourse is seeing an ever-increasing number of opinions that criticise or sometimes even repudiate the contemporary global capitalism as a malfunctioning, unjust and even inefficient system (Mazzucato, 2017). That raises the question: Is shutting ourselves in within national economies and public ownership the right answer, considering that, as it seems, the globalised world is here to stay and the globalisation process cannot be reversed, if only for the couple of reasons astutely identified by A.K. Koźmiński (Kołodko and Koźmiński, 2017), namely:

- financial and capital markets – economy virtually can no longer function without being part of the global cash flow cycle;
- technological dominance which enforces a global standard that is unattainable to closed economies;
- "mandatory economies of scale" – when producing for our own, domestic needs, we are unable to make the most of the production cost optimisation (only the United States and China could potentially do that);
- the existence of global regulations that make possible a harmonised market operation, for example telecom, air traffic and partly even financial market.

Another important area of the state's impact on the sphere of real economy and also on the standard of living of citizens is the scope and quality of services supplied as part of public policies implemented to satisfy and address a hierarchy of human needs, and the scope of vital public goods to satisfy these. The trend based on decentralisation, free market services and profit-maximising management with respect to public services proved to be quite inadequate. Current processes are heading towards a higher rank active state model and the attendant new economic paradigm, i.e. centralisation, return to national ownership (through buyback) and an approach that enforces social prosperity. This requires a reflection on a new method of supplying those services to ensure that the process will not become inefficient from the perspective of the supreme goal. When interpreting the processes presently taking place in Europe, the partial incorporation of the welfare state concept and the ensuing far-reaching state interference with the economic life may soon generate a new trend whose first impulse will come from public finance rather than from financial markets.

As the state's role increases, it is becoming ever-more important to work out the right procedure to take decisions on how to allocate its resources and how to implement public service tasks, also taking account of the supranational nature of some measures taken already today, for example in the European Union. Most of all, though, as pointed out by many researchers (e.g. Stiglitz, 2004;), the global phenomena currently taking place have not – as yet – led to the emergence of an efficient system for coordinating economic policy with the implementation of public services which are of interest to all countries. Therefore, it is worth asking ourselves whether – or rather – how to face those challenges, which will be probably increasingly noticeable in the coming years. Environmental protection, security issues, e-commerce migration and global digital companies – these are processes and entities that will gain importance, and no country will be able to tackle them alone.

These days, active and practical state action is a fixture of economic deliberations. With such an approach in place, public finance and the related science is gaining significance, and the process of formulating new scientific concepts is still underway (Postuła, 2017). Trends involving opposite or very similar assumptions as to the direction of state intervention are cropping up. There are at least several of them at the moment. Two of them, with quite divergent propositions, deserve our attention: new nationalism, contradicting the idea of globalisation, and new pragmatism, to which, according to the researchers associated with this trend, the global economy is very dear.

In response to the aforementioned crisis of globalisation and to the practical failures of neoliberalism, the last couple of years have seen a major radicalisation of the analytical concept of economic nationalism and the ever-more obvious efforts to put it in effect. Nationalist trends and measures referred to as economic nationalism are already visible all over the world and have marked nation state policies quite heavily. They can be hardly found in Community measures as, in many aspects, their functioning contradicts the nationalist idea. The European Union provides an opportunity for a different approach to the processes taking place, by allowing not only global companies but also the strongest national economies to tap into global open markets.

For most of the 20th century, little research was undertaken to develop a detailed analysis of issues related to nationalism which was being crowded out by globally oriented trends. As observed by M.A. Heilperin (1960), the term was widely used for the first time in the interwar period of the 20th century, but its exact meaning was often hard to identify. It was usually used by liberal economists to describe policies they did not like. As J. Kofman put it (1990), it became everything that did not match the liberal definition of economy and development, usually interpreted in a doctrinaire manner. Meanwhile M. Horsman said that economic nationalism is a nondescript term at best, used more often by its detractors than by its proponents (Horsman and Marshall, 1994). Even though it is a novel concept, it must be explained that nationalism – understood as a pervasive cognitive orientation rather than a consistent ideology – continues to enliven daily political discussions in contemporary democracies (Berezin, 2009; Smith, 2003).

Though the term "economic nationalism" is often associated with economic policy, it started from actions by national authorities aimed only to boost the competitiveness of the domestic industry in the integrated world economy rather than further-reaching policies attributed to it today. There was also the 19th-century economic nationalism which supported autarchy. The first one to follow this mindset was J.G. Fichte, one of the first eminent nationalist theoreticians, whose ideas were strictly related to the "Jacobin nationalism". All nationalists, back then perceived this way from the economic point of view, shared the belief that liberal economic policy – such as free trade – is incompatible with nationalist values because it may cause more negative than positive consequences for national economies.

It is worth noting that political nationalism triumphed in the same period where liberal economic policy became widespread and solidified in the international economic governance. Many proponents of the liberal economic policy in the 19th century were actually nationalists who believed that this policy would strengthen national identity, nation's prosperity and/or their country's power. By pointing out this aspect, providing a link between economic nationalism and the original assumptions of nationalism, we arrive at the final 19th-century economic nationalist trend, which we could call "liberal economic nationalism".

For most of the 20th century, the nationalist ideology rarely emerged in academic discourse or was analysed in scientific literature. Recent years, however, have seen a new interest in the more radical meaning of economic nationalism. Certainly some trends within the contemporary economic nationalism are in favour of non-liberal policy, which certainly is a huge challenge to the goals of economic liberals, as it was in the 19th century. However, many economic nationalists today support liberal economic policy. Even though they are not on the same page with economic liberals, when explaining the rationale behind their actions, "liberal national economists" have worked together with economic liberals to promote the advent of a much more liberal global economy over the last two decades, as did their predecessors in the 19th century. The enduring strength of economic nationalism is visible not only in the continued support for the poorest and for the domestic industry, and in macroeconomic activism in many parts of the contemporary world. It can also be seen in the triumph of liberal economic policies themselves. This is why some scientists refer to new nationalism as a "bastard of neoliberalism" (Kołodko and Koźmiński, 2017). This is perfectly exemplified by the research of F. Trentmann (2009), who emphasised in its results that the British support for free trade in the 19th century also had nationalist roots. Trentmann argues that most of the political support for free trade came from groups that had neither understanding nor interest in the course of liberal theory of trade proposed by D. Ricardo. For them, free trade deserved support because it involved moral and political values such as freedom, free exchange and national progress which were associated with the British national identity. As F. Trentmann (2009) puts it: "Britain's free trade vision was sustained by a contrast between British progress and civilization and foreign reaction and backwardness". Political economy was forged through the close link between national identity and free trade.

It is impossible here to fully explain the currently emerging populist nationalist trends and the support for them, but a couple of factors contributing to a spike in the interest in these ideas are quite self-evident. One of the most important ones is the mounting income disparity and social polarisation, which the low-income groups blame on the processes related to globalisation and on the cosmopolitan elites who have permitted the increase in income disparity through their actions.

Economic nationalism has emerged as a powerful and attractive policy to put emphasis on national interests, achieve economic goals and maintain autonomy of respective countries in the increasingly internationalised world. Understanding how and why this process is happening will have great importance for development and for the ability to offer solutions that will help achieve the social and economic goals more efficiently. The contemporary nationalism is founded on the events described in the history of economic thought and in the resulting theories of economics. One of its foundations is taking measures to ensure orienting the economic policy of the authorities towards the development of national economy. Such an economy should be based on traditional economic theories, which principally dealt with instruments to stimulate the development of national economy. From the political point of view, it is hard to imagine a more appealing economic proposition. Such an assumption seems obvious and reflective of the general nature of economic policy. Can we, though, after so many years of continued globalisation processes, go back to such mentality and take decisions on its grounds that are beneficial to further development? Much to the disappointment of the proponents of such a hypothesis, it must be concluded, however, that this is no longer possible. After all, the globalisation phenomenon meant, among other things, obliterating the differences between respective countries' national economic interests, between foreign and domestic capital, as well as between global and national financial systems.

The spread of the influence of global processes caused a partial "levelling" of variance between the national economic policy and the internationalist economic policy subordinate to the interests of global companies. This process unfolded in respective countries in a manner that was characteristic for a given region. This is especially true of the difference between the economic policy of the Western European countries and that of the CEE countries.

Researchers of nationalism who wrote about the future of this trend anticipated a transformation of the classical nation state amid globalisation and a decline in nationalist sentiment in the coming century. These ideas come, to a great extent, from E.J. Hobsbawm (1992) and E. Gellner (1983) – authors of two classic studies, which are generally considered as the cornerstone of research on nationalism. These have been the most quoted and discussed authors, with the greatest impact on the development of the contemporary definition of nationalism. This is why exploring their thoughts will serve as the basis for defining the terms "nationalism" and "economic nationalism" with respect to the goals set in this Monograph. For latest authors, nationalism is linked to economic development and vice versa. Development, however, like the transition of advanced industrial economies, is so unique that its individual models cannot be the basis for generalisation that would indicate one set of economic circumstances applicable to all of them, allowing us to determine how the economic nationalism came into being.

When a strong sense of national goal supports economic development, the state can appeal to citizen sentiment to organise a collective effort. In *Theorizing Economic Nationalism* (2004), T. Nakano wrote that to mobilise economic resources, create an integrated national market and effectively implement an economic policy, a country's elites must make use of common cultural resources and national loyalty. The trust resulting from loyalty to a strong national identity may strengthen economic growth, gathering citizens around a set of nation-wide goals. That is why in the contemporary history, the central meaning of the state as a factor of economic change is related to a sociological element, which nationalist ideologies may complement or even strengthen.

Seeking protection against forces that are beyond the control of the population, citizens all over the world are increasing looking to the state. This is how the phenomenon that is currently often referred to as nationalism comes into existence. Lincoln said that "The legitimate object of government is to do for a community of people, whatever they need to have done, but can not do, at all, or can not, so well do, for themselves – in their separate, and individual capacities" (*Lincoln on Purpose . . .*, no date). Obviously no individual or community can withstand the forces of global capital, and western governments reluctantly offer means of protection to employees, for example through increasing employee rights and unionisation. Citizens, in a quest for a strong government that will defend them, are, however, at risk of surrendering to the state too much control over their lives. As a matter of fact, there is no certainty that a strong national government's policy will be better for them than the one that suits multinational corporations or international communities such as the European Union. Moreover, history shows that the fear of global capital may be misused by unscrupulous politicians to unleash a spiral of fear of other nations and build international tensions. Nationalism was revived largely in the connection with the demise of neoliberal theories, which brought about the crisis of 2007–2008.

Neoliberalism is much more hostile to nationalism, or even to the concept of national economy, than most of its 19th-century liberal predecessors. Its followers have promoted over the last two decades a liberal economic policy, arguing it will bring benefits such as GDP growth, good national trade balance, lower unemployment rate, higher national productivity and higher rate of domestic savings. They have been able to do so because a banal and deeply rooted nationalism, which evaluates economic ideas mostly in terms of their impact on a nation rather than humankind as a whole, remains the dominant discourse of our age (Reich, 1992; Levi-Faur, 1997; Pickel, 2003).

If economic nationalism remains a strong force, what challenge is posed by economic liberalism in the contemporary world? Nineteenth-century experiences suggest that there is no unambiguous answer to that question. As we have seen, the political substance of economic nationalism was very diverse in that time. Some economic nationalists questioned liberal economic policy while others supported and strengthened it. This diversity partly stemmed from the fact that different economic nationalists placed emphasis on different nationalist values such as a pursuit of national prosperity, search for national rule or promotion of national identity and culture. The differences also resulted from disparate contexts in which they were situated. Similarly, the specific substance of national identities in respective countries affected the way nationalist values translated into economic preferences of their citizens. It can be observed, for example, that the nature of British national identities in the 19th century encouraged many citizens to perceive free trade as a reflection of national moral and political values. In other countries, however, this association had a different resonance. The lesson to be learnt from this story is that in the contemporary times, there will be many political projects under the banner of economic nationalism, of which some will question economic liberalism and others will not. For those unfamiliar with economic nuances, this assumption may seem self-evident and reflective of the overall nature of economic policy. As a matter of fact, the centuries-old tradition of national economic policy has been greatly undermined in European countries, though to varying extent.

In parallel with the far-reaching integration process in the European Union, the revival of new nationalism can be observed. Will this new nationalism strive to limit the significant impact the European Union has on Member States, if only through coordination of the ongoing economic processes? Will it be possible to combine interests of 27 Member States if nationalism is the leitmotif of their national policies? Another question is to what extent this decision would be optimal from the point of view of social and economic development of those countries? This does not seem a good direction, especially that – as mentioned before – soon it will probably lose its present momentum. It would be therefore advisable to keep looking and ask ourselves what alternative would ensure further growth; whether it exists already or is only now being forged in the scientific and practical discourse.

There are three arguments to back up government intervention through proactive industrial policy (Sauvant, 2008):

- greater security resulting from a lesser dependence on foreign supplies,
- protection of industries of strategic economic importance, such as those that create new jobs and ensure high value added, and
- intervention in sectors characterised by high barriers of entry and externalities.

Arguments of neoprotectionism include a number of ideas, the most important of which are strategic trade policy and dynamic comparative advantages achieved thanks to industrial policy. The use of various tools aimed to help domestic businesses (subsidies) is, as a rule, justified by the non-existence of perfect competition (Brander and Spencer, 1984; Rodrik, 2004). The pandemic situation has shown, however, that another justification is also the need to limit income disparity. Meanwhile, developing comparative advantages through industrial policy is understood as abandoning the passive acceptance of the existing production structure and trying to influence this structure and modify the industrial activities to ensure the best possible protection of the country's interests (Grossman and Helpman, 1990). Monopolist competition, barriers of entry and economies of scale often make free market conditions seem like a fiction.

In such an environment, cluster companies emerge, businesses are internationally dependent and the industrial policy supports the development of sectors deemed valuable to the national economy. Economic patriotism – a specific form of state intervention – is understood as a selective discrimination in favour of businesses that are domestic or "territorially defined". Even before the advent of 2008, intervention was favoured due to the specificity of international production networks and the existence of fragmented global value chains (GVC), which blur the division line between the domestic and the foreign, and the growing role of intangible assets or the threat of middle income trap (Szalavetz, 2015). Since the crisis of 2007–2008, we can observe a "post-neoliberal transition" in the global political economy (Schmalz and Ebenau, 2012). Most economists still believe in free market competition, but they do not seem to consider government neutrality as the best solution (Chwieroth, 2007). Public intervention appears to be a preliminary condition for economic recovery following the crisis of 2007–2008 (Cohen-Setton and Vella, 2010) and during the Covid-19 pandemic. Moreover, it was already 20 years ago that researchers pointed out (Persson and Tabellini, 2002) that public spending is used to look for a political consensus on behalf of those responsible for managing public affairs rather than encourage economies to change their structure, improve productivity and stimulate growth. It is beyond dispute that those in power, most of whom are politicians, are mostly focused on being re-elected and on maximising their political power, and these goals make public spending management inefficient. It can be concluded that scientific research has demonstrated that the post-crisis stagnation is a very strong case for increasing public investments. It is justified by multiples which imply a significant correlation between public spending and production.

As a consequence of the crisis of 2008 and the pandemic one of 2020, we have witnessed various innovative forms of state intervention. Covid-19 is another crisis to strengthen the great "global interdisciplinary debate" featuring representatives of nearly all academic, political, professional and social communities. Diverse positions are naturally voiced but to discuss their different aspects in detail would go beyond the scope of this Monograph (Acemoglu and Molina, 2021; Bowles and Carlin, 2020; Rodrik, 2020).

Under the aegis of economic patriotism, some countries obstructed the activities of foreign companies, while some others facilitated their economic activities on their territory. In some cases, support for native, domestic businesses, however, was just a political rhetoric, reduced to empty declarations. Nevertheless, in the measures taken and in discussions, one could note the perceived role the state is to play in the economy. The economic situation obliged scientists and political decision-makers to rethink their approach in involving public administration in market processes. The views of J.M. Keynes gained new popularity and government intervention as a counterbalance to excessively developed markets became desirable (Giles et al., 2002), but state aid in the post-crisis reality remains controversial. Some are of the opinion that the meaning of state is weakening in the globalised world, and governments could instead play only an auxiliary role, while others see it quite differently. According to the latter, success on the international arena usually stems from cooperation of state and market. Bregman, who makes references in interviews to historical experiences and to the findings of their flagship work, believes that the pandemic may be a turning point the humanity needs (Bregman, 2020). According to Rediker (2015), the "rules, norms and tools of state involvement in capitalism itself" are being increasingly exceeded in the contemporary world. A more desirable model of market capitalism assumes that the state plays a major role in driving results to develop national interests (Reuters, 2015). This means that the term "state capitalism", previously charged with negative emotions, seems outdated now. The new "state capitalism" stands for a more sophisticated state involvement in the economy and it can be called *State Capitalism 2.0*, where governments intervene in markets using subtler tools. A new perspective on the state–market relationship has revealed the need to abandon the generally accepted dichotomy between these two concepts. In reality, in some situations market is dominant, while the state prevails in others. The state is personified not only by the government but also by various institutions, regulatory and supervisory bodies. It should be, therefore, easier than ever for the state to stimulate relevant actions (interventions), preventing undesirable changes thanks to a better supervision (e.g. frauds in the banking sector), while ensuring stable economy and lightening the burden to the society by reducing the public debt. This is a difficult combination and, as regards the role of the state in the market, one that will not be easy to put in practice without a breakthrough, a radical change or the emergence of a new paradigm.

On the one hand, the Covid-19 pandemic and its global spread gave rise to a gamut of new challenges and threats and made it necessary to look for new solutions for difficult problems the world had never faced on such a large and multidimensional scale. This situation, even more than the previous crises, laid bare the errors and imperfections in the functioning of the existing social and economic policy and became a magnifying glass through which its weak points are exposed, imposing the need to re-evaluate even the concepts that were once treated as nothing short of dogmas (Słodowa-Hełpa, 2020).

In the debate on the role and scale of the state in the economy, a very important factor that is discussed is the origin of the funds being redistributed, whether at domestic or EU level. In this context, questions arise as to whether we can afford it, or whether we are doing it at the expense of future periods, when we incur public debt to pay for the measures in place. This is quite interesting, considering that a number of public management solutions and instruments such as: fiscal rules, independent fiscal institutions or medium-term planning, are meant to prevent such a situation. The question is: Do they indeed? I will attempt to answer this question in the following chapters.

When considering the issues related to the growth of public debt as a factor resulting from state intervention in the social and economic life, it is vital to try and determine the level of public debt above which economic growth is jeopardised by public debt (Reinhart and Rogoff, 2010). Research on that subject, held for decades now, does not yield clear findings and lacks broad presentation in the literature. A major part of the studies conducted point to the inability to reach a straightforward conclusion, for example that public debt-to-GDP should amount to 60%. As a matter of fact, essential elements in defining that level include a given country's characteristics, unforeseen events and events that play a significant role and have a major impact on the relationship between the debt growth and the determinants of that growth (Panizza and Presbitero, 2014; Eberhardt and Presbitero, 2015; Tamborini and Tomaselli, 2020). In particular, Tamborini and Tomaselli (2020) argued that debt and its impact on growth cannot at any point in time be evaluated without reference to the entire debt trajectory and the specific state of economy along that trajectory. This is why, in their opinion, it is impossible to conceptualise one general economic law that would explain the relationship between debt and growth and determine the critical level of public debt. Responsible action in that respect is vital, though as empirical research based on historical data shows that public debt has a tendency to stifle growth by increasing uncertainty as to future taxation, crowding out private investment and weakening a country's resilience to shocks (Schilirò, 2019).

Measures aimed to prevent the negative social and economic consequences during and after the pandemic were based on the issuance of securities at both the EU and domestic levels. As a result, public debt increased significantly as virtually all restrictions in the form of fiscal rules were lifted, with a higher public interest given as justification. Scientists (Burriel, Checherita-Westphal et al., 2020) warn that when the crisis is over and we enter recovery for good, debt will remain at a high, above-average level. Those researchers noted that especially in the euro area, where monetary policy focuses on aggregated data that encompass the entire area, and countries with a high level of debt are not well-prepared for this type of measures, large-scale asymmetric shocks can occur, manifested by side effects such as crowding out of private debt in short- and mid-term. This will have a negative impact on potential (long-term) activity of companies, which will fear an increase in taxation to finance the additional burden with debt in the future (Burriel, Chronis, et al., 2020). Yared (2019) emphasised that a long-term trend in debt accumulation seems inconsistent with the theories of optimum strategy for public debt management. He pointed to a threat presented by specific factors such as: ageing population, growing political polarisation, which may explain the long-term trajectory of public debt.

Presbitero and Wiriadinata (2020) questioned the view of Blanchard (2019) of pursuing fiscal expansion in a low-interest rate environment and high debt that stimulates growth. They warned that despite low-interest environment, there is still risk of high public debt, especially due to the differences in interest rate and growth, which are endogenous to the size and dynamic of public debt, as pointed out by Debrun et al. (2019b). Presbitero and Wiriadinata (2020), in turn, highlighted that even before the Covid-19 pandemic, the public debt level was historically high, with many countries experiencing its significant growth. Consequently, fiscal expansion based on funds from debt, adopted in most countries following the Covid-19 crisis, involves a significant risk. Schiliro (2020) points out that the risk inherent in refinancing is of key importance when countries borrow money in financial markets, the main risk being a potential feedback loop between high public debt and risk premium, as demonstrated also by Alcidi and Gros (2019).

In the context of so many questions and dilemmas, in the coming years or even decades, the most promising and also the most demanding research on economic growth and development will involve perhaps various forms of analysis of interactions between human evolution and development process. Conducting research into such a broad and largely unchartered area may revolutionise the understanding of the evolution of human characteristics and their impact on behaviour in general, especially on development process. This may improve the understanding of sources of human behaviours and global inequalities and help design appropriate policies to promote economic development and reduce income disparity (Galor et al., 2020; Słodowa-Hełpa, 2021).

Douglass North, who emphasises that the objective of his research is not only to provide a new outlook on the past but also to incorporate in the economic theory an analytical perspective to help understand economic change, found the neoclassical static allocative efficiency incomplete and often leading to erroneous practical conclusions. He verified his hypotheses based on extremely in-depth historical analyses, encompassing the development of not only the US economy but also the European one. This way he presented long-term processes and "path dependence" as well as the impact on the path of development of institutions undergoing transformation, which ensure either development or persistent stagnation of countries and regions.

Conclusion

The crisis of 2007–2008 and the Covid-19 pandemic have triggered another debate, not only just on whether monetary or fiscal policy or a policy-mix are a more effective mechanism to shorten the duration of a financial crisis and have an impact on the social and economic development, but also on which tools to apply for measures to bring the best results, without denying the impact itself. Few studies can be found in the literature that assess the structure of the fiscal expansion and its effect on the economic growth at the time of the financial crisis in the short term and after the crisis in the long term (Jansen et al., 2008; Baldacci et al., 2009). Though a lot of time has passed since the first symptoms of the crisis manifested themselves, there is still no unanimity among the scientists as to how to implement state measures to provide long-term social and developmental effects to citizens. Should we follow the path of new nationalism, new pragmatism, new casualism or maybe another "new" variety of an existing paradigm? Scientists have proved that during financial crises, fiscal policy is more effective than monetary policy so fiscal expansion may decrease the loss of production, and consumption stimuli may lay the groundwork for rebuilding the economic growth (Gali et al., 2005; Ghosh et al., 2009; Rogoff and Reinhart, 2009; Fetai, 2017).

An analysis of existing theories and claims gives rise to further questions as to whether in EU Member States, policy should be implemented at domestic level or should EU instruments be used to that end. Until recently, the European Union seemed a unique economic and political unity bringing together 29 Member States which, as a whole, occupy a greater part of the continent; a unity, which, through joint action, could fulfil a major part of public service tasks and level developmental differences. Is it possible, though, considering the events taking place and the lack of agreement on many issues among Member States? In June 2016, the British people voted in favour of exiting the European Union, which, on the one hand, showed, in the most vivid way possible, how many problems have accumulated within the EU, and, on the other hand, proved that without reforms, evolutionary changes, the same cannot be solved. The changes happening before our eyes, Brexit, migration, Covid-19, are examples that the EU must be closer to its citizens after all. And hence the high hopes for the results of the Conference on the future of Europe. May this debate not show indifference of citizens as this will mean that the EU project is a project by Euro-elites while more or less national (not to say nationalist) country governments are better positioned to solve citizens' real problems. Governments, which are eager to benefit from EU aid but only in the financial dimension. Meanwhile, the Covid-19 pandemic, i.e. the years 2020–2021 have shown that the European Union is capable of joint action, for example when it comes to pro-health measures, ensuring vaccines to Member States' citizens and issues that are of importance to European Union citizens. On the other hand, however, National Recovery Plans and other measures for redistribution of public funds have shown that the leading and best heard voice is, sadly, that of national policy rather than supranational, Community policy.

2 Macroeconomic coordination policy tools recommended and assessed at EU level

Introduction

Crises are an inherent part of the ongoing economic and social processes that we are facing today and that future generations will need to solve. With such an approach in mind, we should learn lessons from each crisis to make sure we can prevent any new ones or at least fare better at dealing with them. EU action is visibly informed by that assumption. The quintessence of the measures adopted by the European Commission is the recently enacted MFF 2021–2027, whose flagship programme (and response to Covid-19) is the Resilience and Reform Fund. As the name suggests, the purpose of spending is self-explanatory (Gali et al., 2007). There is another aspect, however, i.e. the innovative method of financing – de facto by incurring common public debt, as presented in more detail in Chapter 1.

The crisis of 2007–2008 was one of the events that made the European Union and other participants of the EU-level public debate aware of the need to strengthen cooperation on economic and budgetary policy. As a result, two main trends have emerged as regards solutions aimed for stronger cooperation: 25 European governments concluded on 29 June 2012, the European Fiscal Compact at the inter-government level, and, as part of the EU legal order, in 2021, they passed a package of relevant regulations, the so-called Six-Pack and Two-Pack. Comparing the significance of the two solutions helps understand the relationships between the Community and inter-governmental integration methods within the EU (Baran, 2013). An analysis of the six-pack shows the effectiveness and the advantage of supranational regulations given that European institutions were able to support it, through their powers and authorities, in accordance with the competences contained in Article 136 of the *Treaty on the Functioning of the European Union* (TFEU), and the Fiscal Compact is largely a repetition of the content of the six-pack (Postuła, 2015). A question arises however as to whether the solutions used by those institutions are effective, ensure the implementation of common fiscal policy and contribute to the social and economic development at the supranational level, also in Member States. Measures adopted during the Covid-19 pandemic have shown different facets of this situation, though the European Union cannot be said to have

DOI: 10.4324/9781003222033-3

failed the test of maturity and prompt action at a time of deep crisis in all spheres of the social and economic life. It is worth going through the instruments aimed to help restore the economic stability after the unstable period in the sphere of health security.

2.1 Economic integration and fiscal policy of EU Member States

The creation of the European Union and of its extended form of economic integration that is euro area was, in the past, and still is based on strictly defined institutional principles resulting from the assumptions underlying its creation. The EU is founded on the free movement of goods, services, capital and labour, which, perforce, greatly limits respective Member States' ability to have an individual economic policy in place, for example due to the impossibility of freely applying instruments such as customs duties, export aids, state aid for domestic enterprises – to be applied only in strictly defined cases – or limits on capital flows. The emergence of the common currency area is another significant element of integration at the currency union level, which is seen as a great value by some, while by others, as curbing the national authorities' ability for economic intervention by moving relevant powers to the supranational level, to which decisions on managing the money supply and interest rates have also been automatically moved (Juncker et al., 2015).

National macroeconomic policy of respective EU Member States was limited to fiscal policy, which is also subject to certain restrictions. First of all, fiscal parameters were set (the levels of public debt and deficit), within which Member States should conduct their national budget policy, aiming to achieve specific levels (Reuter, 2015). Regulations (Stability and Growth Pact along with subsequent additions and amendments – SGP) determine in detail the acceptable debt and deficit limits as well as procedures and possible sanctions for countries that fail to comply with relevant principles. Stability programmes and convergence programmes are, therefore, instruments intended to discipline EU Member States, encouraging their responsible fiscal policy making (Franco, 2005). Such a fiscal policy coordination within the EU has both a theoretical and practical/political rationale, though it does not work as expected in this day and age. In 2021, a heated debate continues at Economic and Financial Affairs Council (ECOFIN) sessions as to whether SGP in its current form is any good. Many findings from research and from the ongoing discussions suggest that the European Union may be in for a reform, including the scraping of the aforementioned fiscal parameters.

In the final conclusions regarding the creation of the euro area, a decision was made that the budget policy of the currency union member states would remain the competence of national governments. This does not mean, however, that the EU will have no influence on it. In fact, as part of the coordination process, relevant principles were laid down, especially those relating to fiscal policy making and avoidance of excessive budget deficit and high debt

(De Grauwe, 2006). Fiscal rules were to play a major role for the centralised monetary policy (Brunila et al., 2001). According to the initiators of the SGP, the great importance of fiscal rules stemmed from the fact that stability in the public finance sector may help minimise the risk of tensions in the monetary policy implemented by the European Central Bank. Solid public finance was also expected to facilitate the use of budget policy in the event of asymmetric shocks (Buti et al., 1997; Buti and Giudice, 2002a). The SGP creators also believe that countries with a low deficit and public debt-to-GDP ratio respond to crisis situations much better than countries with unstable public finance. All of these measures fit squarely with the European Union's efforts aiming to implement economic solutions based on the sustainable development concept. In 2018, a report of the European Commission was published, mapping out

> the challenges and opportunities that the EU faces in developing a sustainable finance policy. It identifies ways in which the financial sector can re-connect with the real economy to support the transition to a more resource-efficient and more circular economy. The group argues that reorienting investment flows into long-term, sustainable projects will also improve the stability of the financial system.
>
> (*Final Report . . .*, 2018c)

The report indicates directions for action aimed to achieve durable and sustainable development based on efforts to combine economic prosperity with environmental and social sustainability (Farah and Gómez-Ramos, 2014). Sustainable development requires a long-term perspective and ensuring long-term financing for the critical infrastructure as well as fast response to any threats that may arise in the long run. As part of these measures, it is concluded that aiming for sustainable development must be supported with a stable financial system (Radu et al., 2011). Action taken in line with the concept of financial stability could contribute to changing the orientation of measures adopted in finance and to strengthening the long-term positive impact on the social and economic development. A special role and importance in this respect is attributed to the public authorities, which use public finance to achieve sustainable development.

Initiatives adopted by public finance institutions to maintain budget stability and public finance stability must be, as a rule, considered in two dimensions: narrow and broad (Krejdl, 2006; Hashimzade and Myles, 2010). In the narrow perspective, public finance stability is defined as measures oriented towards maintaining budget stability. The objective is to keep the budget deficit and public debt at a level below the one set in the Maastricht criteria. The European Union, however, was able to give up, during the Covid-19 pandemic, on such a restrictive approach and suspended the applicability of those parts of SGP in the context of the higher purpose that is prompt action to counteract economic recession (Ardanaz et al., 2021). The ongoing discussions may suggest there probably will be no turning back to their original wording. Meanwhile, the broadly defined concept of budget stability refers to the comprehensive impact of fiscal policy on the value and dynamic of public debt.

G. Keliuotytė-Staniulėnienė (2015) distinguishes between three approaches to how public finance stability is identified:

- in the first approach, fiscal balance is related to solvency – it stands for the current ability to service the debt;
- in the second approach, sustainable fiscal policy is aimed to ensure adequate (as required by relevant laws) debt-to-GDP ratio;
- the third approach is the broadest one as it takes account of both solvency and the limitation on the public debt growth.

It should be emphasised that public finance stability refers to long-term and multiaspect measures, which are determined by a significant impact of external factors such as, for example, business cycle, monetary policy taking account of the current and future cost of money and currency exchange rate.

Considering public authorities' efforts to maintain public finance stability, attention should be also given to the need for public sector to continuously fulfil its basic functions: allocative, redistributive and stabilising, as well as to stave off long-term imbalance in public finance (Rutkauskas, 2015; Stiglitz, 2003). This can be achieved by developing an effective public expenditure and revenue system for public finance sector. Another thing of great significance is the level of fiscalism measured as the ratio of public finance sector revenues and expenditure to GDP. In the light of the above discussion, a question arises as to whether the fiscal policy solutions currently applied at both domestic and EU levels, make it possible to use this instrument to achieve purposes contained in the concept of building sustainable development (Kopits, 2016). In this context, it is important to examine whether instruments applied at EU level not only contribute to the issues related to budget stability and public finance stability but also take account of the elements required for the achievement of sustainable development and financial stability. Obviously the analyses being conducted must acknowledge that in the Covid-19 pandemic period, most solutions related to the fiscal instruments used at EU and domestic level were temporarily suspended or replaced with less restrictive ones. Such course of action was fully acceptable and recommended by international institutions such as International Monetary Fund, OECD and World Bank.

Researchers and economic thinkers are unanimous in pointing out the principal goals of the economic and social policy of state authorities. These include supply of public goods, income redistribution (secondary distribution of the national income) and alleviating temporary or cyclical business fluctuations (Bhattarai, 2016; Tomkiewicz, 2014). Measures leading to the achievement of those goals are referred to as specific economic functions of the fiscal policy, relating to efficiency, fairness, equity and economic stability (Tanzi, 2005). The fulfilment of all of these state functions and the achievement of economic policy goals defined in the theory of economics are enshrined in the applicable legislation in force, while the material image of the fiscal policy is reflected in the flows of public funds in the form of revenues and expenditures as well as receipts and disbursements (for more detail, see Postuła, 2015). The size of the forecasted, planned and actually implemented flows of public funds reflects the scale of respective governments' fiscal policy (Heitger, 2001). Therefore, ensuring a macroeconomic stability requires adopting a horizon whose length matches at least one full business cycle, i.e. that of several years (from four to six years). A sustainable and stable economic growth is promoted by an anti-cyclical fiscal policy, which enables proper functioning of automatic stabilisers (Hallett and Lewis, 2005). A surplus at times of growth or a deficit at times of economic slump can automatically lead to the mitigating and dampening of the business cycle fluctuations, directly translating into keeping the unemployment rate close to the natural one, and GDP, at a level close to the potential one (Mundell, 2000).

When assessing convergence, what should be taken into account is not only its level but also durability. From the point of view of the budget policy, of essential importance is the fiscal criterion, synthetically defined as the avoidance of excessive deficit, indicated in Article 126 of TFEU as one of the fundamentals of EU Member States' economic policy. The Treaty provisions relating to the avoidance of excessive deficit were further elaborated in the SGP (declaration of 16 December 1996 and in the Regulation of the Council of the European Union of 16 June 1997). Measures introduced back then included the obligation to conduct medium-term convergence and stability plans, including setting a medium-term budgetary objective (MTO) (Fourçans and Warin, 2007; Berg et al., 2012).

The arguments to support the inclusion of the provisions on budget policy coordination to the Community-level legislative regulations were introduced in the TFEU, and then elaborated on in the SGP. The participating countries committed to comply with two quantitative convergence criteria, and to maintain the budget close to balance or in surplus position in the medium term (*Specifications on the Implementation . . .*, 2005; Baran, 2013). The rules introduced in such significant regulations represented an unprecedented solution, so initially it was difficult to assess their impact on the decisions taken in Member States and on the real sphere of the economy. Hence it was impossible to establish their actual effectiveness. At the time the currency union was created, the acceding countries were compliant with the convergence criteria, from the point of view of the existing SGP provisions, even though in half of them debt exceeded 60% of GDP (which the aforementioned provisions allowed). However, time quickly verified the state of actual convergence and the quality of budgetary adjustments, disclosing the short-sightedness of the assumptions of the states' continued willingness and determination to maintain stability in the public finance sector (Baran, 2013). Most countries failed to exploit the good times to carry out solid reforms of the expenditure structure; meanwhile, theory and practice alike clearly suggest that adjustments on the expenditure side are the ones characterised by a higher effectiveness and durability than changes on the revenue side (Buti and Giudice, 2002b). Furthermore, budgetary forecasts for most countries were very optimistic, which is why the initial success in limiting excessive deficits contributed to a wrong assumption that progress in this respect would continue to be visible in the following years, too (Hallett and Lewis, 2005). The next chapter of the Monograph will present own research relating to the quality of forecasts in EU Member States in the period of the last 20 years excluding the Covid-19 period, in which not only macroeconomic indicators but also anything else was hard to predict. When analysing the economic crises it is worth presenting a number of interesting aspects. The economic slowdown in the years 2001–2002 clearly manifested the mounting problems in the euro area. Two largest countries – Germany and France – exceeded the acceptable debt and deficit levels in the public finance (European Commission, 2002, 2005a). sector and – in accordance with the relevant provisions – the excessive deficit procedure should have been launched. It quickly turned out, however, that this was impossible in practice for these countries. Consequently, in 2005, changes were decided on, which meant, in many respects, softening the originally prescribed and programmed fiscal rules.

The changes introduced back then authorised deficit-to-GDP ratio to exceed the 3% reference value in strictly defined cases. At the same time, even though practice had already demonstrated the flaws of relevant provisions, the existing mode of enforcement of budgetary rules was kept and no new disciplining tools were introduced to encourage states to make an extra effort at good economic times. On the other hands, there were also visible attempts to "adapt" the provisions to the new realities and to strengthen their effectiveness (Baran, 2013). One of them was the change in the significance attributed to respective elements of the budgetary rules system. In the first years of the euro area functioning, a key role was played by nominal convergence criteria, especially the rule relating to the budget deficit, compliance with which was – and still is to date – the fundamental condition for participating in that area. Since 2005, the numeric rule of MTO has gained clearly greater importance, though not introduced as another Maastricht and still acting as an auxiliary rule. The core assumption was that the achievement of MTO, i.e. a certain level of structural balance (from then on, varying for respective countries) would help ensure fiscal stability in Member States, while leaving some space for active budgetary policy, especially when it comes to public investments, and secure the public finance sector against excessive deficit in case of an economic downturn (Codogo, Favero, 2003; Murova and Khan, 2017). This assumption proved, however, far from the measures adopted in practice because, as was the case of other principles of the European economic coordination, no mechanisms were established for its enforcement. As a consequence, rules set at EU level were still of little effect, with most Member States continuing an expansive approach to budgetary policy. Meanwhile, in accordance with the 16th recital in the preamble to the Council Directive on requirements for budgetary frameworks of the Member States, rules should have a documented effectiveness. Strong numerical fiscal rules should come with well-specified target definitions and monitoring system, and the assessment of compliance with them should be based on a reliable and objective analysis carried out by bodies that are independent of the fiscal authorities. Therefore, according to the European Commission, what is necessary for a rule to be effectively introduced and used is the functioning of independent fiscal institutions (this problem will be discussed in more detail further in the Monograph) (Larch, 2016; Barbier-Gauchard et al., 2021).

Another effort to improve public finance consists in placing a strong emphasis on introducing medium-term perspective in budgetary planning (Bernanke, 2010). In addition to previously indicated factors, the multiannual nature of budgetary processes is, ironically, suggested by the poor flexibility of the size and structure of respective expenditures being subject to the annual planning procedure. The comparison of subsequent annual budgetary documents reveals their significant similarity. This is also confirmed by the provisions of the 20th recital in the preamble to the Council Directive on requirements for budgetary frameworks of the Member States (Holscher et al., 2017). While highlighting the importance of passing the budget law every year, they also point out that most fiscal measures have implications that go way beyond the annual budgetary cycle (Schaechter et al., 2012).

The insufficient effectiveness of the SGP implementation ultimately led to it being significantly revised in November 2011 by introducing the economic six-pack (Postuła, 2015). Legislative changes related to the principles of fiscal policy were confirmed and clarified in the Treaty on Stability, Coordination and Governance in the Economic and Monetary Union of March 2012 (effective as of 1 January 2013). The existing fiscal criterion relating to deficit (3% of GDP) and public debt (60% of GDP) limits was elaborated on. An obligation was introduced to reduce debt, on average, by one twentieth per year of the exceeded percentage points; structural deficit reduction must amount to 0.5% of GDP per annum until the MTO is achieved, with a possibility to deduct the costs of pension reforms from the deficit. Moreover, a fiscal rule must be introduced to respective EU Member States' national law enforcing a proper general government structural balance (or the achievement of a MTO) (European Commission, 2012a). To improve public finance quality, and following the post-2007 events, to limit the possibility of public finance crisis, respective countries' legislation has introduced relevant limitations to be adhered to by legislative and executive authorities alike. These limitations are structured as legal solutions to strengthen the quality and predictability of the fiscal policy by means of the so-called fiscal or numerical fiscal rules (according to the EU legislation) (Portes and Wren-Lewis, 2015).

In addition to the reformed Growth and Stability Pact, another document intended to strengthen fiscal policy coordination was the inter-governmental Treaty on Stability, Coordination and Governance agreed upon by 25 EU Member States (without Czech Republic and the United Kingdom) in 2012 and especially the so-called *Fiscal Compact* being part of the Treaty. Fiscal

Compact specified, among other things, the requirement regarding the maximum structural deficit level at 0.5% of GDP.

The structure of solutions resulting from the reform of the SGP and of the regulations contained in the six-pack and two-pack with respect to the application of fiscal rules, medium-terms budgetary frameworks and independent fiscal institutions provided for similar treatment of all EU countries irrespective of whether or not they were members of the Economic and Monetary Union. Admittedly, the Fiscal Compact imposed more rigorous requirements on the euro area countries, but the fact that most non-EMU countries fully acceded to in on a voluntary basis warrants the conclusion that these regulations should have a similar impact on the implementation of respective fiscal instruments, whether or not a given country is an EMU member state. Taking account of the above, a comparison can be drawn as to the strength of respective fiscal instruments between euro area countries and EU Member States where national currency is in use (Franek and Postuła, 2020).

To assess the state of fiscal policy and the manner in which its goals and functions are pursued, reliable, timely, full and understandable information must be available. Shortage of information in this area is an obstacle to civil society development, decreases the accountability of public authorities, and, consequently it means there is a democratic deficit (Nucci, 2007). Transparency requires the functioning of correct accounting and statistical reporting systems. One of the ways transparency can be increased is by integrating efficiency information (performance budgeting) in budgeting procedures. When introducing in 2011 some changes to the wording of regulations making up the SGP, a decision was made to greatly extend the common rules governing detailed public finance management procedures. To improve the quality of these processes in EU countries is the aim of the aforementioned Council Directive 2011/85/EU of 2011 on requirements for budgetary frameworks of the Member States. The term "budgetary frameworks" is to be understood as a set of arrangements, procedures, rules and institutions that underlie the conduct of budgetary policies of general government. EU Member States were obliged to enact regulations necessary to implement the recommendations of this directive by the end of 2013. In practice, this document is a unique compendium of solutions successfully used by countries with the most advanced public finance management systems (Keliuotytė-Staniulėnienė, 2015). Its main recommendations relate to statistics and accounting, forecasts, numerical fiscal rules, medium-term budgetary frameworks (MTBF) and transparency of public finance. Regulations contained in this directive are largely consistent with the areas of public finance reform identified earlier on the basis of OECD research (Schick, 2010). In summary, it can be said that the European Union responded to various kinds of crises by loosening fiscal discipline as part of the solutions available at the Community level and recommended implementing different public finance management instruments at domestic level (see Figure 2.1)

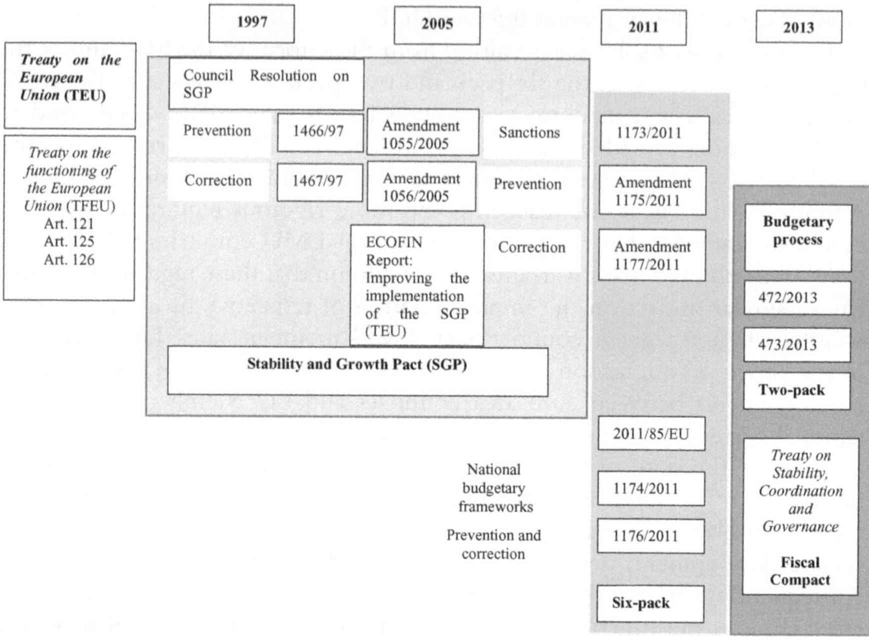

Figure 2.1 Evolution of the Stability and Growth Pact in the European Union

Source: Franek and Postula, 2019 based on Šehović (2015).

It is hard to debate the advisability of implementing this kind of solutions, but it is worth checking to what extent such solutions are implemented by respective countries and assessed by the European Commission.

2.2 Medium-term planning documents as reliable tools for assessing the financial situation of EU countries

Multiannual planning in the public sector has a long history throughout which the function and role of this instrument have changed in individual countries. In the years 1970–1980, MTBF served only as the main instrument for identifying new government programmes and allocating funds to them in future budgets. With such an approach in place, a number of essential issues were not taken into account and some drawbacks would arise such as a tendency to overestimate the economic growth and public resources that can be redistributed in a given period as well as public institutions' perception of forecasts as part of medium-term frameworks as an authorisation to spend money. As a result, any updates involving a decrease in outlays were very difficult, even when it became clear that the economic assumptions were overoptimistic. A perfect example of a country grappling with such problems would be the United

Kingdom, where multiannual spending programmes were presented until 1982 in real rather than in nominal values. When economic growth and inflation accelerated or fell, the forecasting of expenditure was automatically adapted to the changing macroeconomic conditions. Expenditure caps were introduced in the annual budget in 1976 and until 1982 they existed in parallel with multiannual expenditure. In the following period, medium-term financial planning in real terms was replaced in the United Kingdom with expenditure estimates expressed in nominal prices to ensure consistency with a given year's budget. Such a presentation was entirely abandoned in 1995. Since 1998, forecasts have been presented in the form of a three-year budget. Admittedly, these estimates do not include new programmes or major extensions of the existing ones, but their effects in terms of budgetary expenditure planning are similar to those previously known.

Meanwhile, in the United States, some elements of medium-term planning were in use starting from 1960 and became a formal part of the budget process. Currently, medium-term planning in this country is strongly integrated with long-term planning – a full financial projection is presented in the appendices to the federal budget bill, broken down into respective classification items (mostly federal programmes) until 2024. The same perspective applies to presenting the results of the cyclical outcomes assessment conducted as part of reviews of functional spending relating to federal programmes, among other things (that document is also attached every year to the federal budget bill).

Medium-term public finance management did not, however, worked in practice everywhere and in every period. There are examples of countries (e.g. developing countries), where MTBF were prepared (in the years 1970–1980), which did not yield the expected results as they were a relatively ineffective tool for macroeconomic policy and for curbing the expenditure growth, but they merely fulfilled the function of a pilot implementation of sorts, an exercise in budgetary planning, if you will. What can be cited as the main reasons is a major impact of political factors and the absence of medium-term governmental programmes which could serve as a point of reference and an information basis for developing real multiannual financial projections.

Development strategies and programmes, including public investments and public finance consolidation and restructuring processes, have a multiannual horizon. Both material and immaterial effects of the measures as part of their implementation are usually significantly delayed compared to the time they were planned, and they rarely have a timespan of just one budget year. The EU Council Directive on requirements for budgetary frameworks of the Member States imposes the obligation to found the budgetary planning on reliable and effective MTBF with at least a three-year timespan (Mourre et al., 2013). In compliance with that directive, medium-term frameworks include multiannual deficit and debt objectives, spending and revenue forecasts, a description of measures as well as an assessment of the impact of the adopted timespan on the long-term public finance stability. Each subsequent budget law should be consistent with MTBF. Such an approach can be found in essence in measures adopted by respective countries.

Ever since the beginning of the EU existence, Member States have declared commitment to having a responsible economic policy in place, one conducive to stable and sustainable development for the association as a whole (Rebelo, 1993). A good functioning of the entire community requires, however, an adequate level of actual convergence consisting in levelling out the differences in the social and economic development between respective regions and Member States, in aiming for the alignment of business cycles, etc.

The variable structure of national documents developed on the basis of historical data largely results from the diversity of their problem areas, functions and implementation periods. To a great extent, this is also related to the absence of universal models (which is characteristic of modern public management methods). Following an in-depth analysis, it seems, however, that the introduction of some nationwide standards in this domain increases the consistency of social and economic programming and the informational and analytical value of the documents being developed, especially those of strategic importance to a given state (Wynen et al., 2016). The effectiveness of financial planning is contingent on the quality and efficiency of the management system as a whole (Young and Grant, 2015; Speklé and Verbeeten, 2014). Management is a process oriented towards formulation and implementation, and then – which is of special importance – an evolution of strategies to ensure an organisation's perfect adaptation to the surrounding conditions and the achievement of its strategic goals (Weerakkody et al., 2016; Hausner, 2013). The principal functions of strategic management in public finance include analysing the external environment (diagnosis, analysis, *ex ante* evaluation), forecasting the directions of change and development of processes and phenomena taking place in it, analysing the situation and the existing opportunities within the public finance sector, updating and verifying the adopted solutions throughout their functioning (adaptation to the dynamically changing environment) and evaluating performance against goals (*ex post* evaluation, among others) (Van Ravensway and Hamlin, 2015; Laihonen et al., 2014).

The use of medium-term forecasts to properly define public debt rules at the very beginning of the budget preparation process helps assess if the expenditure (and revenue) policy is consistent with the government's medium-term financial objectives and with the expenditure ceilings adopted by the same (Xerri et al., 2015). This guarantees an early warning about the need to make changes to the expenditure or revenue policy to anticipate any medium-term threats to fiscal policy. Another essential function of forecasting is providing assistance in the development of proposed policy changes. Analyses of the changes in the direction of expenditure may be based on an agreed multiannual cost of each new initiative. This provides the certainty that decisions on new proposals are not taken on the basis of limited information on the costs sustained in the first year only; it is worth relying in this respect on historical data from the relevant past period.

When it comes to EU-level planning, in April of every year, euro area countries submit stability programmes to the European Commission and Council, while non-euro area countries provide convergence programmes. These programmes must contain a state's MTO and information on how it will be achieved. They also include an analysis of the outcomes of changes to the main economic assumptions relating to the state's fiscal position. This means that a unilateral analysis of the fiscal side has been replaced, over the last couple of years, with a much more versatile perspective. Convergence/stability programmes are now presented, as part of the European semester, together with the national reform programmes and the new thing is that further to Covid-19 there are also national recovery programmes, which must be compatible with those mentioned above as well as with national climate and energy plans. In other words, a holistic approach is now much appreciated, and, because of the times we live in, fiscal policy will, for a good couple of years, probably be "one of" rather than the main point of reference. It can be therefore concluded that this is a very significant qualitative change compared to the past.

All the programmes mentioned are checked by the European Commission. If the nominal convergence criteria are not met, the European Council – based on the Commission's recommendations – will launch the excessive deficit procedure (EDP). EDP imposes on a country the obligation to present the corrective actions planned to improve the condition of public finance and may impose different sanctions for non-compliance. Sanctions refer to a greater extent to euro area member states, but there are also possibilities to apply them to a non-euro area country.

Solutions as to the application of MTBF vary substantially across EU countries. Undoubtedly, the six-pack provided a strong impulse for their introduction, which can be clearly seen when comparing data from 2009 and 2019 for the European Index on the quality of MTBF, which will be discussed in more detail further in the subchapter (see Figure 2.2).

In most cases, MTBF are prepared by the government and presented to the parliament for information purposes at best. In some countries, they are, however, approved by the parliament (e.g. Austria, Czech Republic, France, Greece, Latvia, Sweden). A detailed overview of solutions for the use of MTBF in respective EU countries can be found in paper by Jankovits and Sherwood (2017) and in the report published by European Union Independent Fiscal Institutions (2018).

The diversity of the existing arrangements is well exemplified by the Netherlands, Finland and Sweden. The Netherlands is a good example of a credible political commitment, which is not formalised, i.e. there is no law or parliamentary resolution on creating MTBF. At the beginning of the government's term of office, the newly created coalition may choose to revise earlier budgetary frameworks. Then, the government sets budgetary assumptions for the following four years, which are defined in the agreement between parties to the coalition. These assumptions include separate expenditure ceilings for social security, healthcare and other government spending. There is always a

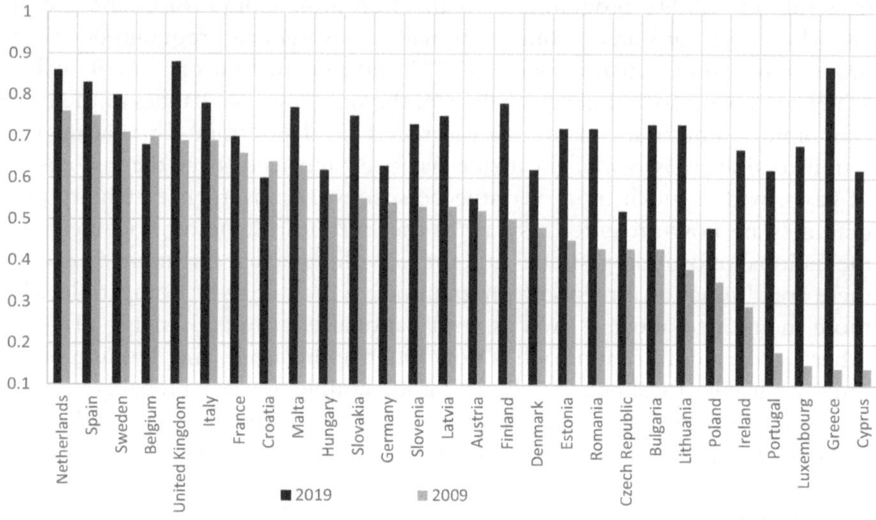

Figure 2.2 Index on the quality of medium-term budgetary frameworks in EU Member States in 2009 and 2019

Source: own elaboration based on data from the European Commission.

possibility to renegotiate the coalition agreement and raise the ceilings, subject to the reservation that the sources of finance for these increases must be first identified.

In case of Finland, there is no legally binding requirement, either. Finland's current fiscal frameworks are based on multiannual expenditure ceilings. The overall purpose of the government's programme translates into the government's decision on expenditure ceiling for the four-year parliamentary term, which are defined in real terms. The government programme is a public agreement between coalition partners, which is submitted to the parliament in the form of government's statement. The preparation and publication of the programme are mandatory. This is why, though not legally binding, it remains very important from the political point of view.

Sweden is another interesting case. Since 2010, Swedish government has been legally obliged to set expenditure ceilings for three subsequent years. This is formally done in the draft budget law presented in the autumn of the year preceding the three-year period. Expenditure ceilings for the central government are set at nominal values and remain unchanged. Though there are no formal obstacles for the Swedish parliament to reassessing the established ceilings, there is a strong expectation that ceilings will be used until the change of government. If a risk of exceeding the approved ceiling is detected during a year, the government is obliged to take measures to avoid this, even though there is no formal procedure to enforce corrective measures, except for the cost of lost reputation.

The time horizon covered by these frameworks usually corresponds to the three-year period indicated as a minimum in the Directive 2011/85/EU, though there are countries that use a four-year period (e.g. Denmark, Estonia, Finland, Germany, Greece, Italy, Luxembourg, the Netherlands, Portugal). Usually frameworks are of the rolling variety, meaning that every year their period is extended by another year. For Finland, the Netherlands and the United Kingdom, the plan has a fixed timeframe, which follows the duration of the parliamentary term.

MTBF also differ in terms of the degree of detail. By way of example, in Sweden and Finland, the main attention is given to the projections of total expenditure of the central government. In several countries, the multiannual ceilings are set at the level of respective ministers (Cyprus, Greece, France, Ireland, the United Kingdom). There are also cases where the first years of a multiannual plan are shown in greater detail than the following years. This is what happens in France, where the overall expenditure ceiling is set for respective subsectors in a five-year horizon, but the first three years are covered by expenditure ceilings assigned to 30 government subsector divisions.

OECD study results reveal that forecasts and medium-term plans are usually updated annually. Only in six countries the update of these plans is conducted every two to three years instead. The scope and complexity of medium-term plans in respective countries always stem from their past experiences with medium-term forecasting. The success and efficiency of the procedures used is mostly related to maintaining the balance between better predictability and adequate flexibility. In most cases, the pivotal element of the medium-term plan is forecasting expenditure, both obligatory/fixed and flexible.

An argument in favour of the annual revision of medium-term plans is the ability to use them as the basis for preparing an annual budget law. This solution is characterised by a sufficient flexibility resulting from the possibility to adapt, on a yearly basis, to the changing internal and external circumstances. A yearly frequency of the update also enables a proper response where priorities change as a result of the parliamentary election and helps limit the negative consequences of the so-called budget games, for example launching costly investment projects while earmarking minor funds in the current annual budget. This was a commonly used tactic in a centrally planned economy but in a market economy, too, there is a risk of it being applied to the budget. All changes of budget plans and forecasts, irrespective of their causes, are made in keeping with the medium-term perspective.

In 27 OECD countries, medium-term planning is a task of the executive branch of government, but in 10 of those countries, medium-term plans are approved by the parliament. A 2018 OECD paper discusses the principles of medium-term budgetary planning which determine the success of those processes. These principles are as follows: conservative expenditure and revenue planning, support for limiting expenditure, plan complexity to strengthen its reliability, simplicity to make the plan understandable to citizens and legislative bodies, consistency with development strategies and transparency of the annual expenditure changes compared to previous plans.

An issue of key importance is the degree of the linkage between multiannual frameworks and the annually enacted budget. The closest ties can be observed in Scandinavian countries. Though in Finland the expenditure ceilings in place refer to real amounts (meaning that the inflation rate has an impact on the final expenditure), in both Sweden and Finland the public expenditure ceiling set in the medium-term frameworks may be modified only in the event of change of government. The interesting news is that these ceiling are not legally binding so they are the result of political arrangements (coalition agreement), but in both countries, the cost of lost reputation is emphasised as the principal safeguard against exceeding the agreed ceilings. Similar solutions are in place also in the Netherlands, where, even though some provisions were introduced into its law due to the need to implement the EU Directive, in practice, these measures are secondary in nature and follow the political agreement. In countries such as Germany, Croatia, Slovakia and Slovenia, government is in no way bound by ceilings set out in the MTBF and can, at any point, scrap them without being obliged to offer explanation to the public. Poland is in the group of countries (some other being Czech Republic, Spain, France, the United Kingdom), whose governments can, at their discretion, change, during a given year, the expenditure ceilings set in the multiannual plan. This means that MTBF are presentational in nature for most EU countries.

Using the above information retrieved from surveys from Member States, European Commission's Directorate General for Economic and Financial Affairs developed an index on the quality of medium-term budgetary frameworks (*MTBF Index*), which is annually updated (since 2006) and published on its website. The index takes account of the existence and characteristics of national MTBF as well as of the preparation, and status of stability and convergence programmes. It captures the quality of MTBF through five criteria: 1) coverage of the targets/ceilings included in the national medium-term fiscal plans; 2) connectedness between the targets/ceilings included in the national medium-term fiscal plans and the annual budgets; 3) involvement of national parliament in the preparation of the national medium-term fiscal plans; 4) involvement of independent fiscal institutions in the preparation of the national medium-term fiscal plans; and 5) level of detail included in the national medium-term fiscal plans (European Commission, 2020b). The grading scale for respective criteria is provided in Appendix 1 (Table 2.1).

Certain problems with using this type of indicators to assess complex institutional aspects should be borne in mind: they cannot take account of all factors and characteristics underlying different budgetary frameworks and they identify the existence of specific normative solutions rather than measuring the actual implementation of MTBFs and their effectiveness in the context of the national budget process. Despite those limitations, an approach involving numerical indices is gaining quite a popularity because of their simplicity, even at the expense of some oversimplifications (Franek and Postuła, 2020). Meanwhile, the European Commission is working systematically on perfecting the methodology in use. Last change in that respect took place in 2015.

Table 2.1 The value of MTBF index in the European Union countries in the years 2010–2019.

Country/Year	*2010*	*2011*	*2012*	*2013*	*2014*	*2015*	*2016*	*2017*	*2018*	*2019*
Austria	0.52	0.52	0.52	0.52	0.52	0.60	0.60	0.55	0.55	0.55
Belgium	0.70	0.70	0.70	0.70	0.70	0.68	0.68	0.68	0.68	0.68
Bulgaria	0.54	0.54	0.54	0.54	0.75	0.73	0.73	0.73	0.73	0.73
Cyprus	0.14	0.14	0.14	0.35	0.56	0.67	0.67	0.62	0.62	0.62
Czech Republic	0.43	0.43	0.43	0.43	0.43	0.33	0.33	0.40	0.53	0.53
Germany	0.54	0.54	0.54	0.64	0.64	0.48	0.48	0.48	0.63	0.63
Denmark	0.41	0.41	0.62	0.62	0.62	0.62	0.62	0.62	0.62	0.62
Estonia	0.72	0.72	0.72	0.72	0.72	0.67	0.67	0.72	0.72	0.72
Greece	0.57	0.64	0.71	0.71	0.71	0.87	0.87	0.87	0.87	0.87
Spain	0.75	0.75	0.84	0.84	0.84	0.83	0.83	0.83	0.83	0.83
Finland	0.50	0.50	0.50	0.50	0.50	0.73	0.73	0.78	0.78	0.78
France	0.74	0.74	0.82	0.82	0.82	0.70	0.70	0.70	0.70	0.70
Croatia	0.64	0.64	0.64	0.64	0.64	0.60	0.60	0.60	0.60	0.60
Hungary	0.37	0.37	0.37	0.47	0.47	0.45	0.45	0.62	0.62	0.62
Ireland	0.29	0.38	0.57	0.57	0.57	0.67	0.67	0.67	0.67	0.67
Italy	0.79	0.79	0.79	0.79	0.79	0.78	0.78	0.78	0.78	0.78
Lithuania	0.23	0.23	0.54	0.54	0.69	0.73	0.73	0.73	0.73	0.73
Luxembourg	0.15	0.15	0.15	0.15	0.59	0.73	0.73	0.68	0.68	0.68
Latvia	0.53	0.53	0.53	0.95	0.95	0.75	0.75	0.75	0.75	0.75
Malta	0.72	0.72	0.72	0.72	0.72	0.77	0.77	0.77	0.77	0.77
Netherlands	0.76	0.95	0.95	0.95	0.95	0.80	0.80	0.85	0.85	0.85
Poland	0.35	0.43	0.43	0.43	0.43	0.43	0.43	0.48	0.48	0.48
Portugal	0.18	0.46	0.55	0.64	0.64	0.62	0.62	0.62	0.62	0.62
Romania	0.96	0.96	0.96	0.96	0.96	0.72	0.72	0.72	0.72	0.72
Sweden	0.71	0.71	0.71	0.71	0.80	0.80	0.80	0.80	0.80	0.80
Slovenia	0.53	0.53	0.53	0.53	0.53	0.63	0.73	0.73	0.73	0.73
Slovakia	0.55	0.55	0.55	0.55	0.55	0.75	0.75	0.75	0.75	0.75
United Kingdom	0.69	0.69	0.69	0.69	0.69	0.88	0.88	0.88	0.88	0.88

Source: European Commission, Directorate-General for Economic and Financial Affairs.

2.3 Fiscal rules as an instrument to support fiscal discipline

Fiscal rules have come to rely on legal and constitutional basis over the past 150 years (Günaydın and Eser, 2009). The evolution of fiscal rules can be divided into three main periods. In the first one, some lower-level governments in countries such as the United States and Sweden adopted the golden rule and declared an obligation to have a balanced budget (Morris and Schuknecht, 2007). In the second one, after World War 2, a number of industrialised countries, including Germany, Italy, Japan and the Netherlands, adopted balanced budget rules to support their stability programmes. Those rules were similar to the golden rule but reserved the right to finance deficits from specific funds – chiefly from central banks. In the third period – which can be also referred to as the current period – fiscal rules including restrictive balanced budget rules were adopted by many countries (Budimir, 2017). In Europe, fiscal rules took effect in 1992, together with the Maastricht Treaty. The number of countries implementing fiscal rules has significantly increased since the 1990s. In the early 1990s, the largest number of fiscal rules were in use at lower tiers of government – at the local and regional level. Perhaps this can be explained by the tendency to impose limitations on subnational government to ensure both better coordination between respective levels of government and a more efficient control of their activities. In 1990, fiscal rules were used in only seven countries (Germany, France, the United States, Luxembourg, Spain, Japan, Italy). Since the mid-1990s, however, an increasing number of fiscal rules imposed on all government levels can be observed. Currently, nearly 100 countries use fiscal rules (Blume, Voigt, 2011).

Fiscal rules are seen nowadays as an element of transparent fiscal policy. Of major importance in this case is the increased predictability of public sector activities (Poterba, 1994). Indirectly, compliance with the rules may also make it necessary to carry out essential systemic reforms. The identified goals of the rules must be consistent with their structure and so with their scale of impact. Rules often lay the groundwork for the fiscal policy, are intended to discipline public finance and limit its imbalance as well as support sustainable economic growth (Kopits and Symansky, 1998; Lupu et al., 2018). At EU level, as mentioned in Chapter 1, two principal rules are in place, as defined in the Maastricht criteria, i.e. public debt rule and public finance deficit rule. Euro area Member States are obliged to comply with them while the other EU countries should aim for compliance (Wickens, 2000). Compliance with the fiscal criterion of nominal convergence should, in the medium and long runs, support social and economic development at the level of EU Member State as well as enable the processes of nominal and real convergence within the Community (Wyplosz, 2012).

The implementation of a desirable and rational fiscal policy is to be backed by relevant legal solutions. The example of Greece demonstrates that years of major deviations from compliance with the rules lead the economy astray (Von Hagen and Wolf, 2006). The current attempts at verifying those rules over a decade into their use by a relatively large group of countries (over 20 countries declare to use them) are especially significant and desirable.

The effectiveness of public debt rules depends on the determination of their authors, on the goals set, on a number of structural characteristics, and especially on the way they are monitored and enforced (Hallerberg et al., 2007). In addition, the functioning of public debt rules can be accompanied by negative outcomes for the quality of public spending, and the same potential "traps" as those observed for deficit rules – especially with reference to the stabilising function of public finance (Bova et al., 2014). Like other fiscal rules, public debt rules ought to be applied over a medium-term perspective, have a stabilising effect on the economy and reduce the potential pro-cyclicality of the government action (IMF, 2017). Efficiency of this type of rules lies, to a great extent, in the policy coordination at all administration levels involved in setting the budgetary targets, which helps counterbalance the possible pro-cyclical effects of government debt. An anti-cyclical definition of public debt rules may be strengthened by an "escape clause" by means of discretionary revenues (Bova et al., 2015).

Based on the analysis of fiscal rules databases, a general tendency can be seen whereby most countries that use fiscal rules have more than one rule. Firstly, this is due to a specific group of countries using supranational fiscal rules, as can be observed in EU Member States, which are obliged to apply the budget deficit rule and public debt rule. Secondly, this stems from the growing awareness that the use of one fiscal rule only entails some weaknesses and does not allow more complex and comprehensive impact on public finance consolidation. Consequently, many countries introduced national rules as a complement to the supranational fiscal rules used. Undoubtedly, the most important breakdown of the rules is the one classifying them by their intended scope, i.e. the indicator underlying the structure of a given rule (Table 2.2).

In reality, there is a major variability of methods used to design fiscal rules worldwide (Eyraud et al., 2018). Addressing the concerns over the lack of capacity for adaptation to shocks, respective countries introduced flexibility elements to their budgetary frameworks, such as cyclically adjusted budgetary targets, well-defined escape clauses in the event of unforeseen shocks and investment-friendly regulations, which are rules that exclude capital expenditures from numerical targets imposed on fiscal aggregates (Guerguil et al., 2017). This type of rules are becoming increasingly popular all over the world. Before 1995, fewer than 15 countries had adopted at least one such flexible characteristic whereas by 2015 their number had risen to 52. By that time, 57% of the countries with an implemented fiscal rule had adopted at least one flexible function, often more than one at the same time. For example, 60% of the

Table 2.2 Fiscal rules by their scope.

Type of fiscal rules	*Structure*		
Budget balance rules	Balanced budget rule	Golden rule	Budgetary deficit ceilings (nominal or as % of GDP)
Debt rules	Debt ceiling in nominal terms	Debt ceiling as % of GDP or budgetary revenues	Debt ceiling related to repayment capacity
Expenditure rules	Nominal expenditure ceiling	Real expenditure ceiling	Nominal or real expenditure growth rate
Revenue rules	Tax burden as % of GDP	Rule based on change of tax rates	Scope of allocation of extra budget revenues

Source: own elaboration based on European Commission (2009). Public Finances in EMU 2009. *European Economy*, no. 5, European Commission; Luxembourg: Office for Official Publications of the European Communities. Retrieved from: http://ec.europa.eu/economy_finance/publications/pages/publication15390_en.pdf.

countries with fiscal rules containing correction clauses also have investment-friendly regulations or cyclically adjusted targets or both (Ardanaz et al., 2021).

Ever since the beginning of the pandemic, the EU and its Member States have introduced unprecedented measures to protect human life and livelihood. In response to the Covid-19 pandemic and as part of the coordinated EU approach, some EU countries introduced budgetary measures aimed to increase the healthcare capabilities, stop the pandemic and provide help to individuals and sectors particularly affected by its effects. The EU supported national efforts to respond to the health crisis and alleviate the effects of the economic slump.

The medium- and long-term consequences of the Covid-19 pandemic will largely depend on how quickly the economy is rebuilt in Member States, which, in turn, will be conditioned on the measures adopted by Member States to alleviate the social and economic consequences of the crisis, with the help of the EU. Member States should benefit from the recovery package, which will help finance the key reforms and investments aimed to boost the growth potential and resilience of the economy. Having these factors in mind, fiscal rules in the years 2020–2022 are not applicable in the context of higher goals such as preventing the deepening of the economic recession. In February 2020, the European Commission started its economic governance review, in which EU principles visibly play the leading role. The crisis caused by the Covid-19 pandemic drew the attention away from efforts to ensure solid fiscal balance. In March 2020, the European Council launched a clause allowing a deviation from the regulations contained in the SGP. Such an approach is quite contrary to the one adopted after the crisis of 2007–2008, where in the following years, the European Union introduced the six-pack as a system of tools to discipline Member States (Figure 2.3).

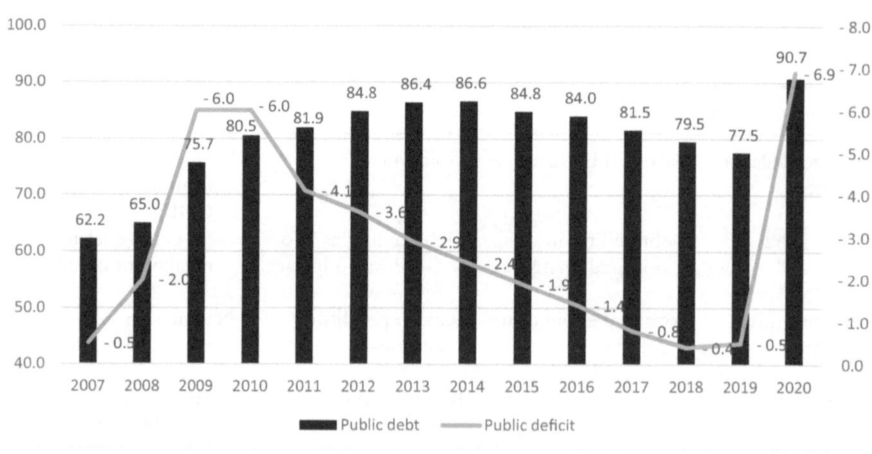

Figure 2.3 Public debt criterion and budget deficits in the European Union 2007–2020 (i.e. taking account of the consequences of both crises)

Source: Eurostat

The public finance situation in Member States has definitely deteriorated (see diagram 2) and the measures adopted vary from country to country, but it is too early now to form a judgment on these developments. What matters, however, is the need to bear in mind the opinions voiced by the International Monetary Fund (2021).

> The covid-19 pandemic and the global economic contraction will put rule-based fiscal frameworks to the test. The severity of the shock will likely result in a temporary large deterioration in the fiscal deficit and public debt. Many countries are already activating escape clauses to deviate or suspend the fiscal rules. It will be important to ensure the use of this flexibility is temporary and done transparently, including explaining the size of the deviation and process to return to the rule, to preserve the credibility of the fiscal framework.

It is well documented in the economic literature that the existence of a fiscal rule in a country is correlated with fiscal discipline measured with fiscal balance (Tapsoba, 2012; Friedrich et al., 2018). This correlation, however, is complicated by endogeneity (more disciplined and prudent governments have a tendency to adopt fiscal rules) or by a reversed causality (many fiscal rules are adopted post-crisis). Furthermore, discipline is mainly determined by the actual strength of the rule rather than by its sheer existence (Bergman et al., 2016). To ensure greater fiscal discipline, fiscal rules need to be adequately designed (strong and effective) (Caselli and Reynaud, 2020).

The strength and quality of a fiscal rule is assessed by the Fiscal Rule Index (FRI) used by the European Commission. It is a commonly applied quality metric for fiscal rules, with its value calculated on the basis of data submitted yearly by all EU Member States in questionnaires developed by the European Commission. Based thereon, the European Commission has prepared, since 1990, a dataset relating to the properties of national fiscal rules in EU countries.

This dataset contains data on all types of numerical fiscal rules used at respective administration levels in all EU Member States, collected for the first time in 2006 and updated on a yearly basis (European Commission, 2007a, 2007b). The scope of information covered by the questionnaire includes the description and definition of the fiscal rule and its coverage, legal form, monitoring bodies, correction mechanisms in case of deviation from the rule as well as experience with compliance with the rules. The method to obtain the final index value that is comparable for all Member States is divided into several stages leading to the calculation of the FRI. The International Monetary Fund uses a similar calculation method for establishing the strength of fiscal rules (Kumar et al., 2009; Schaechter et al., 2012).

The analysis involves fiscal data, economic growth dynamics and Human Development Index, formulating seven questions on the observed (or not) cause end effect relationships. Answers to those questions help verify if a fiscal criterion has been correctly used (or deviations were correctly applied), irrespective of the purely formal need to meet the adopted Treaty obligations. They also indicate the economic effectiveness of the rules applicable as part of the Maastricht criteria. The effectiveness reflects the extent to which the objectives set in convergence programmes or stability programmes have been met and to which the policy, fiscal policy in this case, achieves what it has intended, in the form of relevant macroeconomic indicators (Guerguil et al., 2016). Effectiveness indicators for selected budgetary frameworks basically focus on measuring changes in the main fiscal indicators (especially Maastricht criteria), which reflect the purposes of the solutions introduced by the directive.

However, performance metrics alone (macroeconomic indicators in this case) do not provide information on the causality – on whether the use of 2011 solutions has brought about specific outcomes. Economists apply the concept of alternative scenario to determine what would happen had those solutions not been used. The effectiveness of budgetary frameworks should be measured as a change compared to such alternative scenario (Moździerz, 2015). Yet when analysing and assessing the effectiveness of budgetary frameworks, an alternative scenario cannot be applied as there are too many other factors, for example those related to the specificity of respective EU Member States or to the public finance regulations used by them. Such factors cannot be separated from the analysis to show only the effectiveness of the solutions relating to budgetary frameworks.

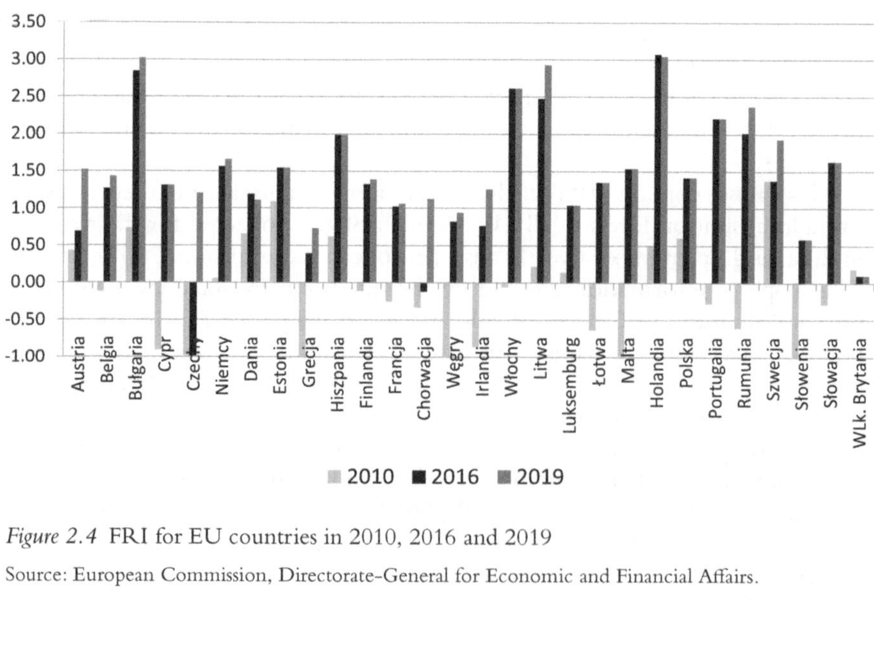

Figure 2.4 FRI for EU countries in 2010, 2016 and 2019

Source: European Commission, Directorate-General for Economic and Financial Affairs.

2.4 Independent fiscal institutions

The economic practice of the second half of the 20th century and of the beginning of the 21st century shows the existence of long-term shortcomings in the fiscal policy, chiefly manifested by excessive deficits and public debt, even at good economic times. The democratic system and the electoral cycle have formed an excessive tendency for a pro-cyclical fiscal policy, which limits a potential effectiveness of automatic stabilisers. Another thing worth noting is the specific challenges for public finance, especially present in the European Union countries, related to the long-term process of population ageing and to the consequences of a single monetary policy as part of the monetary union. Introducing independent fiscal institutions as a complement to the governmental bodies responsible for the fiscal policy is a way to remedy these problems and to improve the quality of the fiscal policy. Moreover, European Fiscal Board (EFB) was established by Commission Decision (EU) 2015/1937 in October 2015 and became fully operational in October 2016. The European Commission largely took the lead in defining the mandate of the EFB, bypassing Member States. EFB's responsibilities include preparing and publishing a yearly report in autumn and providing an assessment of the prospective fiscal stance appropriate for the euro area – every summer as part of the annual cycle of the European semester. Within its mandate, the EFB also provides ad hoc advice to the Commission President as requested. In 2019, Commission President Juncker approached EFB for the first time to prepare an ad hoc evaluation of six-pack and two-pack reforms (European Fiscal Board, 2019). The debates held in 2021 show that the role of EFB in fiscal policy making in Member States may significantly increase in the future.

As part of research into improving the quality of public expenditure, OECD working groups and experts worked out a definition of an independent fiscal institution, which provides fiscal policy monitoring and guidance. First and foremost, they concluded that the functioning of such an institution needs to have a proper legal basis and it should have in its employment non-partisan economics, finance and management professionals.

According to the broadest definition worded by the European Commission (EC), Independent Fiscal Institutions are non-partisan public bodies, other than the central bank, government or parliament whose tasks include production of macroeconomic forecasts for the budget, monitoring compliance with fiscal rules and/or advising the government on fiscal policy matters. They are financial institutions financed by public funds, but they are functionally independent, especially vis-à-vis the government. In its definition, EC also admits the possibility of these tasks being fulfilled by national Courts of Auditors.

The substantial interest this type of institutions enjoys among international organisations stems from the fact that – especially in the context of changes in the governance situation following the last crisis – there is a marked tendency among OECD countries to establish independent fiscal institutions, usually referred to as fiscal councils or parliamentary budget offices. According to the

OECD definition, the task of fiscal councils as independent fiscal institutions is to increase pressure towards maintaining fiscal discipline, raise the quality of debate on public finance and promote budget transparency and accountability. The functioning of this type of institutions is treated as one of the ways to strengthen independent oversight and responsibility over the government's fiscal policy and/or to enhance the credibility of the budget forecasts conducted.

The interest in the advantages and benefits of establishing independent fiscal institutions actually has a much longer tradition. In the mid-1990s, economic theoreticians voiced the view that countries should take advantage of the good operating practices of independent central banks, and develop similar solutions for fiscal policy. It was the growth of deficit and public sector debt that triggered the discussion on independent fiscal institutions. First, governments tried to strengthen the fiscal rules. In many cases, however, the rules turned out to be an insufficient instrument, so they were strengthened by the operation of independent fiscal institutions, whose independence was to guarantee the effectiveness of the policy. The creation of these institutions was to reassure the external environment that the fiscal policy is evaluated by independent bodies. In euro area countries, new regulations require Member States to base their draft budgets on independent macroeconomic forecasts and to indicate which independent bodies check the compliance with national fiscal rules. Independent fiscal institutions were established relatively recently also in non-European countries, for example in Canada, where such bodies were put in place at the country's own initiative. This was not due to any association agreement but to a conviction that such a solution needs to be applied. These institutions were established to increase the transparency of the fiscal policy and to strengthen the legislator's role in the budget process. In addition to this new generation of independent fiscal institutions, there are also other institutional solutions such as: Congressional Budget Office (CBO) in the United States, Belgian High Council of Finance (HCF) and the Netherlands Bureau for Economic Policy Analysis (CPB) (Możdzierz, 2015).

When analysing the available data referring to the topic in question, it is worth noting that starting 2013, most OECD counties have had an independent fiscal institution or are in the process of establishing one. Their number doubled from eight in 2007 to 16 in 2012. The role and structure of these bodies vary significantly across countries. Some are established as part of a statutory executive body, while others were put in place through legislative efforts. The operating costs differ, too. For example, the US CBO has the largest budget – USD 45 million and a staff of ca. 250, while the Irish *Fiscal Advisory Council* costs EUR 1 million a year. Three institutions have their budgets linked to multiannual financial programmes, increasing their independence and helping shield them from political pressure (Australia, the Netherlands and the United Kingdom).

In most cases, independent fiscal institutions prepare official forecasts in the field of broadly defined fiscal policy, especially macroeconomic forecasts. Others are tasked with preparing forecasts that are alternative to those developed by executive bodies (the United States and Canada), while yet some others are only expected to express opinions on governmental forecasts (France); last but not least, there are those (Australia) that play no role in the macroeconomic forecasting process. In addition to macroeconomic forecasting, typical tasks of independent fiscal institutions can be said to include analysing budget proposals submitted by executive bodies, checking compliance of the fiscal targets with fiscal regulations and analysing the financial consequences of the new legislative analyses.

A fiscal institution's independence is the key to success measured with the effectiveness of its activities. The independence is reflected by a clear definition and identification of factors that ensure it, such as:

- management members selected on the basis of their achievements and technical competence, clearly set limit on terms of office (preferably independent on the electoral cycle), well-defined criteria and procedure for staff dismissal and recruitment control;
- ability to establish its own work programme as part of its mandate, with an authority to proactively create reports and analyses;
- separate budget and multiannual financial plan;
- guaranteed access to information on government's activities.

The last factor refers to the internal functioning of independent fiscal institutions and is decisive for the transparency of their operations. The opinions given by these institutions on fiscal policy help build credibility of the exchange of information with the society. The impact of independent fiscal institutions on the fiscal policy making is significant and does not stem from legal constraint, sanction or other penal measures. This impact should largely consist in having a public debate as this is the way to raise awareness of voters, who may exert pressure on the government to conduct its fiscal policy in a transparent and responsible manner.

All of the independent fiscal institutions operating within OECD countries publish reports of their activities at the end of every year, making information available to the media and other interested parties. A great opportunity for preparing independent fiscal institutions' reports is afforded by legislative discussions on the budget preparation, principles underlying the budget policy, fiscal policy objectives and its macroeconomic framework as well as fiscal risk. A great majority of independent fiscal institutions submit their reports to the parliament and/or bring interested parliamentary bodies up to speed even when there is no such formal requirement. When independent fiscal institutions operate directly within the legislative body, they naturally have more frequent contacts with legislative committees. In other cases, they undertake great efforts to contribute to the debate already at the legislative stage rather than as late as at the executive one.

Independent fiscal institutions (fiscal councils) are the most widespread form of delegating the tasks of forecasting, monitoring, analyses and/or advice on fiscal policy. This is a predominant solution in EU countries, where 12 independent fiscal institutions operate. Those with the longest-standing history were established even before the EU's creation, but their tasks have truly risen to importance after 2007, i.e. after the outbreak of the financial crisis.

Some analogies to the operation of independent fiscal institutions could be found in the 1970s when collegiate bodies grew in importance in managing autonomous monetary policy in the light of the problems with the growing inflation rate. Nevertheless, the position of those institutions greatly differs from the role of decision-making bodies in central banking.

The issue of greatest importance, often addressed in the literature, is to ensure independence both to the members of independent fiscal institutions and to the employees of their analytical back office. The key aspects here include the organisational separation of those bodies, the ability to conduct independent analyses (especially as part of forecasting tasks), the scope and quality of the information provided and the channels of communication with the government, parliament and the society at large.

The staff employed at an independent fiscal institution in the form of a fiscal council (both direct members and analytical employees) is very diverse. For full members of fiscal councils, it is emphasised that selection principles meet the independence criteria accepted in a given country whereas the remaining individuals mostly belong to the civil service: they are officials at ministries, at the parliament, at auditing bodies or even at central banks. Fiscal council members, however, have a limited freedom when it comes to choosing their employees, especially independent experts from the academic community. In addition to HR problems, fiscal councils often encounter financial constraints, though expectations as to their work results are very high as a rule.

When it comes to the organisation of independent fiscal institutions, it should be noted that there are three dominant models – though this is not a closed catalogue of solutions – where the implementation of specific tasks may focus on:

- dedicated fiscal councils,
- parliamentary budget offices,
- state audit offices.

The Directive on requirements for budgetary frameworks of the Member States does not formulate the obligation to establish independent fiscal institutions and much less their specific type, but indirectly it binds Member States to implement tasks that were previously listed as falling into the competence of independent fiscal institutions. Potential tasks of such an institution include, without limitations, using independent macroeconomic forecasts as part of the budget process, preparing *ex ante* and *ex post* fiscal policy evaluations and conducting analyses on the desirable systemic changes in the public sector. In 2013, the European Commission, in its assessment of the measures implemented as part of the economic six-pack, emphasised the need to make fiscal policy compliant with the standards which largely refer to the independent fiscal institutions' scope of activities. The assessment also mentions the possibility of using those institutions (European Commission). The next chapter will feature an assessment of the fiscal solutions introduced as part of the SGP as well as six-pack and two-pack to help draw conclusions as to the effectiveness of these tools.

Only five countries can boast an over-a-decade or decades-long history of independent fiscal institutions' operations. In further seven countries, such institutions have been established over the last couple of years. An analysis of the effective use of an independent fiscal institution looks at the evolution of the fiscal balance measured with the general government sector's deficit and public debt. Those aggregates are compared here for 2000–2012 against the average EU level (EU27) and three groups of countries: five countries with the longest tradition of a fiscal council, seven countries which introduced this solution post-2006 and other EU countries that do not make use of this institution. Countries with a long tradition of having an independent fiscal institution were characterised, until 2006, by an average deficit that was close to the overall EU average; later on, during the crisis, the average for those countries exceeded the 3% excessive deficit threshold only in 2009–2010. Since 2007, the value of this average has been noticeably below the overall EU average. In countries where independent fiscal institutions were established after 2006, the average deficit level has evolved inversely to the EU average, while in the remaining EU countries, the average deficit level has been close to the overall EU average. It seems that the serious deficit increase and the excessively growing debt were at the root of the quest for new institutional solutions in fiscal policy. Unfortunately, positive effects of those changes need more time to be visible.

Until 2008, the average public debt level in the countries with a long-established independent fiscal institution was above the overall EU level. Later on, however, debt was growing at a slower rate than in other groups of countries, and in 2012 it stood at a lower level. The debt growth was most dynamic in the countries where an independent fiscal institution was introduced after 2006, which spurred the search for tools to improve the fiscal policy quality.

The evolution of the average debt, and even more so that of the deficit in the crisis years (since 2007) in the countries with a long tradition of having an independent fiscal institution in place points to the effectiveness of this solution in stabilising and ensuring high quality of the policy pursued. These effects, though, are not readily observable. As a matter of fact, the varied impact of such a fiscal institution on the condition of public finance is linked to the scope of its competence, the degree of independence and accountability, and to the existing back office resources and the accumulated experience. Another factor of importance is the overall state of democratic institutions in a given country and its level of social and economic development.

The only EU country with no independent fiscal institution in place is Poland, and Szpringer (2015) gives an insight into how the discussion on the advisability of establishing it evolved. Some of the independent fiscal institution functions are fulfilled by the Supreme Audit Office (NIK), which was reflected by taking account of the body when calculating the Scope Index of Fiscal Institutions (SIFI). An overview of the latest solutions in the field of independent fiscal institutions functioning in EU countries can be found in papers by Jankovics and Sherwood (2017).

In most EU Member States, independent fiscal institutions were established on the basis of legal instruments. In Estonia, France, Italy, Lithuania, Hungary, Portugal, Slovakia and Spain, these were constitutional provisions or organic laws, while the Croatian Fiscal Policy Committee and the Swedish Fiscal Policy Council were established by the government's decision. Fiscal council members are usually appointed by the Member State's government or parliament. Other institutions that appoint and designate fiscal council members include central banks (Estonia, Croatia, Germany, Portugal, Romania, Slovakia), presidents (France, Hungary, Slovakia), representatives of local authorities (Germany, Austria), chambers of commerce or trade unions (Luxembourg, Austria), audit institutions (Croatia, Luxembourg, Portugal), banking associations (Romania) and academic community (Croatia, Romania, Germany). A fiscal council member usually has a term of office of several years, most commonly five to seven years, the exception being the members of the Dutch Council of State (*Raad van State*), who have a lifelong term of office.

The literature on the subject reveals a consensus suggesting that the existence of the "fiscal guardians" that are independent fiscal institutions is conducive to a greater accountability and an improvement of fiscal transparency backed by fiscal policy analyses, assessments and recommendations produced by these entities. In particular, fiscal institutions can carry out or approve macroeconomic forecasts to inform the work on the budget, counterbalancing the over-optimistic outlook of the governmental forecasts; they can objectively monitor the implementation of budget plans, the compliance with fiscal rules and the achievement of budgetary targets; they can raise the awareness of the short- and long-term costs and benefits of budgetary measures both among the decision-makers and in the society at large and, last but not least, they can assess whether fiscal parameters are adequate in terms of how they comply with the rules and ensure durable fiscal balance.

The European Commission developed a comprehensive body of information on independent national fiscal institutions in EU countries, which is collected by means of a survey conducted since 2006 in all Member States. As part of this survey, information has been collected on the main characteristics of those entities, including their mandate and functions, the composition of their governing bodies, their formal status vis-à-vis the government or parliament as well as their mass media presence and the impact on public fiscal debates. Though in the initial phase, the survey covered a broad spectrum of independent fiscal institutions, in recent years, the database has increasingly focused on the so-called "core fiscal institutions", i.e. those provided with formal authority arising from EU legislation as well as a small number of institutions that fulfil specific tasks related to analysing changes in fiscal policy, providing macroeconomic forecasts or fiscal policy recommendations based on a mandate other than arising from EU legislation. Since 2015, the European Commission's Directorate General for Economic and Financial Affairs introduced SIFI, intended to measure the breadth of tasks performed by independent fiscal institutions. SIFI is calculated only for "core institutions" based on the information reported by the same. The index value is calculated on the basis of six criteria that define the fiscal institutions' scope of activities: 1) monitoring of compliance with fiscal rules; 2) macroeconomic forecasting; 3) budgetary forecasting and policy costing; 4) sustainability assessment; 5) promotion of fiscal transparency; and 6) normative recommendations on fiscal policy. It should be pointed out, however, that while the structure of this index shows the variety of functions fulfilled by independent fiscal institutions in respective Member States, it cannot be treated as a fully adequate tool to assess the effectiveness of their operations. The detailed method for SIFI calculation is presented in the Appendix 1.

Table 2.3 SIFI value in EU countries in 2015–2019.

Institution\Year	*2015*	*2016*	*2017*	*2018*	*2019*
Austria	63.57	63.57	63.57	63.57	63.57
Belgium	53.93	53.93	53.93	55.18	55.18
Bulgaria	30.00	30.00	30.00	30.00	40.00
Cyprus	64.29	64.29	64.29	66.79	66.79
Czech Republic	NA	NA	NA	51.25	51.25
Germany	51.96	51.96	51.96	51.96	51.96
Denmark	46.25	46.25	46.25	46.25	46.25
Estonia	51.43	51.43	51.43	51.43	51.43
Greece	48.57	48.57	48.57	48.57	48.57
Spain	68.93	68.93	68.93	68.93	68.93
Finland	41.79	37.50	37.50	37.50	37.50
France	46.43	46.43	46.43	46.43	46.43
Croatia	25.00	25.00	25.00	25.00	42.50
Hungary	36.43	36.43	36.43	51.43	51.43
Ireland	68.21	68.21	68.21	68.21	68.21
Italy	74.29	74.29	74.29	74.29	74.29
Lithuania	58.21	58.21	58.21	55.71	55.71
Luxembourg	20.00	20.00	20.00	20.00	20.00
Latvia	45.00	45.00	45.00	52.50	52.50
Malta	72.14	72.14	72.14	72.14	72.14
The Netherlands	39.29	39.29	39.29	39.29	39.29
Poland	17.50	17.50	17.50	17.50	17.50
Portugal	66.43	66.43	66.43	66.43	66.43
Romania	69.29	69.29	69.29	69.29	69.29
Sweden	42.86	42.86	42.86	42.86	42.86
Slovenia	20.00	20.00	20.00	20.00	20.00
Slovakia	44.64	44.64	44.64	44.64	44.64
United Kingdom	77.14	77.14	77.14	77.14	77.14

Source: European Commission, Directorate-General for Economic and Financial Affairs.

Summary

Adopting the principle of medium-term perspective in budget planning strengthens the fiscal authorities' capability for planning and maintaining a balanced fiscal path. Multiannual horizon characterises the activities of public finance entities (public interventions) arising from development strategies and programmes as well as public investments and public finance consolidation and restructuring processes. The effects of measures taken in those fields are delayed in time from planning and usually they go beyond one budget year.

The proposition to use fiscal rules largely stems from the acknowledgment of autonomy of the fiscal policy, which remains nearly exclusive prerogative of respective countries' governments. The use of specific rules of public finance management, which do not undermine the fiscal policy autonomy, strengthens the policy rationality and predictability, translating into credibility of the finance situation and of the quality of management in a given country. From the point of view of the policy element which they are directly concerned with, fiscal rules used contemporarily can be divided into the following groups: balanced budget rules, debt rules, expenditure rules and revenue rules.

As part of research into improving the quality of public spending, OECD developed a definition of an independent fiscal institution as a body which offers monitoring and advice on fiscal policy. The functioning of this institution should have a proper legal basis and it should employ non-partisan and apolitical professionals. The definition elaborated by the European Commission points, in addition, to the need to place the independent institution outside the government, central bank and parliament, to guarantee the desirable degree of its independence. According to the EC, the main tasks of this institution include preparing macroeconomic and budgetary forecasts, and monitoring the progress of fiscal policy implementation.

There are three basic organisation models for the operation of independent fiscal institution worldwide: fiscal councils, parliamentary budgetary offices and state audit offices. Data relating to the average public debt and even more so to the average deficit in the crisis years in the countries with a long tradition of having an independent fiscal council in place point to the effectiveness of such institutions in ensuring stability and high quality of the policy pursued. The effects of their activities are not readily observable, though. The impact of independent fiscal institutions on the condition of public finance depends on the scope of their competence, their independence and accountability, and, lastly, on the existing intellectual resources and the accumulated experience.

There are at least two reasons why legislative changes introduced as a response to the consequences of the financial and economic crisis can be viewed as the first attempt to truly strengthen fiscal rules in the EU. Firstly, the decision-making mechanism was improved. (The procedure for voting on imposing financial sanctions became based on the reverse qualified majority voting.) Secondly, an even greater importance was attributed to the MTO rule, which is intended to become a major element of the process of restoring long-term public finance stability. States became obliged to include rules to support MTO implementation in their national regulations and a criterion was set for the evaluation of their progress towards the declared medium-term budgetary targets (analysis of the growth path of the original expenditure adjusted by revenue discretionary measures). In addition, sanctions were stipulated in case a given state fails to make sufficient effort. A formula to calculate MTO was also defined, albeit one that was the least transparent and simple of all fiscal rules (Biraschi et al., 2010).

The debate unfolding amid the pandemic crisis shows, however, that the future may bring us ever new ideas and solutions with respect to amendments to the SGP as regards the fiscal instruments used.

Appendix 1

Table A.1 Scores for respective criteria to calculate the MTBF index.

No.	*Criterion name*	*Criterion scoring scale*
1.	Coverage of the targets/ ceilings included in the national medium-term fiscal plans	• MTBF covers more than 90% of the general government – 3; • MTBF covers between 70% and 90% of the general government – 2; • MTBF covers between 50% and 70% of the general government – 1; • MTBF covers less than 50% of the general government – 0. The score is supplemented by 1 if there is some form of coordination between sub-levels of general government when setting the multiannual targets.
2.	Connectedness between the targets/ceilings included in the national medium-term fiscal plans and the annual budgets	• By law or in practice, the annual budget respects the limits set (deficit/ surplus, expenditure ceilings, etc.) in the medium-term fiscal plans which cannot be exceeded in any circumstance – 4; • The annual budget can only deviate at a disaggregated level from the medium-term fiscal plans provided that the nominal budget balance is unchanged (i.e. additional spending is matched by a revenue increase or by a decrease in another spending item) – 3; • The annual budget, including headline balance objectives, can only deviate from the medium-term fiscal plans in a specific set of predefined circumstances (e.g. change in expenditure on pensions/unemployment benefits, substantial change in the macroeconomic forecast, new government coming to power, etc.) – 2;

No.	*Criterion name*	*Criterion scoring scale*
		• The annual budget can deviate from the medium-term fiscal plans, but possible deviations must be publicly explained – 1; • The medium-term plans are only indicative and possible deviations need not be explained – 0. The score is supplemented by 1 in case the objectives/ceilings included in the national medium-term plans are fixed in advance for a number of years and are not changed. The score is further supplemented by 1 in case there are well-defined actions to be taken in case of deviations from plans (applicable only in cases falling under the first three categories above).
3.	Involvement of national parliament in the preparation of the national medium-term fiscal plans	• The medium-term plans are voted by the parliament – 3; • No vote in parliament, but there is a formal presentation by the government and/or a discussion on the medium-term plans in parliament – 2; • No formal presentation in parliament, but the medium-term plans are sent for information to the parliament – 1; • No interaction with parliament – 0.
4.	Involvement of independent fiscal institutions (IFI) in the preparation of the national medium-term fiscal plans	• An IFI produces/endorses BOTH the macroeconomic AND budgetary multiannual forecasts IFI – 4; • An IFI produces/endorses EITHER the macroeconomic OR the budgetary multiannual forecasts – 3; • An IFI assesses BOTH the macroeconomic AND budgetary multiannual forecasts – 2; • An IFI assesses EITHER the macroeconomic OR the budgetary multiannual forecasts – 1; • There is no IFI involvement in the preparation of the fiscal plans – 0.
5.	Level of detail included in the national medium-term fiscal plans	The score of this dimension is the sum of the elements listed below: • There is a detailed breakdown of the total expenditure and revenue projections based on unchanged policies by main components (1/0); • There is a dedicated section/chapter analysing the policies underlying both total expenditure and revenue projections and/or their main components (1/0);

(*Continued*)

Table A.1 (Continued)

No.	*Criterion name*	*Criterion scoring scale*
		• The impact of the main policies and reforms on the unchanged policy scenario is quantified over the time-span of the plan (1/0); • The medium-term fiscal plan provides detailed explanations on the budgetary impact of alternative macroeconomic scenarios (1/0).

Source: *Medium-term budgetary frameworks database*, European Commission.

Table A.2 Scores for respective criteria to calculate the Fiscal Rules Index.

No.	*Criterion name*	*Criterion scoring scale*
1.	Legal base of the rule	• Fiscal rule is constitutional (including higher than ordinary law – organic law) – 3; • Fiscal rule is enshrined in the generally applicable regulations, e.g. a law – 2; • Fiscal rule is based on a coalition agreement (including Government programme voted in parliament or other written agreements at the level of different administration sub-sectors) – 1; • Fiscal rule stems from a non-formalised political commitment – 0.
2.	Room for revising objectives set in the rule	• The target of the rule, as defined in its establishing act, cannot be changed or temporarily suspended by the Government except in well-defined situations (i.e. escape clauses) – 3; • Subject to parliamentary approval, the Government can either temporarily change the target or it is mandated to decide on the target (in case the target is not defined in its establishing act) – 1; • The government can change the target of the rule at any time without parliamentary approval – 0.
3.	Rule monitoring	**Criterion 3a. Nature of the body in charge of rule monitoring and the correction mechanism** • Monitoring by an independent fiscal institution – 3; • Monitoring by an auditing institution and/or parliament – 2; • Monitoring by the ministry of finance or other government body – 1;

No.	*Criterion name*	*Criterion scoring scale*
		• No monitoring of the rule (no report systematically assessing compliance) – 0. **Criterion 3b. Real-time monitoring (quarterly or more frequent)** • Real-time monitoring is widely used – 1; • Real-time monitoring is widely used in case a risk of non-respect of the rule is detected through the real-time alert mechanism – 0.5; • No real-time monitoring takes place – 0. **Criterion 3c. Nature of the body in charge of monitoring the correction mechanism in case of deviation from the rule** • An independent authority (independent fiscal institution or auditing institution endowed with appropriate mandate) – 3; • An auditing institution and/or parliament – 2; • The ministry of finance or other government body – 1; • No correction mechanism – 0. **Criterion 3d. Role of the independent body in providing/endorsing macro/budgetary forecasts** • There is an independent body providing or endorsing the official macroeconomic and budgetary forecasts on which the annual budget is prepared – 2; • There is an independent body providing or endorsing the official macroeconomic or budgetary forecasts on which the annual budget is prepared – 1.
4.	Correction mechanisms in case of deviation from the rule	• The correction mechanism is triggered automatically and there are pre-determined rules framing the nature/size and/or timeline of the correction – 4; • The correction mechanism is triggered automatically or there are pre-determined rules framing the nature/size and/or timeline of the correction – 2; • The state authorities are obliged to take or present corrective measures before the parliament or the relevant authority identified in the regulations, but without a predefined timeline for such action and with no pre-determined rules framing the nature/size and/or timeline of the correction – 1; • The state authorities are not obliged to take or present corrective measures and there are no pre-determined rules framing the nature/size and/or timeline of the correction – 0.

(*Continued*)

Table A.2 (Continued)

No.	*Criterion name*	*Criterion scoring scale*
5.	Resilience to shocks or events outside the control of the government	The score of this dimension is simply the sum of the elements defined below: • Does the rule contain clearly defined escape clauses which are in line with the SGP? (1/0) • Is there a budgetary margin defined in relation to the fiscal rule (i.e. the planned spending targets are set at a lower level than the expenditure ceilings) or a safety margin linked to the MTO which is enshrined in national legislation? (1/0) • Are targets defined in cyclically adjusted terms or do they account for the cycle in any way (e.g. ceilings defined over the cycle) (1/0) • Are there exclusions from the fiscal rule in the form of items that fall outside authorities' control at least in the short term (e.g. interest payments, unemployment benefits)? (1/0)

Source: *Fiscal rules database*, European Commission.

Table A.3 Computation of SIFI index.

$$SIFI_{n,t} = \sum_{a=1}^{6} TK_{a,n,t} \star C_{TKt} \star W_{a,h}$$

$SIFI_{n,t}$ – index for institution *n* at year *t*
$TK_{a,n,t}$ – task *a* completed by institution *n* at year *t*
C_{TKt} – legal force coefficient for task TK at year *t*
$W_{a,h}$ – weight associated to task TK_a (*h* being the type of weighing scheme)
Tasks (TK_a)
1) monitoring compliance with fiscal rules
2) macroeconomic forecasting
3) budgetary forecasting and policy costing
4) analysis of long-run sustainability of public finance
5) promotion of fiscal transparency
6) normative recommendations on fiscal policy

TK scores for tasks 4, 5 and 6 take the value of either 0 or 1 (0 – no activity in the field, 1 – activity in the field). TK scores for tasks 1, 2 and 3 show greater variability depending on the specifics of the task at hand: score of 0, 1 and 2 is possible for those tasks. In addition, there is a possibility to increase these scores. For task 1, a bonus point is obtained for the institution's involvement in triggering correction mechanism and for monitoring of all the rules for the general government level. For task 2, it is possible to score a bonus point for having in place a reconciliation procedure in case of diverging forecasts. For task 3, a bonus point is given when opinion on the advisability of legislative proposals is prepared on the basis of quantitative policy costing. C_{TK} coefficient takes the value of 1 for tasks stipulated in legal remit, value of 0.5 for the fiscal institution's own-initiative tasks if completed regularly, and 0.25 for tasks completed occasionally.

Weights $W_{a,h}$ are assigned as provided in the table below.

Weighting scheme taken into account in the computation of SIFI depending on the role of the independent fiscal institution.

Tasks	*Role of the independent fiscal institution in a given country*			
	Neutral	*Advisory body*	*EU-oriented*	*Fiscal authority*
Monitoring compliance with fiscal rules	16.7	50	30	15
Macroeconomic forecasting	16.7	20	25	20
Budgetary forecasting and policy costing	16.7	0	20	20
Analysis of long-run sustainability of public finance	16.7	15	10	5
Promotion of fiscal transparency	16.7	15	5	10
Normative recommendations on fiscal policy	16.7	0	10	30
Total	**100**	**100**	**100**	**100**

Neutral – equal weights for all tasks;
Advisory body – weights favour consultative tasks;
EU-oriented – weights favour mandatory tasks for euro area member states;
Fiscal authority – weights favour tasks more directly linked to fiscal policy making.
Source: *Independent fiscal institutions database*, European Commission.

3 Public finance management in EU regulations and its effectiveness

Introduction

The previous chapter of the Monograph presents many initiatives taken by the European Union with a view to implementing economic solutions based on the sustainable development concept. A good example of such measures would be the initiative prepared and published by the High-Level Expert Group (European Commission, 2018a) which

> maps out the challenges and opportunities that the EU faces in developing a sustainable finance policy. It identifies ways in which the financial sector can re-connect with the real economy to support the transition to a more resource-efficient and more circular economy. The group argues that reorienting investment flows into long-term, sustainable projects will also improve the stability of the financial system.

This document indicates directions for action aimed to achieve durable and sustainable development based on efforts to combine economic prosperity with environmental and social sustainability, as thoroughly reflected in the assumptions of the EU New Financial Perspective adopted in 2021. Neither theoreticians nor practitioners dispute the fact that sustainable development requires adopting a long-term perspective, ensuring long-term financing for the critical infrastructure and responding to long-term threats (Gopalakrishna and Leelavathi, 2011). It is also believed that the sustainable development goal must be supported by sustainability finance. Measures taken as part of that concept could contribute to changing the orientation of actions pursued in the area of finance and to strengthening the activities that generate a long-term positive impact on the social and economic development. A key role and importance in this respect is attributed to public authorities, which can use public finance to achieve sustainable development.

Actions taken by public finance institutions to maintain fiscal sustainability and public finance stability must be, as a rule, considered along two dimensions: narrow and broad. In a narrow perspective, public finance stability is defined as actions oriented towards maintaining fiscal sustainability.

DOI: 10.4324/9781003222033-4

Their goal is to maintain budget deficit and public debt below the level set in the Maastricht criteria (Postuła et al., 2018; Debrun et al., 2019a). This means that the broadly understood concept of fiscal sustainability is directly connected with the fiscal policy and with the value and growth rate of public debt.

When contemplating public authorities' efforts to maintain public finance stability, attention should be also given to the need for public sector to continually fulfil its fundamental functions: allocative, redistributive and stabilising, and to prevent long-term public finance imbalance. This can be achieved by developing efficient expenditure and revenue systems for the public finance sector. Against the backdrop of the above discussion, a question arises as to whether the public finance management instruments currently applied at domestic and EU level can be used to achieve the goals inherent to the concept of building sustainable development. In this context, it is important to examine whether the instruments applied and, as emphasised in the previous chapter, evaluated by the European Commission (European Commission, 2014a, 2019a; European Fiscal Board, 2019) as part of:

- fiscal rules,
- medium-term planning,
- and independent fiscal institutions,

adopted at EU and domestic level contribute to fiscal sustainability and public finance stability (Eyraud et al., 2017; Darvas et al., 2018; Constâncio, 2020).

3.1 Analysis of the reliability of member states' forecasts submitted to the European Commission

Fiscal sustainability is the ability to take decisions based on reliable macroeconomic forecasts. It is therefore worth asking ourselves whether forecasts that enable a medium-term assessment of the adopted budgetary frameworks can be indeed reliable. As a matter of fact, it turns out that in many cases forecasts differ greatly from reality. One could cite the example of euro area accession of Greece which shortly after the verification and revision of statistical data no longer met the Maastricht criteria. Forecasts presented by Greece were unrealistic. To assess the extent of that phenomenon, forecasts presented by Member States to the European Commission between 1995 and 2020 have been examined and the data contained therein, compared to the results obtained in reality. The analysis results are presented in Table 3.1.

The analysis of forecasts has initially been treated binomially, dividing them into two groups depending on whether the values they describe are higher or lower than the actual performance and on their actual departure from the anticipated values. Based thereon, a conclusion has been reached on whether the forecasts analysed can be considered as a reliable source of information on the situation in a Member State.

Table 3.1 Percentage distribution of accuracy scores for forecasts of the main parameters describing fiscal policy in the year *n* for the year *n*+1.

Indicators	*Actual value compared to the forecast (year n+1)*	*Number (N)*	*Share (%)*	χ^2	*p*
GDP growth	Faster than forecast	51	35.4	12.25	0.99
	Slower than forecast	93	64.6		
Public revenue (% of GDP)	Higher than forecast	68	47.2	0.44	0.505
	Lower than forecast	76	52.8		
Public expenditure (% of GDP)	Higher than forecast	89	61.8	8.03	0.005
	Lower than forecast	55	38.2		
Borrowing needs (% of GDP)	Higher than forecast	85	59.0	4.69	0.030
	Lower than forecast	59	41.0		
Public debt (% of GDP)	Higher than forecast	91	63.2	10.03	0.002
	Lower than forecast	53	36.8		

Source: own elaboration.

An analysis based on the χ^2 test has revealed that the period analysed, i.e. from 1995 to 2016, saw major divergences in the accuracy of forecasts for the year n+1 for GDP growth ($\chi^2 = 12.25$; $p < 0.001$). The indicators have shown that the real GDP growth was in 64.6% of cases slower than the countries anticipated in the forecasting documents submitted. Meanwhile, no divergences have been found in revenue forecasts ($\chi^2 = 0.44$; $p = 0.505$). The analyses have also successfully demonstrated statistically significant divergences with respect to the public expenditure level ($\chi^2 = 8.03$; $p < 0.01$), i.e. it has been shown that in the period analysed, the expenditure was 61.8% higher than planned. Such a deviation in the actual expenditure has translated into statistically significant divergences in terms of respective countries' borrowing needs ($\chi^2 = 4.69$; $p < 0.05$). In 59% of cases, they were higher than assumed in the previous year's forecasts. There was also a statistically significant predominance of underestimated public debt forecasts ($\chi^2 = 10.03$; $p < 0.01$), which resulted, among other things, from higher deficit. The latter was in 63.2% of cases higher than assumed the year before.

Similar analyses have been conducted also for forecasts covering two subsequent periods (i.e. n+2). Their results are presented in Table 3.2.

It has been demonstrated that divergences occurred in the accuracy of forecasts for the year n+2 as regards economic growth ($\chi^2 = 17.94$; $p < 0.001$), because GDP was in 67.6% of cases slower than anticipated in medium-term documents prepared by respective countries. Like in n+1, no divergences have were demonstrated, either, for the year n+2 for revenue forecasts ($\chi^2 = 0.83$; $p = 0.631$) or statistically significant divergences have been demonstrated in the public expenditure forecasts ($\chi^2 = 16.56$; $p < 0.001$). In the period analysed, public expenditure reflected in reporting documents was in 66.9% of cases higher than forecast. Next, statistically significant divergences have been demonstrated in terms of borrowing needs ($\chi^2 = 15.23$; $p < 0.001$), which in

Table 3.2 Percentage distribution of accuracy scores for forecasts of the main parameters describing fiscal policy in the year n+2.

Indicators	*Actual value compared to the forecast (year n+2)*	*Number (N)*	*Share (%)*	χ^2	*p*
GDP growth	Faster than forecast	47	32.4	17.94	0.000
	Slower than forecast	98	67.6		
Public revenue (% of GDP)	Higher than forecast	67	46.2	0.83	0.361
	Lower than forecast	78	53.8		
Public expenditure (% of GDP)	Higher than forecast	97	66.9	16.56	0.000
	Lower than forecast	48	33.1		
Borrowing needs (% of GDP)	Higher than forecast	96	66.2	15.23	0.000
	Lower than forecast	49	33.8		
Public debt (% of GDP)	Higher than forecast	105	72.4	29.14	0.000
	Lower than forecast	40	27.6		

Source: own elaboration.

66.2% of cases were higher than assumed in forecasts for the year n+2. There was also a statistically significant predominance of negative forecasts of public debt ($\chi^2 = 29.14$; $p < 0.001$). Higher than expected deficit occurred in 72.4% of forecasts developed in the year when convergence programme or stability programme was submitted. The results of χ^2 tests have also revealed that forecasts for two subsequent years were definitely less realistic than forecasts for the following year.

As a next step, it has been checked for all countries whether there were any correlations between the forecast for the following year and the forecast for two subsequent years. The purpose of the analysis has been to test whether where the forecast for the following year exceeded the actual result, the forecast for two subsequent years also exceeded the actual level of the variable in question. To that end, McNemar's tests have been conducted for dependent measurements. Table 3.3 presents the percentage correspondence between forecasts prepared for one year and for two subsequent years. The analyses have yielded statistically insignificant results. This means that there was no statistically significant difference between forecasts for one year and for two subsequent years, with forecasts overlapping in most cases. Only for public debt, its lower-than-forecast growth for the following year overlapped in 66% of cases with its lower-than-forecast growth for two subsequent years.

Next, analyses have been conducted with a breakdown by year analysed to check the correlation between the nature of the forecast and the period in which it was prepared. This has helped determine the years in which the forecasts were very optimistic, and those in which they were highly pessimistic. The χ^2 test results for forecasts prepared for the year n+1 are presented in Table 3.4.

The analyses have demonstrated a statistically significant correlation between the years in which growth forecasts were prepared and the nature of these

Table 3.3 Percentage distribution of correspondence between forecasts of the main parameters describing fiscal policy in the years n+1 and n+2.

Indicators	*Actual value compared to the forecast (year n+2)*	*Corresponding (year n+2)*	*Not-corresponding (year n+2)*	*p*
GDP growth	Faster than forecast	15%	85%	1.000
	Slower than forecast	91%	9%	
Public revenue (% of GDP)	Higher than forecast	76%	24%	1.000
	Lower than forecast	18%	82%	
Public expenditure (% of GDP)	Higher than forecast	10%	90%	1.000
	Lower than forecast	84%	16%	
Borrowing needs (% of GDP)	Higher than forecast	89%	11%	1.000
	Lower than forecast	19%	81%	
Public debt (% of GDP)	Higher than forecast	13%	87%	0.424
	Lower than forecast	66%	34%	

Source: own elaboration.

Table 3.4 Percentage distribution of forecasts of fiscal policy indicators for the year n+1 broken down into years.

Year n+1	*GDP growth (%)*		*Public revenue (% of GDP)*		*Public expenditure (% of GDP)*		*Borrowing needs (% of GDP)*		*Public debt (% of GDP)*	
	Faster than forecast	*Slower than forecast*	*Higher than forecast*	*Lower than forecast*	*Higher than forecast*	*Lower than forecast*	*Higher than forecast*	*Lower than forecast*	*Higher than forecast*	*Lower than forecast*
2007	82	18	71	29	29	71	24	76	29	71
2008	6	94	67	33	83	17	78	22	67	33
2009	0	100	33	67	89	11	100	0	100	0
2010	67	33	50	50	75	25	83	17	92	8
2011	39	61	44	56	44	56	44	56	50	50
2012	17	83	33	67	56	44	67	33	83	17
2013	11	89	39	61	67	33	56	44	67	33
2014	53	47	41	59	71	29	53	47	53	47
2015	41	59	41	59	59	41	53	47	53	47
$\chi 2$	43.49		9.64		18.17		23.28		23.98	
p	0.000		0.291		0.020		0.003		0.002	

Source: own elaboration.

growth forecasts (GDP $\chi^2 = 43.49$; $p < 0.001$). In 2009, the GDP growth indicator was lower than forecast in 100% of cases, which evidently resulted from the financial crisis that was raging that year. Similarly, in the following years – 2012 and 2013 – most countries had a lower GDP than assumed in annual forecasts, which represented an opposite trend to that of 2007, for which GDP growth forecasts turned out to be conservative (overcautious).

There was also a correlation between the years and the nature of public expenditure forecasts ($\chi^2 = 18.17$; $p < 0.05$). In 2008 and 2009, in most countries, the level of public expenditure was higher than assumed in annual forecasts. Meanwhile, in 2007, as many as 71% of the countries had lower-than-forecast expenditure, which could have also resulted from the higher economic growth rate entailing a stronger fiscal consolidation.

When it comes to the forecasts of borrowing needs, there was also a temporal correlation ($\chi^2 = 23.28$; $p < 0.01$). In 2009, borrowing was higher than forecast in 100% of the countries, whereas it was only in 2007 that in most countries borrowing was lower than assumed in forecasts.

Another thing that changed over time is the accuracy of public debt forecasts ($\chi^2 = 23.98$; $p < 0.01$). In 2008 and 2009, for most countries, the debt growth was higher than forecast while in 2007, most countries recorded a debt growth that was lower than assumed in the annual forecast.

Meanwhile, no statistically significant correlations have been demonstrated over time for public revenue forecasts ($\chi^2 = 9.64$; $p = 0.291$).

A similar analysis has been conducted for forecasts covering two subsequent years, the results of which are presented in Table 3.5.

Analyses have demonstrated that there was a statistically significant correlation between years and the nature of two-year GDP growth forecasts ($\chi^2 = 55.21$; $p < 0.001$). In 2009, in 100% of cases, the GDP growth was lower than forecast. In 2012 and 2013, most countries also had a lower GDP growth than assumed in two-year forecasts. Meanwhile, higher-than-forecast growth was recorded in most countries in 2007.

Table 3.5 Percentage distribution of forecasts of fiscal policy indicators for the year n+2 broken down into years.

Year n+2	*GDP growth (%)*		*Public revenue (% of GDP)*		*Public expenditure (% of GDP)*		*Borrowing needs (% of GDP)*		*Public debt (% of GDP)*	
	Faster than forecast	*Slower than forecast*	*Higher than forecast*	*Lower than forecast*	*Higher than forecast*	*Lower than forecast*	*Higher than forecast*	*Lower than forecast*	*Higher than forecast*	*Lower than forecast*
2007	94	6	63	38	31	69	25	75	31	69
2008	16	84	53	47	58	42	68	32	63	37
2009	0	100	61	39	94	6	100	0	100	0
2010	67	33	44	56	78	22	78	22	100	0
2011	25	75	58	42	67	33	83	17	83	17
2012	17	83	33	67	61	39	56	44	61	39
2013	6	94	28	72	78	22	67	33	89	11
2014	39	61	28	72	72	28	61	39	72	28
2015	53	47	53	47	65	35	65	35	65	35
χ^2	55.21		10.78		18.03		24.62		29.49	
p	0.000		0.214		0.021		0.002		0.000	

Source: own elaboration.

There was also a correlation between years and the nature of public expenditure forecasts ($\chi^2 = 18.03$; $p < 0.05$). In 2009 and 2010, the public expenditure level was, for most countries, higher than assumed in two-year forecasts, while in 2007, 71% of the countries had lower-than-forecast expenditure.

Forecasts of borrowing needs were also characterised by a temporal correlation ($\chi^2 = 24.62$; $p < 0.01$). In 2009, in 100% of the countries, borrowing was lower than assumed in two-year forecasts and only in 2007, in most countries, the borrowing was lower than forecast.

The accuracy of public debt forecasts changed over time as well ($\chi^2 = 29.49$; $p < 0.01$). In 2009 and 2010, 100% of the countries recorded a higher debt growth than forecast two years before, and in 2007, debt growth was lower in most countries than expected in an annual forecast.

Meanwhile, no statistically significant correlations have been demonstrated over time for public revenue forecasts ($\chi^2 = 10.78$; $p = 0.214$).

It can be therefore observed that there were higher deviations from forecasts, especially negative ones, for two-year forecasts, with forecasts for 2009 straying the most from reality.

Further analyses have been conducted for each country separately and their results are presented in Table 3.6.

First, forecasts for the next budget year have been analysed. It has been demonstrated that there was no statistically significant correlation between respective countries for GDP growth ($\chi^2 = 15.44$; $p = 0.631$) and public debt ($\chi^2 = 23.20$; $p = 0.183$). In terms of these variables, no statistically significant differences between the countries have been found. Differences have been recorded, however, between the countries in terms of public revenue ($\chi^2 = 63.24$; $p < 0.001$). For Austria, Luxembourg and Slovakia, the planned revenue was 100% lower than the actual one while for Cyprus, Ireland, Malta and the Netherlands, planned revenue was 100% higher than the actual one. Then differences in the public expenditure growth have been demonstrated ($\chi^2 = 49.90$; $p < 0.001$). Expenditure was higher than planned in the period analysed for Greece, Slovakia and Spain. The most lower-than-forecast expenditure has been observed, however, in Cyprus, the Netherlands, Malta and Germany. Analyses have also revealed differences between the countries in terms of borrowing needs ($\chi^2 = 37.18$; $p < 0.01$). Higher-than-forecast borrowing has been recorded in Greece, Belgium, Slovenia, Spain and Portugal. Meanwhile borrowing was lower than assumed in the annual forecast for Germany, Luxembourg, Estonia and Austria.

A similar analysis has been conducted for two-year forecasts, the results of which are presented in Table 3.7.

Also in this case, no statistically significant correlation has been demonstrated between the countries for GDP growth ($\chi^2 = 15.31$; $p = 0.640$) and public debt ($\chi^2 = 27.07$; $p = 0.077$). Meanwhile, differences have been demonstrated between the countries in terms of public revenue ($\chi^2 = 50.89$; $p < 0.001$). For Austria, Germany, Luxembourg and Slovakia, the revenue planned for two subsequent years was usually lower than the actual one, and for Malta and the

Table 3.6 Percentage distribution of forecasts of fiscal policy indicators for the year n+1 broken down into respective countries.

Countries	*GDP growth (%)*		*Public revenue (% of GDP)*		*Public expenditure (% of GDP)*		*Borrowing needs (% of GDP)*		*Public debt (% of GDP)*	
	Faster than forecast	*Slower than forecast*	*Higher than forecast*	*Lower than forecast*	*Higher than forecast*	*Lower than forecast*	*Higher than forecast*	*Lower than forecast*	*Higher than forecast*	*Lower than forecast*
Austria	29	71	0	100	71	29	29	71	100	0
Belgium	38	62	12	88	75	25	87	13	87	13
Cyprus	17	83	100	0	0	100	67	33	67	33
Estonia	25	75	50	50	50	50	25	75	75	25
Finland	25	75	25	75	62	38	62	38	62	38
France	12	88	37	63	87	13	75	25	75	25
Greece	0	100	40	60	100	0	100	0	80	20
Spain	37	63	50	50	100	0	87	13	62	38
The Netherlands	37	63	100	0	12	88	62	38	37	63
Ireland	38	63	100	0	50	50	50	50	62	38
Lithuania	50	50	50	50	87	13	62	38	50	50
Luxembourg	37	63	0	100	50	50	13	88	50	50
Latvia	29	71	43	57	71	29	57	43	43	57
Malta	75	25	100	0	25	75	50	50	50	50
Germany	37	63	37	63	25	75	12	88	25	75
Portugal	57	43	43	57	86	14	86	14	100	0
Slovakia	37	63	0	100	100	0	50	50	50	50
Slovenia	50	50	37	63	75	25	87	13	75	25
Italy	25	75	75	25	50	50	75	25	62	38
χ^2	15.44		63.24		49.90		37.18		23.20	
p	0.631		0.000		0.000		0.005		0.183	

Source: own elaboration.

Netherlands – in 100% higher than the actual one. Next, differences have been demonstrated compared to the public expenditure growth (χ^2 = 38.64; p < 0.01). In the period analysed, expenditure was 100% higher than planned for France, Greece and the Netherlands, while most lower-than-forecast expenditure has been observed for Cyprus and the Netherlands. Analyses have also demonstrated difference between the countries in terms of borrowing needs (χ^2 = 30.71; p < 0.05). Higher borrowing than assumed in two-year forecasts has been demonstrated for Luxembourg and Germany, and lower – for France, Greece, Spain and Belgium.

Further analyses have focused on the actual differences between the forecasts and the real values of variables rather than on the dichotomisation of variables. First, it has been verified for all countries whether the differences between the forecasts and the actual values followed a specific trend. To that end, a number of regression analyses have been conducted (see Table 3.8).

Table 3.7 Percentage distribution of forecasts of fiscal policy indicators for the year n+2 broken down into respective countries.

Countries	*GDP growth (%)*		*Public revenue (% of GDP)*		*Public expenditure (% of GDP)*		*Borrowing needs (% of GDP)*		*Public debt (% of GDP)*	
	Faster than forecast	*Slower than forecast*	*Higher than forecast*	*Lower than forecast*	*Higher than forecast*	*Lower than forecast*	*Higher than forecast*	*Lower than forecast*	*Higher than forecast*	*Lower than forecast*
Austria	38	62	0	100	88	12	62	38	100	0
Belgium	25	75	25	75	88	12	88	13	88	12
Cyprus	14	86	86	14	14	86	71	29	71	29
Estonia	25	75	25	75	75	25	50	50	88	12
Finland	25	75	25	75	75	25	62	38	62	38
France	14	86	57	43	100	0	100	0	100	0
Greece	0	100	50	50	100	0	100	0	100	0
Spain	38	62	38	62	100	0	88	12	88	12
The Netherlands	25	75	100	0	25	75	62	38	62	38
Ireland	38	62	88	12	62	38	50	50	62	38
Lithuania	50	50	50	50	75	25	62	38	62	38
Luxembourg	50	50	12	88	50	50	13	88	62	38
Latvia	38	62	50	50	62	38	62	38	38	62
Malta	71	29	100	0	29	71	86	14	57	43
Germany	43	57	14	86	43	57	29	71	29	71
Portugal	29	71	57	43	71	29	86	14	86	14
Slovakia	38	62	13	88	87	13	50	50	62	38
Slovenia	38	62	38	62	62	38	75	25	75	25
Italy	12	88	62	38	62	38	75	25	88	12
$\chi 2$	15.31		50.89		38.64		30.71		27.09	
p	0.640		0.000		0.003		0.031		0.077	

Source: own elaboration.

It has been demonstrated that for forecasts for the year n+1, there was an observable GDP growth trend (t = 2.03; p < 0.05). Based on the coefficient β = 0.17, it can be said that over time the GDP growth was higher than forecast in the previous year. A trend has been also identified for borrowing needs (t = 2.33; p < 0.05). The coefficient β = 0.19 suggests that over time the actual borrowing became lower than forecast.

Further analyses have been conducted with a breakdown by country. This is intended to check the specific distribution of forecasts in every country. Due to the large number of data, the tables (see also Tables 3.9 and 3.10) describe and present only the statistically significant results.

For annual forecasts, a statistically significant GDP growth trend has been demonstrated for Cyprus (t = – 4.40; p < 0.05) and Greece (t = – 3.94; p < 0.05). Based on standard coefficients β (– 0.91 and – 0.92, respectively), it has been found that over time the GDP growth was lower than forecast in the

Table 3.8 Results of regression analyses for trends observable in the forecasts of fiscal policy indicators.

Indicators	*Years*	*B*	*SE*	*β*	*t*	*p*	R^2
GDP growth	*n+1*	*0.24*	*0.12*	*0.17*	*2.03*	*0.044*	*0.03*
	n+2	*0.06*	*0.12*	*0.04*	*0.47*	*0.640*	*0.00*
Public revenue (% of GDP)	n+1	–0.42	0.32	–0.11	–1.31	0.192	0.01
	n+2	0.00	0.18	0.00	0.00	0.997	0.00
Public expenditure (% of GDP)	n+1	0.16	0.13	0.11	1.27	0.206	0.01
	n+2	0.16	0.09	0.15	1.79	0.076	0.02
Borrowing needs (% of GDP)	n+1	0.11	0.10	0.09	1.06	0.290	0.01
	n+2	0.35	0.15	0.19	2.33	0.021	0.04
Public debt (% of GDP)	n+1	–0.15	0.21	–0.06	–0.72	0.472	0.00
	n+2	0.00	0.49	0.00	–0.01	0.993	0.00

B – unstandardised coefficient; *SE* – standard error; *β* – standardised coefficient; *t* – *t*-Student statistics; *p* – statistical significance; *R* – determination coefficient.
Source: own elaboration.

Table 3.9 Results of regression analyses for trends observable in the forecasts of fiscal policy indicators for the year n+1.

Indicators for the year n+1	*Countries*	*B*	*SE*	*β*	*t*	*p*	R^2
GDP growth (%)	Cyprus	–1.18	0.27	–0.91	–4.40	0.012	0.83
	Greece	–1.71	0.43	–0.92	–3.94	0.029	0.84
Public revenue (% of GDP)	Latvia	1.14	0.31	0.85	3.66	0.015	0.73
	Slovakia	0.84	0.12	0.95	7.27	0.000	0.90
Public expenditure (% of GDP)	Cyprus	0.73	0.17	0.90	4.23	0.013	0.82
	Italy	0.36	0.12	0.76	2.88	0.028	0.58
	Slovakia	0.71	0.24	0.77	3.00	0.024	0.60
Borrowing needs (% of GDP)	Cyprus	–1.30	0.33	–0.89	–3.88	0.018	0.79
Public debt (% of GDP)	Cyprus	5.74	1.35	0.91	4.27	0.013	0.82
	Ireland	–5.21	1.76	–0.77	–2.96	0.025	0.59

B – unstandardised coefficient; *SE* – standard error; *β* – standardised coefficient; *t* – *t*-Student statistics; *p* – statistical significance; *R* – determination coefficient.
Source: own elaboration.

previous year. The ever decreasing GDP growth was strongly correlated with the passage of time. Then, it has been demonstrated that a trend was also present in the public revenue forecasts for Latvia ($t = 3.66$; $p < 0.05$) and Slovakia ($t = 7.27$; $p < 0.001$). Coefficients β (of 0.85 and 0.95, respectively) suggest that over time the planned revenue became much lower than the actual one. With respect to the public expenditure analysis, a statistically significant trend has been demonstrated in annual forecasts for Cyprus ($t = 4.23$; $p < 0.05$),

Table 3.10 Results of regression analyses for trends observable in the forecasts of fiscal policy indicators for the year n+2.

Indicators for the year n+2	*Countries*	*B*	*SE*	*β*	*t*	*P*	R^2
GDP growth (%)	Ireland	2.50	0.94	0.74	2.67	0.037	0.54
	Malta	1.16	0.42	0.77	2.74	0.041	0.60
Public revenue (% of GDP))	Greece	1.24	0.34	0.88	3.67	0.021	0.77
	Ireland	–0.81	0.31	–0.73	–2.60	0.041	0.53
	Portugal	0.43	0.15	0.79	2.88	0.035	0.62
	Slovakia	1.37	0.28	0.89	4.91	0.003	0.80
Borrowing needs (% of GDP)	Cyprus	–1.32	0.51	–0.76	–2.61	0.048	0.58
	Malta	0.52	0.06	0.97	9.35	0.000	0.95
Public debt (% of GDP)	Cyprus	7.49	0.97	0.96	7.73	0.001	0.92
	Luxembourg	–1.63	0.48	–0.81	–3.37	0.015	0.65
	Slovenia	4.07	0.79	0.90	5.13	0.002	0.81

B – unstandardised coefficient; *SE* – standard error; *β* – standardised coefficient; *t* – *t*-Student statistics; *p* – statistical significance; *R* – determination coefficient.
Source: own elaboration.

Italy (t = 2.88; p < 0.05) and Slovakia (t = 3.00; p < 0.05). From year to year, expenditure in those countries was higher than planned in the annual forecasts, as concluded on the basis of relevant coefficients β (0.90, 0.76 and 0.77). For Cyprus, a trend has also been demonstrated for annual borrowing needs (t = – 3.88; p < 0.05). Based on the coefficient β = – 0.89, it has been determined that, from year to year, deficit was increasingly higher than forecast. Meanwhile, in terms of public debt forecasts, a trend has been demonstrated for Cyprus (t = 4.27; p < 0.05) and Ireland (t = – 2.96; p < 0.05). From year to year, public debt for Cyprus (β = 0.91) was higher than planned, and for Ireland (β = – 0.77) – lower than planned.

For two-year forecasts, a trend has been demonstrated in the GDP growth for Ireland (t = 2.67; p < 0.05) and Malta (t = 2.74; p < 0.05). Based on coefficients β (0.74 and 0.77, respectively), it has been determined that over time the GDP growth for these countries was higher than that in the two-year forecast. Next, it has been demonstrated that there was a trend in public revenue forecasts for Greece (t = 3.67; p < 0.05), Ireland (t = – 2.60; p < 0.05), Portugal (t = 2.88; p < 0.05) and Slovakia (t = 4.91; p < 0.01); for Greece (β = 0.88), Portugal (β = 0.79) and Slovakia (β = 0.89), the planned revenue became over time much higher than the actual one, while for Ireland (β = – 0.73) – much lower than the actual one. For Cyprus (t = – 2.61; p < 0.05) and Malta (t = 9.35; p < 0.001), there were trends with respect to borrowing needs: in Cyprus (β = – 0.76) deficit was, from year to year, increasingly higher than planned, and in Malta (β = 0.97) – increasing lower than planned. When it comes to public debt forecasts, a trend has been demonstrated for Cyprus (t = 7.73; p < 0.01), Luxembourg (t = – 3.37; p < 0.05) and Slovenia (t = 5.13; p < 0.01). From year to year, public debt for Cyprus (β = 0.96) and Slovenia

($\beta = 0.90$) was higher than planned, and for Luxembourg ($\beta = -0.81$) lower than planned.

The next stage of the analysis has been to calculate modules from the forecast deviations to check for which countries the forecasts (both annual and two-year forecast) were the most accurate and for which ones, the least (see Tables 3.11 and 3.12).

Annual forecasts for the GDP growth were the most accurate for Austria, with an average forecast error of 0.95%, whereas the least accurate annual forecasts have been observed for Finland and France, where errors stood at 4.26% and 5.26%, respectively. For two-year forecasts, the most accurate ones were also those prepared for Austria (1.13%), and the least accurate ones, for France (10.07%) and Finland (7.48%). When analysing public revenues for both annual and two-year forecasts, the most accurate were the forecasts for Austria, with errors of 0.86% and 1.41%, respectively. The least accurate annual revenue forecasts were those for Germany (3.37%), and the least accurate two-year forecasts – for Cyprus (6.50%). When it comes to public expenditure, the most accurate annual forecasts were those for Portugal (1.54%) and Estonia (1.59%), and two-year forecasts, for Ireland (1.68%). Meanwhile, the least accurate forecasts of annual public expenditure were prepared for Greece (7.26%), and two-year forecasts, for Cyprus (7.79%). Borrowing needs were predicted with the greatest accuracy for Spain (0.79%), Portugal (0.89%) and Slovenia (0.89%), and when it comes to two-year forecasts, for Spain (0.92%). The least accurate forecasts of borrowing needs have been observed for Greece (7.83%), and when it comes to two-year forecasts, for Greece (7.77%) and France (7.65%). The most accurate annual forecasts for public debt were those for Lithuania (2.91%) and Austria (2.93%), and two-year forecasts only for Austria (3.91%). Meanwhile, the least accurate annual forecasts of public debt were those for Greece (16.24%), and among two-year forecasts, those for Italy (26.88%).

The planning processes in place in respective countries are based on different public management instruments which have an impact on their structure, the stability of public finance and on the economic development they help achieve. Consequently, as a next step, a decision has been made to analyse the effectiveness of the solutions recommended in the Budgetary Frameworks Directive as a remedy to the crisis of 2007–2008 proposed by the European Union. Analyses have been conducted on the basis of data from all EU Member States for 2004–2020 to be found in Eurostat and European Commission databases, with minor exceptions if data were unavailable for such a time horizon. One such exception is the index that measures the strength of independent fiscal institutions (Wyplosz, 2019) which is only available for the last eight years. A decision has been made to apply, in the evaluation of the effectiveness of public management instruments, indicators that measure correlations between assessment indices for those instruments, i.e. Fiscal Rule Index, Fiscal Rule Strength Index, Medium-Term Budgetary Frameworks Index, Scope Index of Fiscal Institutions, and the levels of public debt-to-GDP, public finance deficit-to-GDP and economic growth measured by GDP. Indeed, it seems relevant to

Table 3.11 Ranking of average deviations from the actual values in forecasts of fiscal policy indicators for the year n+1.

GDP growth (%)		*Public revenue (% of GDP)*		*Public expenditure (% of GDP)*		*Borrowing needs (% of GDP)*		*Public debt (% of GDP)*	
Country	Variation	Country	Variation	Country	Variation	Country	Variation	Country	Variation
Austria	0.95	Austria	0.86	Portugal	1.54	Spain	0.79	Lithuania	2.91
Malta	1.22	Malta	1.00	Estonia	1.59	Portugal	0.89	Austria	2.93
Ireland	1.26	Portugal	1.06	Malta	1.79	Slovenia	0.89	Belgium	3.08
The Netherlands	1.54	Cyprus	1.40	Germany	2.01	Lithuania	1.09	Malta	3.36
Germany	1.56	Greece	1.45	Austria	2.01	Malta	1.14	Portugal	3.61
Spain	1.60	Finland	1.67	Slovenia	2.27	Slovakia	1.30	Spain	3.78
Slovakia	1.70	Latvia	1.99	Latvia	2.42	Belgium	1.34	Cyprus	5.25
Portugal	1.81	Belgium	2.08	France	2.44	Latvia	1.50	Slovakia	6.56
Latvia	2.03	The Netherlands	2.08	Belgium	2.45	Germany	1.87	Estonia	6.68
Belgium	2.31	Slovenia	2.20	Italy	2.54	Luxembourg	1.89	Germany	7.51
Cyprus	2.74	Lithuania	2.21	Luxembourg	2.55	Austria	1.98	The Netherlands	7.60
Italy	2.83	France	2.22	Lithuania	2.58	Cyprus	2.14	Ireland	7.88
Greece	2.85	Italy	2.26	Cyprus	2.61	Estonia	2.36	Slovenia	8.11
Lithuania	3.03	Luxembourg	2.42	Slovakia	2.85	Italy	2.57	Latvia	8.23
Luxembourg	3.13	Estonia	2.46	Spain	3.13	The Netherlands	2.84	Finland	8.46
Estonia	3.69	Ireland	2.62	Finland	3.56	Ireland	3.00	Italy	9.95
Slovenia	3.96	Slovakia	2.63	Ireland	3.87	Finland	3.27	Luxembourg	10.09
France	4.26	Spain	2.96	The Netherlands	4.06	France	3.93	France	10.45
Finland	5.26	Germany	3.37	Greece	7.26	Greece	7.83	Greece	16.24

Source: own elaboration.

Table 3.12 Ranking of average deviations from the actual values in forecasts of fiscal policy indicators for the year n+2.

GDP growth (%)		*Public revenue* (% *of GDP*)		*Public expenditure* (% *of GDP*)		*Borrowing needs* (% *of GDP*)		*Public debt* (% *of GDP*)	
Country	Variation	Country	Variation	Country	Variation	Country	Variation	Country	Variation
Austria	1.13	Austria	1.41	Ireland	1.68	Spain	0.92	Austria	3.91
Slovakia	1.38	Portugal	1.61	Slovenia	2.74	Slovenia	1.07	Belgium	6.10
Ireland	1.40	Greece	1.73	Lithuania	2.78	Belgium	1.45	Spain	6.48
Spain	1.69	Italy	1.95	Austria	2.91	Luxembourg	1.67	Malta	6.96
Greece	1.82	Slovenia	2.13	Portugal	2.93	Malta	1.71	Estonia	7.40
Portugal	1.91	Malta	2.20	Luxembourg	3.08	Lithuania	2.20	Slovenia	9.67
The Netherlands	1.97	Belgium	2.33	Malta	3.34	Slovakia	2.20	Ireland	9.76
Malta	2.15	Slovakia	2.40	Belgium	3.40	Ireland	2.39	Lithuania	9.87
Latvia	2.55	Germany	2.44	Italy	3.51	Portugal	2.43	Finland	10.90
Belgium	2.73	Luxembourg	2.49	Slovakia	3.81	Cyprus	2.49	The Netherlands	11.09
Estonia	2.84	The Netherlands	2.57	Latvia	3.86	Estonia	2.49	Portugal	11.59
Cyprus	2.89	Lithuania	2.61	Spain	4.19	Austria	2.50	Cyprus	12.70
Lithuania	3.57	Finland	2.70	The Netherlands	4.48	Latvia	2.68	Germany	13.02
Italy	3.70	France	2.82	Finland	4.83	The Netherlands	2.95	Latvia	13.90
Slovenia	4.09	Latvia	2.88	Greece	5.32	Italy	4.31	Luxembourg	14.66
Luxembourg	4.13	Spain	3.69	Germany	5.67	Finland	4.38	Slovakia	17.16
Germany	4.56	Ireland	3.90	Estonia	6.03	Germany	5.31	Greece	17.46
Finland	7.48	Estonia	5.42	France	6.30	France	7.65	France	19.97
France	10.07	Cyprus	6.50	Cyprus	7.79	Greece	7.77	Italy	26.88

Source: own elaboration.

determine whether EU Member States making use of the increasingly highly rated public management tools have more stable public finance, i.e. whether the solutions introduced by the EU have an actual impact on the debt and budget deficit levels while not causing the GDP growth rate to slow down (Lledo et al., 2017). In this part of the Monograph, research is conducted for the European Union as a whole rather than for individual countries because from the point of view of community management it seems relevant to check whether the model has worked "globally", while in respective countries the effectiveness of relevant solutions might have been affected by single events. A decision has been made to conduct research using dynamic models which also take account of the time shift.

The reason why dynamic models have been chosen is that they are often used by economists in studies where factors of significance include the existence of long-term stability, the pace at which such balance is reached and the resulting delayed response to exogenous shocks. To analyse the phenomenon in question, ADL models (*Autoregressive Distributed Lags models*) seem the most appropriate. In addition to lags in the response variable, ADL models also take account of lags in independent variables among explanatory variables. In statistical terms, the case for including lags in the response variable in the model is that such a model has undoubtedly better statistical properties, often manifesting themselves in eliminating the autocorrelation. This is achieved at a relatively low cost of having to estimate just a couple of parameters more. Meanwhile, the economic case for choosing this type of models is that it addresses the need to take account of the significant inertia inherent in macroeconomic phenomena.

As the first research step, an analysis has been conducted to determine whether the data collected and their scope make it possible to use the ADL model and obtain reliable research results. For the index of public management instruments and selected macroeconomic indicators, the diagnosis has proved unequivocally positive, meaning they can be analysed using this test (see Table 3.13).

Upon confirming that the set of research data and their variation can be used for further modelling, first an attempt has been made to estimate the impact of the medium-term planning implemented in EU countries on the selected macroeconomic indicators. Each analysis has been conducted on the basis of two dynamic estimation models that are characteristic of the ADL test.

3.2 The impact of medium-term planning on the economic growth rate and selected fiscal indicators

As the first step, attempts have been made to demonstrate how the implementation of medium-term planning measured with MTBF index affects the macroeconomic indicators selected for the analysis. One such indicator is Gross Domestic Product growth indicator, which will be treated as a variable dependent on MTBF. To analyse this correlation, a panel ADL model

Table 3.13 Parametric assessment of the analysed variables relating to assessment indices for public management tools and selected macroeconomic indicators.

Details	*SIFI*	*MTBF*	*FRI*	*FRSI*	*Public debt-to-GDP*	*Public finance deficit-to-GDP*	*GDP growth*
Mean	50.20594	.6077378	.1235882	.590215	61.07952	−2.590632	1.011642
Standard variation	16.98307	.189226	.4199146	1.035543	36.28624	3.67372	3.989576
Coefficient of variation	.3382681	.3113612	3.397691	1.754518	.594082	−1.418079	3.943665
Skewness	.3102829	−.770111	3.608166	.2107377	.9975029	−1.635517	−.3869701
Kurtosis	2.200954	3.480874	17.95423	2.457838	4.199147	11.85768	8.264819
Median	51.42857	.6387227	0	.615337	54.3	−2.3	44409,00
Min 5%	20	.1819671	−.068555	−.985529	44450,00	−9.2	−6.6
Max 5 %	74.28571	.8666667	1.208061	2.599744	131.4	44198,00	44321,00
N	137.00	360.00	392.00	392.00	459.00	459.00	335.00

Source: own elaboration.

has been estimated, where independent variables included a response variable delayed by two periods, and exogenous variables: one from the current period and one delayed by four periods. Statistically insignificant variables have been eliminated using the backward stepwise method, arriving at a relevant model, which points to the existence of correlations in different periods (see Table 3.14).

The research results are very interesting and confirm the high significance of medium-term planning for the economic growth measured by GDP growth across the Community. Analyses have demonstrated that a one-unit increase in the index on the quality of MTBF in a given current period will cause the EU-level GDP growth to go up, on average, by 1.86947 unit, *ceteris paribus*. Meanwhile, a one-unit MTBF increase over one period will cause the GDP rate to grow by 8.1044 units over a long-term period.

A similar positive effect of the use of high quality medium-term budgetary planning has been demonstrated for the level of public debt-to-GDP. The model tests conducted reveal, like in the previous case, that a one-unit increase in MTBF over one period will cause the public debt-to-GDP ratio to go down by 86.903 units over a long-term period. In the model, MTBF from two periods back has a significant impact on the debt growth. A one-unit MTBF growth two period before will cause debt in the current period to go down by an average of 14.7531, and a one-unit MTBF growth in one period will cause the public debt-to-GDP ratio to go down by 61.34 units over a long-term period (see Table 3.15).

What has come as a complete surprise is the results of ADL panel modelling for the impact of medium-term planning on the Community-level public finance deficit-to-GDP ratio. In model analyses, the results have revealed that MTBF from the current period has a significant impact on the deficit level, i.e. when MTBF rises in a given period by one unit, the deficit increases by an average of 8.62188 units. Meanwhile, a one-unit MTBF increase in one period will cause public finance deficit to rise over a long-term period by an average of 20.41469 units (Table 3.16). Such results are astonishing because one

Table 3.14 Dynamic two-step estimation model for the impact of medium-term planning on the GDP growth.

Asymptotic standard errors

	Coefficient	*Standard error*	*z*	*p-value*	
GDP growth (n–1)	0.0582178	0.00745765	7.806	<0.0001	***
MTBF	1.86947	0.699972	2.671	0.0076	***
MTBF (n+2)	5.76316	0.729623	7.899	<0.0001	***
Residual sum of squares	*1972,051*		*Residual standard error*	*2.819897*	

Source: own elaboration.

Table 3.15 Dynamic panel estimation model for the impact of medium-term planning on public debt-to-GDP.

Asymptotic standard errors					
	Coefficient	*Standard error*	*z*	*p-value*	
Public debt-to-GDP in the previous year (n–1)	1.05075	0.0236316	44.46	<0.0001	***
Public debt-to-GDP two years before (n–2)	−0.291264	0.0226540	−12.86	<0.0001	***
Const	0.734303	0.0566741	12.96	<0.0001	***
MTBF (n+2)	−14.7531	2.63971	−5.589	<0.0001	***
Residual sum of squares	*5651.43*		*Residual standard error*	*7.359156*	

Source: own elaboration.

Table 3.16 Dynamic panel estimation model for the impact of medium-term planning on the public finance deficit-to-GDP in the European Union.

Asymptotic standard errors					
	Coefficient	*Standard error*	*z*	*p-value*	
Public finance deficit in the previous period (n–1)	0.577663	0.0282424	20.45	<0.0001	***
MTBF	8.62188	0.888404	9.705	<0.0001	***
Residual sum of squares	*3588,085*		*Residual standard error*	*3.359060*	

Source: own elaboration.

generally recognised positive characteristic of medium-term planning is that it ensures responsible, anti-cyclical fiscal policy, which has not been confirmed by the research, though.

As a next step, regression models have been used to conduct dynamic tests for each country separately, measuring the correlation between MTBF and the indicators previously selected for analyses. The results obtained are quite heterogeneous and for some countries they cannot be deemed representative, as highlighted in the descriptions later.

Austria has legal solutions relating to medium-term planning enshrined in its constitution and a reference to the same is made in the budget law every year. Solutions regarding federal-level multiannual budgetary planning are implemented by means of the Federal Financial Framework Law (BFRG) and the Strategy Report. The former sets binding public expenditure ceilings broken down into five expenditure categories representing the main spheres of government action on the central level, while the Strategy Report contains political declarations of intent as well as annotations relating to revenue, among other things. The statistical research conducted has demonstrated that such a medium-term planning model has a positive impact on the economic growth in Austria, i.e. an increase in the MTBF index in a given year is not reflected by a higher GDP growth, but in the following periods a one-unit increase causes economic growth rate in the following years to grow by 11.8 units in the period n+1, 10.5 units in the period n+2 and 10 units in the period n+3. Expenditure ceilings in selected categories provide a positive stimulus for economic growth, though, unfortunately, a similar correlation cannot be observed for public deficit measured in relation to GDP. The dynamic panel model has demonstrated that a one-unit increase in MTBF in the current period causes public finance deficit to grow by 14.2 units, while in the following period n+1 there is no statistically significant correlation between these variables, and a growth of 10.3 and ca. 21.7 units is observable in n+2 and n+3, respectively. When it comes to the impact of this instrument on the public debt level, one notes that better planning in a given year may contribute to public debt-to-GDP ratio decreasing by up to 52.4 units, which is very beneficial from the point of view of public finance stability.

Belgium applies medium-term planning only as an auxiliary formula, this process not being integrated with the annual budget law. A relatively low effectiveness of this solution is confirmed by the research conducted. Based on the information presented to the European Commission, it can be concluded that only the existence of a rolling three-year framework in Belgium is reported, applicable to the central government, with no mention of local government or social insurance sectors. The aforementioned research has indicated that this type of public finance management instrument has a negative impact on the economic growth rate in n+2, i.e. at a one-unit MTBF growth, the GDP growth rate falls by 35.4 units. As for fiscal indicators, i.e. debt and public finance deficit, it has been difficult to model, based on the available data, any significant correlations that could lead to binding interpretations.

In Bulgaria, medium-term budget forecast has been converted into a real instrument of medium-term forecasting and planning in the form of a three-year rolling budget planning with a two-step annual budget procedure. The first step ends on 15 April with the approval of a medium-term budget forecast for a three-year period and with the Council of Ministers updating the Government Debt Management Strategy. The deadline for the second stage is 31 October, when the Council of Ministers has to submit draft state budget law with the updated medium-term budget forecast. The regulations implemented in Bulgaria stipulate that "the parameters of the approved state budget bill shall comply with the parameters of the updated medium-term budget forecast". Such an approach to shaping medium-term budget frameworks may have a positive impact on the economic growth rate, as confirmed by research results indicating that a one-unit MTBF increase in a current year causes this macroeconomic indicator to rise by 4.9, and by as much as 12.1 in the following period. When it comes to the impact on fiscal indicators, no positive effect of MTBF on the public finance deficit has been recorded; an improvement of that indicator has no impact on reducing the deficit, quite the contrary, actually. It is clear, however, that the use of such a solution to determine medium-term fiscal frameworks has an impact on public debt, i.e. a one-unit MTB growth in the year n+1 causes public debt to decrease by 43 in the year n+2 and by 27.3 units in the year n+3.

Cyprus is one of the countries which approach medium-term planning as an administrative issue: an instrument that is directly required by EU directives but not necessarily one to be applied in practice on a mandatory basis. Such an approach is reflected in the general provision of the local law whereby the budget policy is based on the adoption of a multiannual budget planning horizon aimed to meet the medium-term budget target. In that situation, conducting statistical research is doomed to fail by definition. However, certain positive aspects can be found, too as the extensive room for improvement of this instrument results in a major potential for a positive impact in reducing the public debt-to-GDP ratio in the period n+1 by 43 units.

Czech authorities have integrated medium-term planning with the annually prepared budget law. An MTBF proposal is submitted with the budget law to the Chamber of Deputies, which establishes the expenditure framework for the years n+1 and n+2 aimed to cover total expenditure from the state budget and state funds; a revenue forecast is also submitted. More detailed regulations specify the contents of the public sector strategy document and its integration into the budget process. The research conducted has revealed that for Czech Republic, medium-term planning may have a positive impact in reducing public finance deficit-to-GDP ratio, i.e. a one-unit improvement in the MTBF index in the period n+1 may help bring this indicator down by 14.5 units with all other assumptions remaining the same. By contrast, no correlation has been observed between this process and the public debt amount in Czech Republic. A relatively low correlation, a negative, to boot, has been noted for the impact of medium-term planning and the economic growth indicator.

In Germany, the federal government and the federated states have adopted a five-year fiscal planning horizon. Detailed forecasts of general government revenue and expenditure are published in the Stability Programme, in the Federal Finance Ministry's Financial Report and in its monthly reports (Truger and Will, 2013). German authorities affirm in strategic documents that medium-term financial planning is a general point of departure for the next planning cycle. The report by the federal government and by federated states details changes compared to the previous planning cycle in the attached documentation on medium-term financial planning. Model tests have demonstrated no correlations between MTBF and the levels of the fiscal indicators analysed; meanwhile, a one-unit increase in this index may contribute to the economic growth going up by 8.8 units.

In Denmark, the budget law introduces binding multiannual expenditure ceilings for three main public subsectors, i.e. central government, municipalities and regions. These ceilings relate to nominal upper caps on the actual expenditure. Danish authorities believe that the agreed ceilings in each sector ensure a clear accountability for keeping expenditure under control and support compliance in each of them. Expenditure ceilings must be approved by the Danish parliament and they apply to a period of four years. Ceilings for the new fourth year are established yearly based on an updated medium-term macroeconomic projection. Relevant ceilings cover a wide array of public expenditure: the ceiling for the central government includes operating costs, expenses on income transfers not related to unemployment, subsidies and foreign transfers while expenditure ceilings for municipalities and regions include servicing/operating costs. As revealed by the analyses conducted, the proposed expenditure ceiling-based solutions have a positive impact on the economic growth rate and contribute to lowering the public deficit (by up to 17 units in the period n+2) and public debt (by up to 23 units in the period n+3) in relation to GDP over a two- or three-period horizon.

Estonia has put in place a rolling system for creating medium-term documents which are adopted in the form of the State Budget Strategy. This document is enacted on a yearly basis in May. It sets the fiscal policy objectives for the coming three years and is the basis for developing draft state budget for the following three years. The State Budget Strategy is approved by the government upon request of the Minister of Finance seven months before the beginning of a budget year. A dynamic model has demonstrated that MTBF in Estonia has a minor impact on the macroeconomic indicators selected for the analysis. This result comes as no surprise considering the structure of the process which makes it relatively non-binding on the fiscal policy in place.

Greece is one of those countries whose fiscal results and public finance management instruments in use have urged the European Union to introduce Community-level legal regulations. The current national legislation stipulates that a medium-term fiscal strategy plan (MTFS) is a medium-term document containing a revenue and expenditure forecast for two previous years, current year, budget year and three following years. MTFS lays down the main political priorities and directions, the fiscal commitments undertaken for the following period and consequently the fiscal ceilings, detailed targets, timelines and implementation indicators for expenditure control and gradual deficit reduction and, last but not least, expenditure ceilings for each area within the central government throughout the duration of MTFS. At the planning stage, MTFS takes account of medium-term targets for the general government (total public deficit, primary general government deficit, public debt) and its subsectors, macroeconomic prospects and economic developments. In accordance with the law, MTFS is submitted to the Ministerial Council by mid-April and to the parliament to be adopted no later by mid-May each year. The plan can be updated if the macroeconomic environment has undergone a significant change. A dynamic model has demonstrated that in this case MTBF does not have a significant impact on the macroeconomic indicators selected for analysis.

When it comes to Spanish solutions, it is hard to identify any highly detailed information on medium-term planning because the local law only contains a general provision whereby fiscal policy shall be based on medium-term objectives. Such a solution is possible to implement but it is difficult to assess its effectiveness based on *ex post* statistical data.

Another group of countries analysed includes Finland, the Netherlands and Sweden, which implemented, as early as in the 1990s, medium-term planning solutions into their public management processes. In Finland and Sweden, this came as a response to a serious economic and financial crisis which spurred the introduction of MTBF as the benefits of an enhanced fiscal discipline proved even more visible under the circumstances, hence there was a strong political will to adopt them. In the Netherlands, the main motivation for extending the budget planning horizon beyond one year was the awareness that expenditure grows at an irregular pace and tax cuts would only be possible if the expenditure growth was subject to a specific limit. Most documents relating to medium-term planning are prepared on a continuous basis, with the next year added from year to year. However, in some cases (Finland, the Netherlands), planning documents cover a specific period beyond the budget year and are not extended on an ongoing basis. Here are a couple of examples to illustrate the degree of detail observed in planning documents. Sweden and Finland have focused on setting global expenditure ceilings for the central government. In the Netherlands, in addition to the expenditure ceiling for the central government, there is a separate ceiling for the social security system and another one for the healthcare system. Member States use many solutions involving the so-called discretionary measures and excluding certain public expenditure groups from expenditure ceilings. For example in Finland, cyclically sensitive expenditure (such as interest payments and unemployment benefits) is excluded from the ceiling but increases in cyclical spending resulting from a change in eligibility criteria or regulation of certain social allowances are included. In the Netherlands, unemployment expenditure usually does not exceed the ceiling but, for pragmatic reasons, this item was excluded from the ceiling during the last economic and financial crisis. Solutions adopted by Finland with respect to medium-term planning seem very effective in how they impact the public debt level as the research conducted has demonstrated that a one-unit increase in MTBF in the period n+1 causes the debt-to-GDP to fall by 14.9 units, and in the period n+3, by as many as 20 units. Meanwhile, as for the impact on the GDP growth, it is observable, too, as in the period n+1, a one-unit MTBF growth may cause the GDP growth to accelerate by as much as 13.8 units. The budget process in the Netherlands is currently based on a four-year cycle with minimum annual adjustments. The government adheres to the expenditure frameworks which set the general expenditure to be incurred during its term of office. These frameworks are usually developed by a new government by way of initial budget memorandum based on multiannual expenditure estimates which, in turn, are derived from prudent economic development scenarios presented by an independent planning office. Thanks to this approach, a positive correlation can be found between the MTBF indicator value and the economic growth in this country, i.e. a one-unit increase in the index causes economic growth in the following period to grow by 12 units. As for Sweden, its authorities forecast all main expenditure and revenue items for at least three years, and the Swedish parliament also approves the expenditure and revenue levels for the years following the upcoming budget year. The research conducted using a dynamic model has not demonstrated statistically positive correlations between the MTBF index and debt- and deficit-to-GDP ratios, i.e. a one-unit increase in this index in the period n causes, respectively, a drop in public debt in the period n+2 by 113.2 units, and a one-unit increase in MTBF in the period n+2 causes an increase by 73.8 units. When it comes to deficit, research has shown major variation in the results obtained, for example in the period n+1, public finance deficit may grow by 13.3 units as the quality of medium-term planning increases, whereas the correlation is reversed in the following periods.

France is a country often quoted as a model when it comes to its approach to modern forms of public finance management in many areas, for example medium-term planning solutions. French authorities have included relevant provisions in the country's constitution, which stipulates that multiannual public finance guidelines shall be set as part of performance-budgeting process. The multiannual public finance planning acts, first adopted in February 2009, represent the main element of multiannual planning in France. These laws define expenditure ceilings for the state at a disaggregated level and for governmental subsectors over a three-year horizon as well as the minimum annual amount of additional revenue from the new fiscal solutions being implemented. The exemplarity of the French solutions has been also confirmed by statistical research: a one-unit MTBF growth in the period n+1 will cause public debt-to-GDP ratio to decrease by 3.2 units and the GDP growth to accelerate by 8.3 unit.

Hungary's regulations include a provision on medium-term planning based on which the government lays down the planned state budget revenue and expenditure as well as budget balance for three years, to be updated as needed in line with budget and macroeconomic trends. As part of this framework budget set in a relevant law, funds for budget sectors are presented for at least three years in clear and quantitative terms. Despite the three-year perspective described earlier, Hungary's current budget framework focuses on planning, with government action planned one budget cycle ahead. To change this approach, the authorities have stipulated in the new legislative framework that the total revenue and expenditure will be set three years ahead. However, this would not necessarily mean imposing any limitations on the government. Revenue and expenditure as aggregates can be modified only to the extent justified by macroeconomic circumstances. The lack of concrete binding solutions makes it, in this country, too, impossible to establish in a reliable manner the impact of MTBF on macroeconomic parameters.

Irish authorities declare that regulations are being elaborated that will serve as the legal basis of the existing multiannual expenditure ceilings. The Irish medium-term budget framework is fully consistent with the Irish stability programme, as can be read in governmental documents from that country. Medium-term ceilings/targets can be adjusted in response to changes in the parameters set in relevant regulations or another public strategy document (e.g. change in expenditure on pensions and unemployment benefits). This means that they are relatively non-binding and are only presentational in nature, which involves no positive impact on the economic growth rate or fiscal parameters in this country.

Italy is one of the countries to have been the hardest hit by the crisis of 2007–2008, both in the economic sphere and in public finance. As such, the country has undertaken a number of measures to improve the public management process. The reform proposed in 2009 changed regulations to coordinate the Italian budget timetable with the European semester. As a result of these efforts, the Economic and Financial Document (Documento di Economia e Finanza – DEF) is at present a key material on the rolling medium-term budget framework which the government submits every year to the parliament in April. In October, the budget package consisting of the Budget Law and Stability Law is submitted to the parliament by the government. The Stability Law contains, for three reference years, qualitative and quantitative measures intended to achieve the fiscal targets set in DEF (and in each September update thereof). The appropriateness of the approach to the planning process and of the many efforts aimed to increase the efficiency of these measures has been confirmed by the results of the dynamic model testing conducted for that country. To quote but one fact, if MTBF increases by one unit in the period n+2, the economic growth rate can be observed to accelerate by 33 units in the period n+3.

Luxembourgish authorities admit that from the point of view of the EU law and of the provisions of the budgetary framework directive, medium-term budgetary framework is not used. At the moment, the MTFS is based on the stability programme. Moreover, the government undertakes efforts to ensure consistency between the medium-term validity period of the forecast macroeconomic variables and the annual budget. There is also a need to strengthen the top-down budget procedures as part of the budget cycle. There are even no detailed regulations on medium-term planning but the ongoing improvement of this process may contribute to the positive correlation, i.e. a one-unit MTBF growth in Luxembourg may cause public debt-to-GDP ratio to go down by 3.2 units in the following period.

Lithuanian authorities report that the current MTBF is adopted by the parliament together with the budget and defines the total state revenue and expenditure for the coming three years. Hence, the authorities believe this is compliant with Chapter 5 of the directive. The Law on the Approval of

Financial Indicators of the State Budget and Municipal Budgets is prepared and approved in accordance with the Law on Fiscal Discipline, which means that considering the anticipated state budget growth, expenditure may not exceed the ceilings set in the Law on Fiscal Discipline. Meanwhile, in Latvia, the Medium-Term Budgetary Framework Law (MTBFL) has been adopted as one of the fiscal planning instruments. MTBFL is based on the following main principles: a three-year time horizon is set on a rolling yearly basis and it contains rules determining expenditure ceilings. MTBFL was first prepared with the Draft Budget Law of 2013 for 2013–2015 and included medium-term budget objectives and priority development areas as well as maximum state expenditure (by each ministry and by other central state institutions).

Poland has detailed multiannual planning solutions in its public finance law, at both central (Multiannual State Financial Plan – WPFP) and local levels (Multiannual Financial Forecast – WPF). The Multiannual State Financial Plan is the foundation for government-level medium-term budget planning. It was introduced following an in-depth analysis of tools of that kind functioning in other countries. The Polish multiannual planning model is similar to the model that has been successfully used for many years in Finland. The creation of WPFP was made possible by applying experience in medium-term planning and performance budgeting methodology, which has, to date, mainly consisted in presenting findings. The Polish Public Finance Law stipulates that WPFP is developed and adopted as a resolution by the Council of Ministers. The procedure and principles for developing a draft WPFP strengthen the new quality of multiannual planning within state administration, based on the use of the latest public management methods. The principal and pioneering element of the plan is a state budget expenditure forecast broken down by state functions, specifying the targets and the metrics measuring the progress towards their achievement. My own statistical research has demonstrated that such solutions and their ongoing improvement have a good impact on lowering public debt- and deficit-to-GDP ratios, i.e. a one-unit MTBF increase in Poland has a positive effect on those indicators after two years, with an increase of 16 and 39 units, respectively.

Portuguese authorities seem to have a relaxed attitude to medium-term planning, as reflected by the data on the quality of forecasts prepared in this country, presented in the previous subchapter. A budget strategy document (Documento de Estratégia Orçamental) is prepared in the country. In addition, each year, the government submits to the parliament a draft budget law with a multiannual budget programme updated yearly for the following four years, in line with the stability and growth programme objectives. The multiannual budget programme was first prepared and published in April 2012 for the period 2012–2016. It defines caps for expenditure financed from the central government's general revenue and each of its programme budgets. Considering such general provisions used in Portugal for medium-term planning, model testing has proved ineffective as it has been difficult to demonstrate any credible correlations based on quantitative data.

Romania, a former member of the ex-communist bloc, has implemented European solutions by adopting three-year budget planning with deficit and expenditure targets, reimbursable financing and a ceiling for guarantees. The Fiscal and Budgetary Strategy is a public policy document that lays down the fiscal and budget objectives and priorities. It contains forecasts for the main expenditure and revenue items as well as a description of key policies having an impact on fiscal targets. A draft annual budget presented to the parliament is compliant with the fiscal rules and with the Fiscal and Budgetary Strategy. Romanian authorities, in their national documents and in those submitted to the European Commission, state that the President of the Council of Ministers and the Minister of Finance are committed to publicly address any discrepancies between the annual budget and MTBF within a defined timeframe. Dynamic model testing has demonstrated that MTBF applied by the Romanian authorities does not have a positive impact on the public debt and budget deficit levels. Quite the opposite – even a one-unit improvement in the MTBF index in a given period n+1 may cause deficit to grow by 12 units and debt, by 7.6 units in the period n+2.

Further two EU Member States are Slovenia and Slovakia, which joined the Community in the same year 2004. As these are countries from the same region, they have nearly identical medium-term planning solutions; in both cases, the MTBF index level identified by the European Commission has no impact either on economic growth rate or fiscal parameters as included in the Maastricht criteria. In Slovenia, a complete budget is prepared by the government for the following year together with a budget for the budget year. Hence, a document is submitted to the National Assembly containing a two-year rolling budget for central government and an overall expenditure framework for general government for the year n+3. These caps, however, are not binding, they can be adjusted from year to year in the light of the current economic developments. The timing and horizon for budget constraints are set as part of medium-term social and financial goals, taking account of the real budget deficit. In accordance with the Public Balance Act, a Budget Memorandum contains guidelines on the economic and fiscal policy and structural reforms as well as measures to be taken on revenue and expenditure side alike. Such a solution can be seen as an element of a presentational approach to medium-term planning as the framework can be modified and is purely informative in nature rather than represent binding guidelines for action to be taken by the government of Slovenia. Meanwhile, in Slovakia, the main component of the fiscal framework is a detailed three-year general government budget, a Budget Act prepared and approved by the government. The first year is binding whereas the remaining years of the multiannual budget are updated on a yearly basis. Medium-term policy projections affecting the general government finance are described in the Stability Programme, but not so clearly in the Slovak MTBF. Unfortunately, the statistical research has failed to demonstrate for those two countries any significant correlation between MTBF and any of the macroeconomic variables analysed.

3.3 Impact of fiscal rules on the GDP growth rate and selected fiscal indicators

Another instrument EU Member States are obliged to implement is fiscal rules, already presented to a certain extent in Chapter 2. The econometric research has been conducted using the same methodology as for medium-term planning, its results being presented in Tables 3.17 and 3.18.

An ADL panel model has been estimated where independent variables are a response variable delayed by 2 periods and exogenous variables: one for the current period and one delayed by 4 periods. Statistically insignificant variables have been eliminated using the backward stepwise method, arriving at the target model. In the model, GDP growth is significantly affected by Fiscal Rules Index from all previous periods. A one-unit increase of Fiscal Rules Index in one period will cause the GDP to grow by 5.116785 units in the long term.

An ADL panel model has been elaborated, where independent variables are a response variable delayed by 2 periods and exogenous variables: one for the current period and one delayed by 4 periods. Statistically insignificant variables have been eliminated using the backward stepwise method, obtaining the first results. In the model, the ratio of public debt growth to GDP in the previous year is significantly impacted by Fiscal Rules Index from all previous periods.

Table 3.17 Dynamic panel model estimation of the impact of Fiscal Rules Index on the GDP growth rate.

Asymptotic standard errors

	Coefficient	*Standard error*	*z*	*p-value*	
GDP growth (n–1)	0.243025	0.0330336	7.357	<0.0001	***
GDP growth (n–2)	−0.191544	0.0113205	−16.92	<0.0001	***
Const	0.566059	0.164766	3.436	0.0006	***
Fiscal Rule Index (n+1)	0.873939	0.171352	5.100	<0.0001	***
Fiscal Rule Index (n+2)	1.63263	0.158975	10.27	<0.0001	***
Fiscal Rule Index (n+3)	0.931009	0.175099	5.317	<0.0001	***
Fiscal Rule Index (n+4)	1.42579	0.176078	8.097	<0.0001	***
Residual sum of squares	*2947.997*		*Residual standard error*	*3.292146*	

Source: own elaboration.

Table 3.18 Dynamic panel model estimation of the impact of Fiscal Rules Index on the public-debt-to-GDP ratio.

Asymptotic standard errors					
	Coefficient	*Standard error*	*z*	*p-value*	
Public debt-to-GDP in the previous year (n–1)	0.980130	0.0410059	23.90	<0.0001	***
Public debt-to-GDP in the previous year (n–2)	−0.266410	0.0373647	−7.130	<0.0001	***
Const	0.493782	0.0626412	7.883	<0.0001	***
Fiscal Rule Index (n+1)	−1.13044	0.299164	−3.779	0.0002	***
Fiscal Rule Index (n+2)	−2.31898	0.327255	−7.086	<0.0001	***
Fiscal Rule Index (n+3)	−2.12742	0.415675	−5.118	<0.0001	***
Fiscal Rule Index (n+4)	−2.96519	0.268431	−11.05	<0.0001	***
Residual sum of squares	*14799.92*		*Residual standard error*	*7.501564*	

Source: own elaboration.

A one-unit increase in the Fiscal Rules Index in one period will cause public debt-to-GDP in the year n–1 to fall by 29.838 in the long term.

Then, statistically insignificant variables have been eliminated using the backward stepwise method, arriving at model 40. In the model, the increase in the public debt-to-GDP in the previous year does not significantly impact the Fiscal Rule Index delayed by 1, 2, 3 and 4 periods. A one-unit growth in Fiscal Rules Index in one period will cause public debt-to-GDP in the year n–1 to fall by 414.13 units on average in the long term (see Tables 3.19 and 3.20).

An ADL panel model has been estimated, where independent variables are a response variable delayed by 2 periods and exogenous variables: one for the current period and one delayed by 4 periods. Statistically insignificant variables have been eliminated using the backward stepwise method, arriving at model 67. In the model, the public deficit growth in the previous period to GDP is significantly impacted by Fiscal Rules Index delayed by 2, 3 and 4 periods. A one-unit increase in the Fiscal Rules Index in one period will cause public deficit in the previous period to GDP to grow, on average, by 1.169346 in the long term.

An ADL panel model has been estimated where independent variables are a response variable delayed by 2 periods and exogenous variables: one for the current period and one delayed by 4 periods. Statistically insignificant variables have been eliminated using the backward stepwise method, arriving at the target model. In the model, the GDP growth is significantly impacted by Fiscal Rule Strength Index from the current period and from all previous periods. When Fiscal Rules Index increases by one unit in the current period, GDP will grow, on average, by 0.621602 units *ceteris paribus*. Meanwhile, a one-unit

Table 3.19 Dynamic panel model estimation of the impact of Fiscal Rules Index on the public finance deficit-to-GDP ratio.

Asymptotic standard errors					
	Coefficient	*Standard error*	*z*	*p-value*	
Public finance deficit in the previous period to GDP (n–1)	0.522822	0.0398976	13.10	<0.0001	***
Const	−1.61152	0.186034	−8.663	<0.0001	***
Fiscal Rule Index (n+2)	0.905092	0.161061	5.620	<0.0001	***
Fiscal Rule Index (n+3)	0.629528	0.211948	2.970	0.0030	***
Fiscal Rule Index (n+4)	0.907790	0.251733	3.606	0.0003	***
Residual sum of squares	*2343.832*	*Residual standard error*		*2.833165*	

Source: own elaboration.

Table 3.20 Two-step dynamic panel model estimation of the impact of Fiscal Rule Strength Index on GDP growth.

Asymptotic standard errors					
	Coefficient	*Standard error*	*z*	*p-value*	
GDP growth (n–1)	0.333453	0.0494986	6.737	<0.0001	***
GDP growth (n–2)	−0.120142	0.0113121	−10.62	<0.0001	***
Const	0.786020	0.146746	5.356	<0.0001	***
Fiscal rule strength index (n+1)	0.621602	0.125247	4.963	<0.0001	***
Fiscal rule strength index (n+2)	0.541428	0.182422	2.968	0.0030	***
Fiscal rule strength index (n+3)	−0.762793	0.200844	−3.798	0.0001	***
Fiscal rule strength index (n+4)	−0.817367	0.184270	−4.436	<0.0001	***
Residual sum of squares	*2870.288*		*Residual standard error*	*3.248466*	

Source: own elaboration.

increase in the Fiscal Rule Strength Index in one period will cause the GDP rate to grow by 6.804924 units in the long term (see Tables 3.21 and 3.22).

An ADL panel model has been estimated where independent variables are a response variable delayed by 2 periods and exogenous variables: one for the current period and one delayed by 4 periods. Statistically insignificant variables have been eliminated using the backward stepwise method, arriving at model 47. In the model, the GDP growth is significantly impacted by the Fiscal Rule Strength Index delayed by 1 and 2 periods. A one-unit increase in the Fiscal Rule Strength Index in one period will cause debt to fall, on average, by 10.1846 units in the long term.

An ADL panel model has been estimated where independent variables are a response variable delayed by 2 periods and exogenous variables: one for the current period and one delayed by 4 periods. Statistically insignificant variables

Table 3.21 Two-step dynamic panel model estimation of the impact of Fiscal Rule Strength Index on public debt-to-GDP.

Asymptotic standard errors

	Coefficient	*Standard error*	*z*	*p-value*	
Public debt-to-GDP in the previous year (n–1)	1.27159	0.0241318	52.69	<0.0001	***
Public debt-to-GDP (n–2)	−0.339281	0.0272820	−12.44	<0.0001	***
Const	6.36394	0.617716	10.30	<0.0001	***
Fiscal rule strength index (n+1)	−1.29902	0.330889	−3.926	<0.0001	***
Fiscal rule strength index (n+2)	0.609616	0.281093	2.169	0.0301	**
Residual sum of squares	*15924.23*		*Residual standard error*	*6.784083*	

Source: own elaboration.

Table 3.22 Two-step dynamic panel model estimation of the impact of Fiscal Rule Strength Index on the public deficit-to-GDP.

Asymptotic standard errors

	Coefficient	*Standard error*	*z*	*p-value*	
Public deficit in the previous period to GDP (n–1)	0.575836	0.0481538	11.96	<0.0001	***
Public deficit-to-GDP (n–2)	−0.230284	0.0334776	−6.879	<0.0001	***
Const	−2.40601	0.239720	−10.04	<0.0001	***
Fiscal rule strength index_2	1.33659	0.312608	4.276	<0.0001	***
Fiscal rule strength index_3	−0.788038	0.340703	−2.313	0.0207	**
Residual sum of squares	*2970.829*	*Residual standard error*		*3.051712*	

Source: own elaboration.

have been eliminated using the backward stepwise method, arriving at model 56. In the model, the deficit growth is significantly impacted by the Fiscal Rule Strength Index delayed by 2 and 3 periods. A one-unit increase in the Fiscal Rule Strength Index will cause debt to grow in the long term, on average, by 0.83819 units.

As a next step, the dynamic panel model method has been used to conduct, for each country, separate analyses of the correlations between the Fiscal Rule Strength Index and the public debt- and public deficit-to-GDP levels as well as those of the economic growth measured with a change in GDP. In the analyses conducted autonomously for each country, it is impossible to determine reliable correlations at domestic level. This stems from the fact that the database for this index is incomplete and the data are available for a relatively limited time horizon, making it impossible to apply it responsibly in econometric research.

In Austria, a number of changes were conducted in 2011, introducing a new system for implementing new fiscal rules, which were extended to apply to the local government sector as well (Eisl, 2020). The country has three main rules in place. The first one is the structural balance rule, in effect since 2017, whereby a lower limit of the total structural deficit of general government sector is set at −0.45% of GDP (−0.35% for the central government and −0.1% for the *Länder* and municipalities). Another one, the expenditure rule, holds that, in accordance with the preventive arm of the European Stability and Growth Pact, the public expenditure growth (excluding discretionary measures) may not exceed the average potential growth and must be consistent with the adjustment path towards the medium-term budgetary objective (Eijffinger and de Haan, 2000). According to the last rule relating to the public debt level, if public debt exceeds 60% of GDP, it should be reduced by 1/20 over three years.

The statistical research conducted has demonstrated that complying with the applicable set of fiscal rules in force may contribute to economic growth in Austria, i.e. in a given year, it can contribute to GDP growing by 1.9 units. No similar correlation has been observed for the budget deficit-to-GDP. A dynamic panel model has revealed that a one-unit FRS increase in the current period will cause the public deficit to grow by 1.3 units, while in the following periods (n+1 and n+2) we can see an increase of 1.7 and 3.1 units, respectively. As regards the impact of FRS on the public debt, research has demonstrated a 7.8-unit decrease in the public debt.

In Belgium, some fiscal rules are very strictly adhered to, while in other cases, there is hardly any link between the target and actual values; hence, there is much room for improvement when it comes to some Belgian fiscal rules. Belgium generally meets its general government budget balance objective at a satisfactory level. The country's annual structural balance of the general government must be at the level of the medium-term budgetary objective (currently 0% of GDP) or respect the adjustment path towards the same as defined in the stability programme, with a bottom limit for the structural deficit set at 0.5% of GDP (Blanchard et al., 2021).

The aforementioned research has demonstrated that Belgian fiscal rules have a positive impact on the economic growth in the base year and in n+3. Like in Austria's case, no positive impact of fiscal rules on the budget deficit-to-GDP has been observed in Belgium. The model applied has demonstrated that a one-unit increase of FRS in the current period will cause the public deficit to go up 1.5 units in the year n+2, and 1.3 units in n+3. As regards the impact of FRS on the public debt, research has revealed a 4.8-unit decrease in public debt in the period n+3.

Fiscal rules in effect in Bulgaria are defined by the Law on Public Finances. The law lays down expenditure, debt and budget balance rules and sets a medium-term budget objective whereby deficit may not exceed 0.5% of GDP in structural terms. This objective may be updated every three years. Moreover, relevant regulations define a nominal ceiling for the general government deficit at 3%. The nominal ceiling for the consolidated debt is 60% for general government. Moreover, the expenditure ceiling (40% of GDP) is supplemented by an expenditure rule derived from the provisions of SGP:

> the average growth rate of budget expenditure for the period of the forecast shall not exceed the forecast average growth rate of the potential Gross Domestic Product until the attainment of the medium-term structural balance target set out in the budgetary forecast.

When it comes to local governments, a cash-based medium-term budget objective has been introduced, along with limitations on debt and debt payment and a requirement for municipalities to set an expenditure ceiling for new commitments. Additional rules limiting debt accumulation and the issuance of guarantees are applicable to the social security subsector and to other entities whose budgets are excluded from the state budget but are included in the Consolidated Fiscal Programme.

The fiscal rules applied in Bulgaria may have a positive impact on the GDP growth rate as the increase in FRS in the period n+1 causes the indicator in question to go up 2.1 units. When it comes to the other fiscal aggregates analysed, namely debt-to-GDP and public deficit-to-GDP, it has been difficult to model, based on the available data, any significant correlations that could suggest any binding interpretations.

In Cyprus, there is a debt rule and budget balance rule with associated provisions for an automatic correction mechanism. The budget balance rule states that the general structural budget position must be in balance or in surplus in the medium term. This rule is met if the annual structural balance of the general government achieves the defined medium-term budget objective (Cebotari et al., 2008). Local authorities are obliged to maintain sustainable annual budgets. The debt rule stipulates that the public debt-to-GDP ratio may not exceed 60%.

The statistical research conducted for Cyprus has yielded similar results to those obtained for Bulgaria. It has demonstrated that the set of fiscal rules in effect in Cyprus may have a positive impact on the GDP growth rate because a one-unit increase in FRS in the period n+1 causes the indicator in question to grow by 2.3 units. When it comes to fiscal indicators, that is public debt-to-GDP and public deficit-to-GDP, it has been difficult to model, based on the available data, any statistically significant correlations that could be the basis for binding interpretations.

Until 2017, virtually no fiscal rules were in effect in the Czech Republic. In 2017, the Constitutional Act on fiscal responsibility introduced three fiscal rules. The first one is a balanced budget rule based on a medium-term objective (MTO) of structural deficit of 1% of GDP. Another one is the debt brake set at 55% of GDP and a debt brake for regional and local governments for which the maximum debt limit stands at 60% of their revenues.

It was challenging to conduct research in the Czech Republic due to the relatively short time the fiscal rules have been in effect. Nevertheless, one can tentatively conclude that the debt rules introduced stand a chance of success as research has demonstrated that in the base year, a one-unit increase in the FRS indicator causes public debt to decrease by 3.4 units.

In Germany, the budgetary policy is based on rules that ensure its stable and effective functioning and are enshrined in the Constitution (Heimberger et al., 2020). The principal fiscal rule in Germany is the debt rule, the so-called debt brake. In accordance with that rule, the state must keep overall finance balanced without revenues from credits (Schoeller and Karlsson, 2021). This rule is deemed satisfied when the structural public debt does not exceed 0.35 % of GDP. The debt brake also functions with respect to *Länder*, where the rule is fulfilled when the structural debt does not go beyond 0% of GDP. In addition, structural deficit of the general government may not exceed the upper limit of 0.5% of the nominal GDP. The social security sector is obliged to maintain nominal balance between all revenue and expenditure. The minimum provision for health insurance in Germany is 25% of the monthly expenditure. The dynamic panel research conducted has demonstrated that this is one of the strongest fiscal rules in EU Member States. A one-unit increase in FRS causes the public debt to go down by 3.4 units in the period n, and by as many as 6 units in the period n+3. When it comes to the impact on the economic growth, none has been defined while for the impact of FRS on the public finance deficit-to-GDP, the research has demonstrated that a one-unit increase triggers a 2.5-unit increase of this ratio.

Like in Germany, Danish fiscal rules are enshrined in the Constitution. The first one is a balanced budget rule based on a MTO that is a structural deficit of 0.5% of GDP. The expenditure rule defines nominal expenditure ceilings for three main budget areas (central government, local government and regions) that are legally binding for four years. In this country, the FRS indicator has a significant impact on the GDP growth rate, i.e. a one-unit increase of this index will cause the economic growth rate to grow by 1.2 units in a given period and by 0.8 units in the period n+2. As regards fiscal indicators, when FRS grows by one unit in a given period, the public debt-to-GDP may fall by 4.5 units whereas in the period n+2, one can expect a 5.2-unit fall. An improvement in the FRS in Denmark has no positive impact on the public sector deficit.

Another country where the issue of fiscal discipline has been dealt with in the Constitution is Estonia. The Estonian Constitution makes it mandatory for the general government to maintain a balanced budget or generate a surplus, taking account of the official macroeconomic forecasts, but it does not provide for specific fiscal rules. The national public finance law indicates that governmental entities may not accumulate debt obligations beyond 40% of their annual income unless they have been authorised to do so by the government. As regards local governments, their activities have been governed since 2012 by the Local Government Financial Management Act. The Act stipulates that local governments must ensure that the operating result, i.e. the difference between operating revenue and operating expenditure, is balanced or positive. Their debt should be below 60% of the budget revenue less funds allocated for specific purposes. Basing fiscal rules on expenditure ceilings has a very positive impact in Estonia, as reflected by the research conducted, on the economic growth rate, i.e. a one-unit increase in FRS may cause the macroeconomic indicator to grow by 3.8 units in the period n+2. Similarly positive effects can be observed for the public finance deficit, i.e. it falls by 1.5 unit in the period n+2 following a one-unit FRS increase in the period n+1.

Greece is a bit of a black sheep of the euro area when it comes to the results of its fiscal policy in place (Athanassio, 2009). In 2014, the Greek law No. 4270/2014 transposed the budgetary framework requirements of the Council Directive 2011/85/EU to the national law. Pursuant to these regulations, a debt rule and a balanced budget rule were introduced. The debt rule stipulates that if the debt ratio exceeds a reference value of 60% of GDP, it must be reduced until the reference value is reached. The gap between the debt and the reference value should be bridged at an annual rate of 1/20th of the average for the last three years. Meanwhile, the balanced budget rule indicates that the structural budget balance must correspond to the MTO (European Commission, 2012a, 2012b, 2012c, 2012d). Econometric research conducted on *ex post* data has not confirmed the correlation between the fiscal rules applied in Greece and the macroeconomic and fiscal indicators under analysis (Arbatli et al., 2020). This may suggest a low effectiveness of the fiscal rules used (Liargovas and Psychalis, 2020).

Spain has a single expenditure rule applicable to all levels of general government (Organic Law, Article 12), which holds that the annual expenditure growth may not exceed the average GDP growth rate (over 10 years) in nominal terms. Moreover, in accordance with the budget balance rule, public administration may not generate structural deficit. Debt rule stipulates that total debt of the public administration may not go beyond the limit allowed by the European Union, i.e. 60% of GDP. Law No. 2/2012 of 27 April 2012 on Budgetary Stability and Financial Sustainability sets a limit for each public administration subsector: Central Administration at 44%, Autonomous Communities at 13%, local communities at 3% and social security at 0%. When looking at the measures undertaken to comply with fiscal rules and the fiscal results, no direct positive correlations can be observed between them. The results have shown that a one-unit increase in the FRS index causes both debt- and public finance deficit-to-GDP to grow.

In Finland, the government, in the beginning of its term of office, sets, by a political decision, the parliamentary spending limits, i.e. the budget expenditure ceiling and the rules governing the procedure for limiting expenditure for the four-year parliamentary term. Central government's and local governments' deficits should not exceed 0.5% of GDP. Since 2015, an additional debt rule has been in place. If the debt-to-GDP ratio does not decrease, corrective measures are to be taken at central government level on the expenditure and revenue side. Finland's only fiscal rule enshrined in the law holds that the

Government sets a MTO for the structural balance of the general government. Such two-pronged approach, based on political decisions on the one hand but, on the other, supported by regulatory measures, seems to be a very efficient example of fiscal rule implementation. This has been confirmed by model research, indicating that a one-unit increase in the SRF indicator will cause public finance deficit to decrease by 0.6 units and the public debt, by 2.7 units in the period n+1. When it comes to the impact on the economic growth rate, it is observed as well: a one-unit increase in SRF means a 2.1-unit decrease in the GDP growth rate.

In France, a golden rule was introduced in 1983 with respect to local authorities which prohibits financing current expenditure through debt. Compliance with the rule is monitored by the prefect supported by regional chambers of auditors. Moreover, the constitutional provisions make it obligatory to set structural balance objectives as a share of GDP. In addition, a revenue rule is also in effect in France, which holds that all unexpected receipts from taxes are to be used towards decreasing the fiscal deficit. Such an approach to fiscal rules generates positive correlations between their improvement and the fiscal outcomes: a one-unit increase in FRS causes GDP growth rate to go up by 0.8 units and the public debt-to-GDP ratio to drop by 2.7 units in the period n+3.

Croatian legislation, starting from 2019, has introduced three rules at the central government level: with respect to balanced budget, expenditure and debt. Balanced budget rule holds that the structural balance expressed as a share of GDP will be realised according to the adjustment plan in order to reach a medium-term budgetary objective. The expenditure fiscal rule in Croatia stipulates that an increase in budgetary expenditure may not exceed a referential potential GDP growth rate plus the expected rate of price increases. The debt rule requires that public debt as a share of GDP may not exceed the reference value of 60%. If the share exceeds that value, the difference between public debt as a share of GDP and the reference value of 60% must be reduced at a rate consistent with the EU law (an average annual reduction by 1/20th). In Croatia, fiscal rules play a minor role in the fiscal policy in place. This has been confirmed by the model research which has demonstrated no significant correlations, given that the fiscal rules were introduced in Croatia to the full extent only three years ago and their effectiveness cannot be yet reliably established.

Hungary has a numerical fiscal rule which is a debt reduction rule enshrined in the Act on the Economic Stability. Its scope covers central government administration, local governments and other authorities classified as government sector entities. It stipulates that as long as public debt exceeds half of GDP, the National Assembly may only pass a central budget law which includes a reduction in the public debt-to-GDP ratio. Hungarian legislation also provides for two balanced budget rules in the context of government sector. The first rule holds that general government deficit may not exceed 3% of GDP, and the second, that the general government balance should be set at a level that makes it possible to achieve the medium-term budgetary objective. Research demonstrates that the FRS index has an impact on the public debt level, contributing to a 2.3-unit reduction of this fiscal parameter in the period n+3. These solutions, however, have a much lesser impact on the level of sector deficit, which goes up by one unit with one-unit increase in SRF and all other factors unchanged.

The Irish Fiscal Responsibility Act of 2012 requires the government to adhere to the balanced budget rule and to the debt rule. According to the debt rule, when the ratio of general government to GDP ratio exceeds 60%, the ratio shall be reduced in accordance with the 1997 excessive deficit regulation until the ratio reaches 60%. The budgetary rule holds that the budgetary position of the general government must be in balance or in surplus, which is determined by reference to the MTO or it must be on the adjustment path towards the MTO – unless exceptional circumstances have arisen as provided in the SGP. The research conducted has demonstrated a poor effectiveness of such an approach as a one-unit increase in FRS in the period n+1 may reduce the public debt-to-GDP ratio by 13.9 units. When it comes to the other fiscal aggregate, i.e. debt-to-GDP, a one-unit increase in FRS may cause deficit to go up by eight units.

Fiscal rules in effect in Italy were enshrined in 2012 in the Constitution which contains a general requirement whereby the government ensures budgetary balance, general government debt sustainability in accordance with the legal order of the EU and a nominal balance of local governments. As provided in the Constitution, the central government budget must ensure balance between revenue and expenditure unless exceptional circumstances are approved by the parliament with an absolute majority (Blanchard et al., 2018). Local government rules are defined in detail by the local law on the implementation of the balanced budget principles. Italian authorities declare that they aim towards strengthening the fiscal discipline by strengthening the set of fiscal rules. With respect to local and regional authorities, the "National Stability Pact" lays down the measures that enable local and regional authorities to contribute to the achievement of public finance objectives. It contains the principles of disclosing cash receipts from borrowing in public statistics (new long-term secured loans and other sources of market financing): the yearly debt servicing must be below the ceiling set as a percentage of revenue collected in the two preceding years. Unfortunately, model research has demonstrated no significant positive impact on the parameters selected for the analysis: the significance of the results obtained is quite minor so it is hard to view them as fully reliable, which is why they are not presented.

In Lithuania, which, in the recent years, has joined the euro area and implemented a number of cutting edge public management solutions, the national law contains a national fiscal rule. It holds that general government finance must be compliant with the MTO of ensuring a surplus or near balance of the general government budget. In addition, if the arithmetical mean of the general government balance from the last five full calendar years shows a deficit, known at a time when the state budget or amendments to it are being prepared, the annual increase in the expenditure of the state budget, Social Security Fund and Health Insurance Fund budgets may not exceed half of the average annual rate of revenue growth for the state budget (not including the EU support measures) for the last five years. With respect to such circumstances, estimations demonstrate no significant correlation between the FRS index and the economic growth rate, while, in turn, they have evidenced a correlation with fiscal parameters, i.e. a one-unit increase in FRS may trigger a deficit-to-GDP growth of up to 4.7 units in the period n and 0.3 in the period n+3, and a 1.5-unit reduction in the public debt-to-GDP ratio.

The Luxembourgish government is obliged by law to maintain an adjustment path towards MTO (a structural deficit equal to or less than 0.5% of GDP). Code de la Sécurité Sociale 2021 and the annual budget balance rule makes it mandatory for each social security fund to maintain reserve funds for healthcare. At the commune level, the Municipal Organisation Act (*Loi Communale*) restricts loans to those intended to fund capital expenditure, but the costs of loan repayment must be financed from the current budget. In this relatively small country that follows EU regulations, fiscal rules have been observed to have a significant positive impact on the GDP growth rate in the short term while in the long run, this type of fiscal tightening may affect the economic growth (a one-unit increase in FRS may result in the GDP rate growing by 2.5 units in the period n and by 3.8 units in the period n+2, and falling by up to 5.5 units in the period n+3). Meanwhile, the research conducted for the purposes of this Monograph has demonstrated no significant correlation between FRS and fiscal parameters in Luxembourg.

The Latvian Fiscal Discipline Law (FDL) contains, among other things, three national fiscal rules. The first one is balanced budget rule which holds that the structural balance may not be below −0.5% of GDP. The FDL provisions require that this rule should be applied when the planned structural balance from the previous year exceeds −1.0% of GDP, but until this rule is satisfied, the structural balance is planned to improve by 0.5% of GDP compared to the previous year. The expenditure rule holds that real expenditure should not grow faster than the potential GDP. Last but not least, the debt rule stipulates that the general government debt-to-GDP ratio may not exceed 60% as of the year end, in accordance with the Council Regulation (EC) No. 2223/96. The estimation has demonstrated that in case of these solutions, there is a relatively low correlation between debt and the economic growth rate. When it comes to fiscal parameters, a one-unit increase in FRS may cause sector deficit to go up by 2.6 units in the period n and by 0.7 units in n+3. Meanwhile, no impact has been observed for the public debt-to-GDP.

Maltese authorities, to strengthen the budget discipline and better integrate the medium-term strategy in budget formulation, implemented national fiscal rules in 2014. Relevant regulations stipulate that if the general government debt-to-GDP at market prices exceeds 60%, this ratio shall be reduced in accordance with the 1997 excessive deficit regulation until it has reached 60%. In addition, the general government sector is obliged to either maintain budget balance or generate a surplus. Therefore, these regulations are not too restrictive compared to other countries that have implemented strictly defined numerical fiscal rules. In this case, Malta founded its solution on EU regulations, especially those contained in the two-pack and it can be indicated that a one-unit increase in FRS may lead to public debt-to-GDP decreasing by 2.1 units in the period n, by 2.2 units in n+1 and by 2.2 in n+3. Meanwhile, the same does not have a positive impact, from the perspective of stable fiscal policy making, on all other indicators selected for the analysis.

The Netherlands can boast a very long history of fiscal rules in use since 1945, which, rather than be enshrined in the law, have been an element of a political post-election agreement. As already mentioned, since 1994, an expenditure rule has also been in place which sets the expenditure ceiling for a four-year parliamentary term. It is applicable to the total general government expenditure. The revenue rule holds that when a medium-term budgetary objective is satisfied and, as a next step, a long-term general government surplus is generated, 50% of that surplus should go towards public debt repayment, with a possibility to finance tax cuts from the remaining 50% of the surplus. The research conducted has demonstrated that in this case, the FRS index has a significant impact on the public debt reduction and a moderate one on the economic growth rate, while having no positive effect on the sector deficit (i.e. a one-unit growth in FRS causes: debt-to-GDP to fall by 2.4 units, GDP growth rate to grow by one unit, deficit-to-GDP to grow by 2.5 units in the period n and by 0.7 unit in the period n+2).

The principal fiscal rules in Poland relate to budget expenditure and public debt. The constitutional debt rule holds that it is prohibited to "contract loans or provide guarantees and financial sureties which would engender a national public debt exceeding three-fifths of the value of the annual gross domestic product". The Public Finance Act additionally sets prudential thresholds for the national public debt-to-GDP ratio. The Polish stabilising expenditure rule came into effect in 2014 pursuant to the provisions of the Public Finance Act. The stabilising expenditure rule is a limitation that defines an absolute expenditure cap for selected entities of the public finance sector. The rule mechanism is based on the assumption that the expenditure amount may grow at a medium-term real GDP growth rate multiplied by the forecast CPI inflation rate. Models have demonstrated that the fiscal rules used in Poland have a positive impact on the public debt level, i.e. a one-unit FRS increase causes this parameter to drop by 5.8 units in the period n and by up to 9.1 units in the period n+3. Research has also revealed no positive impact on decreasing the public finance deficit because as FRS grows by one unit, this fiscal parameter increases, for example, by 3 units in the period n+2. When it comes to the GDP growth index, increases can also be observed, i.e. in the period n+2, a one-unit FRS growth causes the economic indicator to go up by 3.7 units.

In Portugal, at least three different fiscal rules can be distinguished, i.e. budget balance rule, expenditure rule and borrowing ceilings for autonomous regions and local governments. Every year the Budget Law stipulates that the general government budget balance, in ESA terms and adjusted for cyclical effects and temporary measures, cannot be less than the MTO. Any deviation has to be corrected in subsequent years. Moreover, budgets of the administrative public sector, its entities and agencies must be in balance or positive. Based on the assumptions presented by the Portuguese authorities, each of the sub-sectors should contribute "proportionally" to achieving this budget balance target. The post-crisis changes in the approach to fiscal rules introduced in the country have had a positive effect on the effectiveness of these instruments. The least-squares estimation has revealed that a one-unit increase in FRS will contribute to a 7.5-unit debt reduction; a downward effect can be also observed for budget deficit, whose decrease will amount to 1.8 units. When analysing the modelling results, it can also be indicated that a one-unit FRS increase will contribute to the GDP growth rate going up by 0.8 unit in the period n+1 and by 2.6 units in the period n+2.

In Romania, the main fiscal rules were introduced by the Tax Responsibility Law and were implemented to strengthen the fiscal discipline. The law provides that the annual structural deficit of the general government is in balance or in surplus. This principle is deemed satisfied if the annual structural balance of the public administration does not exceed −1% of GDP at market prices or is close to the medium-term budgetary objective in accordance with the adjustment path agreed with the EU institutions. In addition, the provisions of the Law impose limits on the yearly increase in the public expenditure growth and set the maximum allowed public debt ceiling at 60% of GDP. According to the research conducted, such solutions may have a limited effect on the economic growth rate, i.e. a one-unit increase in FRS causes the GDP growth rate to go up by 0.9 units. As regards fiscal parameters, a positive impact has been recorded only for GDP growth, i.e. a one-unit FRS increase will cause the GDP growth rate to fall by 0.9 units.

Swedish fiscal policy is based on public debt rule, expenditure rule and budget balance rule. In accordance with the Budget Act, the government must propose a level of general government net lending based on the regulations that provide that the surplus net lending is to be equal to 1/3% of GDP on average over a business cycle. The current surplus target is in effect until further notice but is reviewed at the end of every second electoral term. The monitoring of the surplus target focuses on comparing the surplus target against the net structural lending. Since 2019, the surplus target has been complemented with the public debt rule to further strengthen the framework and emphasise the fundamental importance of debt to the budget policy stability. The debt anchor is a point of reference for the medium-term consolidated gross debt also known as Maastricht debt. The public debt rule defines that the public debt-to-GDP ratio may not exceed 35%. In addition and also in accordance with the Budget Act, the government is obliged to propose an expenditure ceiling for the national budget and pension system for the following three budget years. Hence, the expenditure ceiling – an upper cap not to be exceeded by expenditure – is established three years in advance. The mere fact that the rules applied cover varied fiscal policy areas suggests high effectiveness of such a solution, but this has also been confirmed by the analyses conducted. A one-unit increase in FRS may cause the public sector deficit in Sweden to go down by 22.5 units and the public debt, by 7.6 units.

In Slovenia, there is a budget balance rule currently in effect, whose design was modelled on the Swiss debt brake formula. The rule stipulates that the maximum level of general government expenditure must be equal to the level of revenue adjusted by a business cycle factor. The business cycle factor is meant to stabilise expenditure around the level of cyclically adjusted revenue. The fiscal rules used in Slovenia may have a positive impact on the GDP growth rate, as a one-unit increase in FRS can cause the indicator in question to go up by 2.25 units. When it comes to debt-to-GDP, in a similar situation it can be reduced by 9.5 units in the period n and by 9.36 units in the period n+2. When it comes to public finance deficit-to-GDP, it would be difficult to model, based on the available data, any significant correlations that could be the basis for binding interpretations.

In Slovakia, public debt rule is used, as part of which general government gross debt brackets are defined (50%–53%, 53%–55%, 55%–57% and 57%–60%). Relevant measures/political sanctions are triggered upon exceeding them. When the ultimate threshold is exceeded, the government must ask parliament for a vote of confidence. The Act also indicates that the general government structural deficit shall be equal to or less than 0.5% of GDP. If the general government debt is much lower than 60% of GDP and the long-term stability risk is low, the structural deficit may not exceed 1% of GDP. In addition, local governments are bound by debt and balanced budget rules. The most effective rule of them all is the one involving measures to limit the public debt growth rate as research has demonstrated that a one-unit increase in FRS causes this parameter to fall by 3.7 units, which has not been observed for public finance deficit.

Even though the United Kingdom is no longer an EU member, it is worth presenting the country's experience in the area of fiscal rules. The balanced budget rule means that government revenue must be high enough to cover all current expenditure. Hence, this rule allows the government to borrow money for capital expenditure (investments) but not to cover day-to-day spending such as administrative expenditure or current costs of public services. The second rule, the net investment rule, makes it obligatory "to limit public sector net investment to 3% of GDP". It permits "public sector net investment (PSNI) to go up to three per cent of GDP, averaged over the standard five-year forecast horizon, provided that interest rates do not rise significantly" (net investment equals capital spending minus depreciation). The government's third fiscal rule suggests that when public expenditure on debt interest (the cost of debt servicing) exceeds 6% of government revenue, it must amend its fiscal forecasts to ensure national debt-to-GDP keeps falling in the following periods. For most of the past two decades, debt interest costs have been less than 6% of the revenue in the United Kingdom due to unusually low interest rates. Earlier on, fiscal rules in the United Kingdom used to determine debt levels (as a share of national income) directly. Then the government adopted instead a rule that restricts the cost of this debt rather than its level. The rationale is that borrowing more to fund investment costs less when interest rates are low, even if it increases the total debt. Since the 2007/08 financial crisis, net debt in the United Kingdom as a share of national income has more than doubled. Own research has confirmed the positive impact of such solutions on the economic growth rate, i.e. a one-unit FRS increase is likely to cause this macroeconomic indicator to go up by 4.5 units in the period n and by 4 units in the period n+2.

3.4 The impact of the functioning of independent fiscal institutions on the economic growth rate and selected fiscal indicators

Independent fiscal institutions are among the instruments that reinforce the measures intended to maintain public finance stability and strengthen the effective impact of the other public management tools, as presented in more detail in Chapter 2. Unfortunately, when it comes to the assessment of how effective these institutions are, the same has been conducted only at the Community level as data from respective countries are very scant and cannot serve as the basis for reliable quantitative research. Consequently, this subchapter presents the results of research for the EU as a whole with respect to the quality of independent fiscal institutions and their real impact on the macroeconomic parameters selected for analysis. As a first step, an attempt has been made to analyse the impact of SIFI on the economic growth rate measured with GDP (see Table 3.23).

An ADL panel model has been estimated, where independent variables include a response variable delayed by 1 period, and exogenous variables: one from the current period and one delayed by 2 periods due to the low quantity of annual observations for the panel. Statistically insignificant variables have

Table 3.23 Dynamic model estimation of the impact of the Scope Index of Fiscal Institutions on the GDP growth rate.

Asymptotic standard errors					
	Coefficient	*Standard error*	*z*	*p-value*	
GDP growth (n−1)	−0.0490751	0.00594814	−8.250	<0.0001	***
Const	2.85441	0.222676	12.82	<0.0001	***
Scope Index of Fiscal Institutions	0.0730802	0.00890820	8.204	<0.0001	***
Scope Index of Fiscal Institutions (n+1)	−0.0661411	0.00641771	−10.31	<0.0001	***
Residual sum of squares	*318.3648*		*Residual standard error*	*1.749628*	

Source: own elaboration.

been eliminated using the backward stepwise method, arriving at the ultimate model, in which the GDP growth is significantly impacted by the Scope Index of Fiscal Institutions delayed by 1 period and its current value. A one-unit increase in the Scope Index of Fiscal Institutions in the current period causes the GDP growth to go up in the same period by an average of 0.0730802 units. Meanwhile, in the long term, the same increase in SIFI in the current period causes the GDP growth to go up by an average of 0.006614 units. The model has a correct number of instruments adopted for model estimation (Sargan's test: p = 0.5654), but its quality is lower than for other models due to the low value of annual observations for panels.

Another correlation analysed is the impact of SIFI on the public debt-to-GDP ratio (see Tables 3.24 and 3.25).

The model research conducted has failed to demonstrate a significant impact of the Scope Index of Fiscal Institutions on the public debt ratio, which is interesting insofar as the fiscal rules, the compliance with which these institutions are meant to safeguard, have a very significant impact on this fiscal index. This makes it even more interesting to analyse whether SIFI has an impact at least on the public finance deficit.

An ADL panel model has been estimated, where independent variables include a response variable delayed by 1 period, and exogenous variables: one from the current period and one delayed by 2 periods due to the low quantity of annual observations for the panel. Statistically insignificant variables have been eliminated using the backward stepwise method, arriving at the final model, in which the deficit is significantly impacted by the Scope Index of Fiscal Institutions in its current value. A one-unit increase in the Scope Index of Fiscal Institutions in the current period causes deficit to go up in the same period by an average of 0.0189075 units. Meanwhile, in the long term, the same increase in SIFI in the current period will cause the deficit to go down by an average of 0.0337 units. The model has a correct number of instruments adopted for model estimation (Sargan's test: p = 0.9996).

Table 3.24 Dynamic model estimation of the impact of the Scope Index of Fiscal Institutions on the public debt-to-GDP.

Asymptotic standard errors					
	Coefficient	*Standard error*	*z*	*p-value*	
Public debt-to-GDP in the previous year (n−1)	1.02551	0.0240995	42.55	<0.0001	***
Const	0.418280	4.54124	0.09211	0.9266	
Scope Index of Fiscal Institutions (n−1)	−0.0155895	0.0573065	−0.2720	0.7856	
Residual sum of squares	*6180.397*			*Residual standard error*	*6.921709*

Source: own elaboration.

Table 3.25 Dynamic model estimation of the impact of the Scope Index of Fiscal Institutions on public finance deficit-to-GDP.

Asymptotic standard errors

	Coefficient	*Standard error*	*z*	*p-value*	
Public finance deficit in the previous period (n−1)	0.438285	0.0206047	21.27	<0.0001	***
Const	0.763988	0.155238	4.921	<0.0001	***
Scope Index of Fiscal Institutions	−0.0189075	0.00322102	−5.870	<0.0001	***
Residual sum of squares	*214.1676*		*Residual standard error*		*1.288493*

Source: own elaboration.

Conclusion

The solutions proposed by the European Union in response to the crisis of 2007–2008 to strengthen Member States' financial stability and stimulate anti-cyclical measures in the current fiscal policy making should be undoubtedly appreciated and seen as a move in the right direction. Extending the financial planning horizon in the public finance sector and the possible ways to carry out this task are among the most important contemporary problems facing the authorities responsible for the fiscal policy (Chadha et al., 2021). A proper approach to this issue requires both theoretical reflection and practical implementation and testing of new solutions and then reviewing their results. Of great importance here is an efficient cooperation between science and practice. Research that uses international examples remarkably extends the possibilities to develop the theory and reduces the time necessary to test specific solutions and revise them, if needed. One should also pay attention to the theoretical proposals related to choosing such multiannual allocative decisions. These decisions should be taken on the basis of objective arguments, above a given budget holder's individual interests, and reflect a consensus on the optimum pro-development budget choices that foster social and economic development. The medium-term strategic financial planning system also requires mastering the difficult art of forecasting the future trends and events, while the diagnosis alone is not enough as it is also necessary to identify and estimate the likelihood of specific situations occurring that could affect the goal achievement process. An analysis of the solutions used in EU Member States draws attention to a number of issues related to medium-term planning and the forecasts presented, i.e. their non-binding nature in the medium-term horizon (Sherwood, 2015). Of course this can be justified by the relatively poor quality of the forecasts presented by Member States to the European Commission, and by medium-term documents being prepared in the format required by the Community rather than one which would be usable in country-level decision-making. Despite these drawbacks, one should obviously appreciate the European Commission's efforts to oblige Member States to look at the measures undertaken as part of their social and economic policy from a perspective that goes beyond one year. The preparation of medium-term documents is aided by fiscal rules, whose aim is to ensure an anti-cyclical fiscal policy is in place to help prepare for crisis times.

The above-listed conditions are, against all appearances, not easy to meet. Simple fiscal anchors, for example expenditure ceiling or deficit ceiling, are not universally applicable and can be used only in specific circumstances. Temporary solutions do not allow building a relevant system that would lend a high credibility to the fiscal anchor. In turn, more complex anchors which limit, for example, the acceptable structural deficit, require adequate calculations. This opens up the possibility of arbitrary estimates, for example of the potential output, making it possible to stretch the anchor estimates to fit the current political situation. A condition regarding the mechanism to ensure sound public finance must be enforceable and thus credible. Consequently, a major problem presents itself: Should the budget rule relate to the deficit or to the public debt level? It seems that, from the point of view of financial markets, it should be about the adequate debt level. On the one hand, financial markets that know the debt structure and the expected deficit are able to define the magnitude of the borrowing needs. On the other hand, considering the assessment of a given country's capacity to carry out the manoeuvre of budgetary consolidation, markets define the maximum debt level which a country is able to finance in the long term. The maximum debt level does not mean a safe level of debt. Turbulence on financial markets and the attendant changes in the risk assessment may, temporarily, reduce respective countries' access to financial markets. A safe level of debt should be set below the maximum level. Hence, a fiscal anchor should have several brackets rather than one threshold. A properly defined debt criterion encourages complementing it with a fiscal deficit criterion. The criterion of public finance or budgetary deficit may be the necessary catalyst for an early introduction of fiscal policy tightening programme. The interaction of both requirements may ensure greater flexibility and speed up the preparation and implementation of a relevant fiscal stability programme. A two-criterion system makes it possible to attach different importance to each of them, for example treat one criterion as an alert mechanism to detect a potential for breakage of the principal anchor. For example, when using public debt index as the anchor, deficit can be treated as something that signals that a given debt level has been exceeded. This signaller should enforce a gradual introduction of specific spending cut plan before the deficit level reaches the values that would make it easy to exceed the thresholds set for public debt indicators. The research conducted on the effectiveness of fiscal rules solutions implemented in the European Union shows that they have a significant impact on the public debt-to-GDP ratio in the medium term, whereas, sadly, they can also have a negative impact on the GDP growth rate. The effectiveness of fiscal rules was to be strengthened by the activities of independent fiscal institutions, intended to impact the long-term financial stability (Blanchard et al., 2021).

Many independent fiscal institutions have already been created and are fully exercising their function (Larch and Branedle, 2018), while in other countries further improvements are being implemented to boost their effectiveness.

In summary, the measures being undertaken to implement public management instruments deserve recognition and these instruments are already enforceable by regulations, but the effectiveness of their functioning depends on the regulatory tools assigned to them by the national government and is limited by resources.

4 The evolution of the role, scale and directions of impact of EU funds

Introduction

The EU membership brings not only measurable benefits to national economies, observable regardless of whether a given country has been a member for a long time or joined more recently, but also makes it possible, in crisis times, to apply emergency financial instruments to intervene in specific economic spheres to alleviate the consequences of the crisis. In some EU Member States, transfers of structural funds are among the main economic growth determinants, which even out regional development disparities, and the scale of their impact is not to be downplayed (Dall'Erba and Gallo, 2007). All citizens of EU Member States benefit directly or indirectly from projects financed from the EU budget, be it through access to a better infrastructure, human capital development or other measures that contribute to social development (Tomasino et al., 2017). Benefits are also reaped by economic operators, in terms of both a growing demand for their services and the emerging opportunities to access a wider market for the goods and services offered by them. Measures and projects financed from the EU budget are a reflection of the priorities set for a given period by the EU. The Treaty of Rome establishing the European Economic Community stipulated that the Community's activity would be financed from own resources, including Member States' national contributions, which would cover the expenditure on Community projects. In recent years, there have been a growing number of proposals, and an ongoing discussion, to establish, in addition to funds contributed to own resources, a common system of supranational taxes, for example digital or climate levy.

In this chapter, addressing the research goals set in the introduction, analyses focus on expenditure and debt instruments not only as elements of support for the implementation of the Community's priorities but also as response to emerging crises. In the analysed period of 1995–2020 and relying on the assumptions of the new financial perspective 2021–2027, six periods can be distinguished in which funds flowed from the EU budget using different expenditure classifications to support measures set out in two strategic documents – Lisbon Strategy and "Europe 2020" strategy (Farole et al., 2011; Radło, 2003) – and as part of emergency post-crisis measures. These funds were usually grouped according

DOI: 10.4324/9781003222033-5

to six or seven (MFF 2021–2027) vast expenditure categories (referred to as Headings) and 31 various policy areas. The EU budget finances measures and projects in the policy areas for which all Member States have agreed to act at EU level. The European Commission uses activity-based management which is then the basis for its accountability for the activities and the budget implemented. Each of the European action areas has a form of a relevant programme logic model. It enables a more in-depth understanding of the mutual relationship between the existing social and economic needs, and the objectives, inputs, processes, outputs and outcomes of intervention put in place to meet those needs. Based thereon, the efficiency of a given intervention is evaluated by the ECA, which will be discussed in the last subchapter of this chapter. In addition to direct effects measured with implementation indicators, measures undertaken by the European Union are of much greater importance when it comes to tapping into Member States' growth potential.

4.1 The scale and key aspects of the EU's financial impact in 1995–2020

In addition to the supranational coordination of activities, which process is presented in detail in the previous chapter of the Monograph, the European Union provides financial support to strategic measures oriented to evening out the disparities between Member States, taking account of the directions set in its long-term policy papers, and in recent years it has also undertaken special measures to counter the effects of occasional crises. Ever-growing funds need to be employed to implement such projects at a scale that would enable the expected changes to be actually made and ensure developmental progress of the states aspiring to fulfil real convergence requirements.

In order to assess to what extent the financing of EU policy and strategic measures has intensified, a basic analysis of budgetary data has been conducted. It has been established that originally – until 1966 – the actual expenditure from the European Community budget was used mainly to cover administrative costs and the so-called other activities, which, in a relevant expenditure classification, included the activities of the European Community of Coal and Steel (established in Paris in 1952), of EURATOM Community (established in Rome in 1957) and of the European Development Fund (also established in Rome in 1957, to aid European countries' former colonies). The funds earmarked for those organisations were, however, incorporated, over time, entirely or partly into respective sectors of budget expenditure. For example, in 1965–1968, the budget of the EURATOM Community was incorporated into the general budget, and its expenses, mainly into "Scientific research" and "Administration". Meanwhile, the budget of the European Community of Coal and Steel was divided: a general part was incorporated into the EEC budget, while the operational part was, until 2002, set aside from the Community budget. The introduction of the Common Agricultural Policy (CAP), starting from 1967, has caused a significant increase in agriculture expenditure.

From 1968 onwards, this expenditure would account for more than 50% of the budget, representing as much as 87% of all Community expenditure in 1970. Since 1992, the share of agricultural expenditure has decreased, fluctuating around 50%, which was due to the growing importance of the structural fund and to the increase in the expenditure earmarked to achieve the related goals.

The first presentation of expenses analysed by the Author, for 1995–2017, relates to the general level of EU's actual budget expenditure presented on a yearly basis (Greenwood et al., 1995). These data point to an extremely dynamic growth (YoY) of the EU budget expenditure from EUR 67 billion in 1995 to EUR 158 billion in 2017, i.e. a 136% increase. It should be made clear that the growth in the analysed period results, to a great extent, from the fundamental factor that is the increase in the number of Member States which these programmatic activities involved as well as the increased number of countries that paid a membership contribution. The analysis conducted has demonstrated that the correlation ratio between the budget value and the number of Member States was 89% and an increasing scale of EU-level redistribution is clearly noticeable, stirring a controversy not only as to the phenomenon itself but also as to the efficiency with which these funds are spent.

An analysis of the collected data indicates that 2004 saw an exponential growth in the expenditure level, by ca. EUR 10 billion compared to the previous year. On the one hand, this phenomenon came at a time the EU enlarged to include 10 new Member States which, admittedly, had already participated in the EU budget through pre-accession funds but not to the same extent Member States do. The increase in actual expenditure in 2013 was also connected to the EU accession of another country – Croatia. On the other hand, the increase in the actual budget expenditure from 1995 has also been largely related to the economic growth (expressed in GDP per capita). As a matter of fact, 2004 saw a major (exponential) increase in this indicator, with the GDP upward trend continuing until 2008. Between 2009 and 2012, we can observe a decline in GDP, directly linked to the post-crisis situation. Meanwhile, in 2014–2015, a clear EU budget reduction was recorded – by ca. 6% compared to the previous year. In 2014, a decrease in GDP growth was also observed compared to the previous year.

To summarise, a dynamic growth in budget expenditure was observed in the period analysed, which was due to the EU enlargement and to the higher economic development level of EU countries. The result of the correlation test for budget expenditure to the GDP growth rate is linked to the membership contribution calculation method and translates into the scale of the available funds falling under the competence of the European Commission. At the same time, the analysis of the GDP level in the EU for 1995–2020 pointed to a dependence between the upward trend in the EU budget expenditure and the economic growth, which is obvious and stems from the way membership contribution is calculated. The latter conclusion will be of particular significance both to the desired general effects (not just direct ones) of the impact of the Community's economic policy on Member States' economies, and to identifying its future directions to be set as part of key strategy documents. From this point of view, the strengthening of the economy will mean accumulating the capital by expanding the Community's fiscal space and thus enlarging the capacity and structural range of tools to enhance the Member States' social progress. Efforts of this kind will result in a sort of "feedback", whose role will be noticed only after the first round of reflection on the EU strategic choices, which will be discussed in the following subchapter. As a matter of fact, a sustainable growth path intended to indirectly ensure a proper quality of life will, from the very beginning, require a synergy between the two spheres – the social and the economic one. The former, rather than be just a passive backdrop and the recipient of the outcomes of higher competitiveness, will act as a pillar to ensure real and durable foundations for this kind of EU's economic expansion. At the same time, the larger number of Member States will mean the need to broaden the scale of impact financed from the EU budget. Brexit and, should it come to that, a potential exit of another country from the European Union will obviously not be without the consequences for the shape of budget packages.

Much attention is often devoted, in the context of analysing and evaluating the overall expenditure from the EU budget, to the discussion of the expenditure related exclusively to the administrative management. Indeed, in the debate held by practitioners, public life observers and scientists, the objection is raised that the growing volume of expenditure distributed at EU level, rather than contribute to the fulfilment of specific goals, is significantly diminished by administrative costs. From the perspective of this chapter's discussion of the efficiency of EU expenditure, it is worth conducting an analysis of the extent to which these claims are true.

As such, statistical research has been conducted for administrative expenses over time, broken down into the analysed time intervals resulting from changes in the EU-level expenditure classification. The results obtained point to the upward trend in administrative expenses, its growth rate being higher than the average growth for other expenditure categories. Consequently, the subsequent sections of this chapter will also look into this category. Even though it is not a priority item, costs sustained in this area diminish the EU's financial capacity, resulting in a limited ability to reallocate these funds to Member States' pro-development projects (spending rigidity).

4.2 Analysis of the structure of the EU's financial impact – directions of 1995–1999 budget expenditure

The first period analysed is 1995–1999, i.e. the five years directly preceding the adoption of the Lisbon strategy. Data from that period are a good comparative basis for changes taking place in the subsequent planning periods for multiannual strategies. It is worth emphasising here that already in those five years, the EU expenditure classification was modified, making it very difficult to measure and compare the effects achieved, which will be discussed further in the chapter.

When embarking on an analysis of the expenditure structure in EU budgets for 1995–1997 and 1998–1999, one should take into account the important phenomenon of structural activities being enlarged since 1998 to include newly created mechanisms, such as: European Agriculture Guidance and Guarantee Funds, Financial Instrument for Fisheries Guidance, European Regional Development Fund, European Social Fund, Community initiatives, fight against fraud, monitoring payment tranches, Cohesion Fund and EOG financial mechanism. As the EU budget had been prepared, until 1999, in the ECU currency (European currency unit), which was replaced 1:1 with euro on 1 January 1999, for the purposes of this analysis, to ensure data comparability, different types of expenditure in respective years have been assigned uniform names, all expressed in euro. It is worth pointing out here that expenditure on training, energy market and research was grouped in the "Internal activities" section of the budget for 1998–1999.

An analysis of the expenditure structure has revealed that in 1995–1999, half of the budget was allocated to expenditure on agricultural policy implementation, which corresponded to the activities underlying the creation of the EU budget, which were launched in previous periods.

Hence, in the period analysed, agricultural expenditure increased from EUR 34.5 billion in 1995 to EUR 40.5 billion in 1999. The largest growth in the expenditure on the agricultural policy and structural operations occurred in 1996 (the analysed period of 1995–1999), when it amounted to ca. EUR 4.5 billion and EUR 5 billion, respectively. In the subsequent years, a greater focus on structural expenditure could be observed compared to expenditure directly allocated to agriculture. An increasing scale of the structural impact can also be noted – with relevant expenditure undergoing a significant increase in 1995–1999, growing to represent a 33% share of the EU budget expenditure. At the same time, it needs to be emphasised that the growth rate of the structural expenditure greatly exceeds that of agricultural policy expenditure, which, in 1996–1999 followed a downward trend compared to the former.

The share of agricultural expenditure is decreasing mainly due to the change in the EU policy, particularly – which is of special significance in the context of our discussions – due to putting a growing emphasis on extending and developing the structural funds. These activities were a prelude to further development of such trends, while creating demand for further intensification and expansion of the financial support as well as strengthening and systematising its policy and strategic underpinnings. Member States needed a clear stimulus – a signpost message from the European Commission that this kind of budget allocation arrangements will be perceived, also in the future, as necessary to ensure the EU's further development, to improve its external competitiveness – and ultimately – to enhance its population's quality of life (Esposito et al., 2017). Furthermore, in the context of the challenges of global competition, it was expected this trend would require further expansion. Those expectations as well as hope for the future led to the adoption of the Lisbon strategy and to its follow-up in the form of the "Europe 2020" policy paper.

4.3 The Lisbon strategy as a stimulus to look for ways to optimise EU budget allocations

The dynamically changing "wandering world" has confronted European decision-makers with a dilemma that is both fundamental and complex – how to meet the above-described EU members' expectations efficiently and also on a solidarity basis (resulting in a pro-development allocation oriented towards structural intervention) and, at the same time, how to use such a mechanism to help all of Europe, effectively and efficiently, join in the contest for the supremacy in global economic competitiveness (Patrizii and Resce, 2015). Though the EU's leading economic centres such as France, Germany or Italy were traditionally and unquestionably held to be the engines of Europe's growth, it would be obviously an inefficient solution to leave all other Member States in the background of this race (where the United States is considered the main competitor and a still unchallenged leader). Especially that these leading European centres of growth, despite their staggering results, did not achieve, in the 1990s, any spectacular developmental leaps that could substantially change the shift of power in the global economy.

Considering the above-described circumstances, 1990s saw an increasingly noticeable lack of vision on how to speed up the development of the whole integration grouping rather than that of only selected group of countries. "The (EU countries') ability to undertake a closer economic cooperation in the area of strategic development" (Białek and Oleksiuk, 2009) was the Community's huge, though still untapped, asset. This is why in a situation where the traditional strategic framework for the EU's economic policy *en bloc* was becoming increasingly outdated and insufficient for all EU countries, in the light of the ever stronger challenges resulting from globalisation, the growing competition in the global economy, and, furthermore, due to new unfavourable conditions in the form of structural barriers to the economic growth in the EU countries and economic slowdown (coupled with a relatively high unemployment rate), a comprehensive debate was launched on the need to set new groundbreaking programmatic directions which could lay the groundwork for the EU's new economic programme (Rodrik, 2021). The innovativeness of the approach then adopted amid this quest consisted in assuming synergies and a comprehensive nature of the identified strategic solutions which became the foundation of an all-out (meaning both economic and social) programme of the European Union (Archick and Mix, 2012). The policy underpinnings of the new strategy, which came to be known as the Lisbon strategy, essentially focused on one thing – strengthening the efforts to actively leverage the advantage of the broadly defined knowledge in promoting economic innovation as the accelerator of long-term economic growth (Hernaus et al., 2016). This was by no means a novel conclusion (in addition, as G.W. Kołodko wrote in "Świat na wyciągnięcie myśli": "each economy is in a way knowledge-based"), as the impact of research and development activities as a determinant of achieving a developmental leap (among others, in productivity) has already been the object of research and expert debates, but what mattered in this respect is the unprecedented, operational way to use this optic in modelling an approach to shaping a strategic framework for the economic policy in the EU. As emphasised by E. Okoń-Horodyńska, before the Lisbon strategy was adopted, "the R&D sector had not been, in practice, in the mainstream of economic policy" and "knowledge carriers were not, in essence, treated as strategic economic growth drivers" (Zachorowska-Mazurkiewicz and Okoń-Horodyńska, 2011; Woźniak, 2012). This very obvious factor was seen as the main mechanism and trigger of development in other areas, among others, in the social, cultural and civilisational spheres.

However, to reach the level of economic development that could be comparable to the US economy, many other challenges must be tackled to overcome the developmental backwardness, for example an optimised use of the labour factor, among others, by increasing the employment rate, participation in the labour market and labour efficiency. The ongoing demographic changes were becoming ever more palpable, making it necessary to undertake efforts to change the prevailing systemic solutions affecting the EU social governance. This involved, among others, proposals to raise the retirement age and activate the unemployed, to reconsider the advisability of keeping unemployment benefits at their current level and to carry out a retirement system reform.

The European Commission also realised that the structure and level of public expenditure must change as well. Until then, there had been a negative correlation between changes in public expenditure and the economic growth rate. Over several decades, expenditure on social transfers and the so-called public consumption had significantly increased in the EU countries, with public investment declining. However, the increasing budgetary burden on the expenditure side, related to social spending, to boot, meant no significant effect of economic expansion could be achieved without a major structural and systemic breakthrough. To arrive at such a shift, though, it was, first of all, necessary to change the philosophy of managing the European Union's economic and social policy, and thus to adopt new, unprecedented solutions at the strategic planning level.

The Lisbon Strategy as a 10-year development plan for the European Union was adopted by the European Council at its session in Lisbon in March 2000. The following assumption was made back then: "the Union has set itself a new strategic goal for the next decade: to become the most competitive and dynamic knowledge-based economy in the world, capable of sustainable economic growth with more and better jobs and greater social cohesion".

The operational objective of the Lisbon Strategy was to lay "the groundwork for the transition to a competitive, dynamic, knowledge-based economy" and to "modernise the European social model".

The first, economic pillar, was to be achieved by means of:

- steadily building an information society;
- preparing the concept for and implementing the European Research and Innovation Area;

- promoting the establishment and development of innovative companies;
- undertaking economic changes to promote the creation of a functional internal market;
- ensuring an efficient and integrated financial market;
- ensuring macroeconomic policy coordination, fiscal consolidation and improving public finance quality in respective EU economies.

The social pillar was to be fulfilled using the following measures (Wamser et al., 2013):

- ensuring proper education for living and working in a knowledge-based society;
- developing an active employment policy;
- modernising social policy;
- promoting social involvement.

Moreover, the environmental pillar was added to these objectives in 2001, which emphasised the need for positive impact on the natural environment of human beings. The Lisbon Strategy's objectives were to be fulfilled by implementing measures such as: (1) a quick transition to a knowledge-based economy through research and innovation development, including increased expenditure on R&D and information society development; (2) liberalising and integrating selected markets and sectors which largely remain unaffected by the single market; (3) stimulating enterprise growth by deregulating the economy and eliminating administrative and legal barriers, providing an easier access to capital and new technologies, ensuring a level playing field and limiting state aid which distorts competition; (4) undertaking a social model change consisting in stimulating labour market participation and employment by increasing labour market flexibility and improving the education model as well as thoroughly rebuilding the social security model; and (5) ensuring conditions conducive to sustainable economic growth, i.e. taking account of environmental factors.

The achievement of the strategy's objectives required a number of economic, social and environmental reforms. The literature on the subject distinguishes between five reform areas meant to ensure Lisbon Strategy implementation, to which funds were allocated from the European Union budget (Żmuda, 2011; Radło, 2002; Wysokinska, 2008):

1) "strengthening economic and social attitudes by completing the implementation of the internal market programme, strengthening competition, ensuring macroeconomic stability and economic openness as well as increasing public expenditure on undertakings that support long-term development;
2) facilitating the diffusion of information and communications technologies in the economy by improving competition on ICT markets and enhancing IT skills;

3) strengthening the innovation by improving the efficiency of R&D expenditure, especially on primary research, as well as by strengthening partnership between research centres/scientific institutions and businesses;
4) human capital investment by improving initial and continuous training systems and stimulating labour market participation;
5) strengthening enterprise and creation of new companies by promoting enterprise, ensuring easier access to capital and simplifying economic activity and tax system regulations".

In quantifiable terms, the ultimate goals to be achieved by the Lisbon Strategy were described by quite ambitious indicators of the "measurable" effects of fulfilling its policy aims. The main planned effects included R&D investment increasing to 3% of GDP coupled with a higher employment rate, to reach 70% for men and 60% for women (above 62% on average). Such ambitious and legitimate goals can hardly be contested, but unfortunately, today it is clear they have not been successfully met.

The introduction of the areas of impact outlined in the Lisbon Strategy essentially sanctioned the action plan adopted by the heads of EU countries at the European Council summit in Lisbon in March 2000. However, the economic goals set out in this strategy could not have been implemented by way of policy proposals only. The Union needed, first and foremost, real sources of financial support for mechanisms that enable the implementation of the economic and social objectives set out in the Lisbon vision of development. It was able to secure these funds with an adequate and consistent support from the Community budget. That is why the priority goals of the Lisbon Strategy implementation were defined as part of the EU budget at the very outset of the process of pursuing these objectives.

The basis for the *Financial Perspective for 2000–2006* was the European Council adopting, at the summit in Berlin in 1999, *Agenda 2000* and structuring based thereon relevant provisions to be later set out in the Lisbon Strategy (Grimm, 2011). The European Commission included in it its proposed reforms of the CAP, changes in regional development financing and the rules of financing the EU enlargement to new Member States. Hence three main objectives were set for the 2000–2006 programming period.

1. Objective 1 – supporting the development of regions that are in the greatest need and are significantly falling behind the rest of Europe, to ensure EU cohesion policy implementation (as part of respective instruments, support was adopted for areas that were eligible for such aid as per detailed criteria of this policy, also indicating other regions than before) (European Commission, 2013; Alegre, 2012; Annoni and Rubianes, 2016).

2. Objective 2 – promoting the economic and social convergence of areas facing structural difficulties and targeting areas undergoing socio-economic change in the industrial and service sectors, declining rural areas, urban areas in difficulty and depressed areas dependent upon fisheries (applicable to European Regional Development Fund financing).

3. Objective 3 – lending financial support to education, training and employment initiatives, supporting both the employed and unemployed, and promoting lifelong learning, equal opportunities and social inclusion (applicable to European Social Fund financing).

In the above context, of greatest significance were the Community initiatives acting as special financial instruments of the EU's structural policy, developed to find common solutions to specific problems affecting the EU as a whole. The key thing was that Community initiatives were (and still are) co-financed from the European Union's budget. To this end, an expenditure category was earmarked referred to as structural funds, meant to ensure a significant value added and complementarity to principal regional programmes such as Objectives 2 and 3. An optimally high reallocation of EU funds to this most valuable part of the budget could have resulted in the adequate strength of reforms whose directions had been set by the Lisbon Strategy (Dall'Erba and Fang, 2017). Unfortunately, due to the status quo, changes in that direction could not have been an actual breakthrough; what was needed was as a properly planned, gradual and consistent policy aimed at a major broadening of the financial foundations (the so-called fiscal space) of the EU's economic and social development. This growth was being impeded by the traditionally stable directions of allocation – competing for funds with structural operations – which resulted from the pre-existing financial commitments and from the implementation principles of the EU policies representing the most significant burden to the EU budget as well as from the still large scale of Member States' own expenditure policies, as discussed in this chapter (Borrás, 2009).

When analysing the budget expenditure structure in 2000–2006, it can be concluded that expenditure on CAP still represented its major share. In 2000, its share was observed to have grown, compared to 1999, from 46% to 48%. In the following years, this share increased to 51% of the EU budget and it was not until 2004 that it visibly dropped to 43%. However, in the coming years, the expenditure on agricultural policy purposes increased, which was caused by the introduction of reforms to CAP as part of *Agenda 2000* focusing on the EU enlargement to include Eastern countries and by the related additional agricultural policy costs. EU undertook a number of measures to limit the operating costs of CAP compared to the prior situation by reducing the prices of basic agricultural products, bringing them closer to global prices and by providing stronger support to actions to reduce the agricultural output. This way the CAP expenditure's share of the budget was successfully diminished.

An equally strong focus is placed in the Monograph on expenditure on structural measures, which represented the second most important group of general budget expenditure (for comparison's sake: 35% in 1999, 33% in 2000, 30% in 2006). The average share of structural expenditure in 2000–2006 was ca. 30%, though it should be pointed out that since 2000, priority objectives and tasks have been included in structural expenditure (which will be discussed further in the chapter).

Having regard to the above-presented general conclusions, it is worth taking a closer look at the results of the expenditure trend analysis by structure. In this respect, as mentioned above, a further increase in agricultural expenditure was observed, which was due to the planned EU enlargement and to an additional agricultural expenditure resulting from the structure of economy of the newly acceding countries (like Poland, for example) (Boboc et al., 2016). Meanwhile, structural expenditure, of greatest importance from the point of view of the EU developmental goals, dropped in 2000 by EUR 3.1 million compared to 1999, this decrease reaching in 2001 as much as EUR 5.1 million compared to 2000. It was only from 2003 onwards that the structural expenditure growth was higher than that of agricultural expenditure – which was the result of EU's deliberate action aimed to reduce the CAP operating costs. This trend was consistently sustained in 2003 (with the increase in structural expenditure amounting to as much as over EUR 5 million, and the expenditure on agriculture going up by only EUR 0.9 million). Despite this qualitative change in the EU budget allocation, the high level of agricultural policy expenditure and the growth trend for this expenditure category continued. As already mentioned on many occasions, this was due, on the one hand, to the planned EU enlargement to include CEE countries, and on the other, to the implementation of Lisbon Strategy tasks as part of *Agenda 2000–2006*, which consisted, among other things, in increasing financing for rural areas. This was true of the most significant tasks that were implemented through rural development policy (so-called second pillar of CAP) in 2000–2006, among which the following should be mentioned:

1) restructuring of farms, oriented to increasing their area and thus enhancing farming efficiency and the competitiveness of agriculture;
2) supporting changes in the output volume and structure, aimed to limit the costly food surpluses;
3) promoting a multifunctional development of rural areas by creating new jobs outside agriculture – in services, tourism, arts and crafts, small business as well as preparing the rural population to work in non-agricultural jobs.

It is assumed that all of the aforementioned actions in this area were also reflected in the Lisbon Strategy, which was oriented towards boosting the competitiveness of the economy, supporting less developed areas and creating new jobs. In this respect, the Community agricultural policy fit squarely into the EU's latest directions of policy and strategic aims. However, irrespective of the continually growing importance of structural instruments, they still continued to represent only a minor percentage of all EAGGF (*European Agricultural Guidance and Guarantee Fund*) expenditure as part of the CAP. Hence, the existing trend solidified – expenditure on direct aid for farmers retained the largest share of CAP structure (Collignon, 2008).

It was also observable in the period analysed that 2002 and 2004 saw an increase in the expenditure on internal policies (EUR 1.2 million in 2002 and EUR 1.6 million in 2004), their largest part being R&D and education expenditure, which was in line with the Lisbon Strategy's guidelines.

The European Regional Development Fund (ERDF) unquestionably had the largest share of structural funds – an average of ca. 57%. This was due to the implementation of Lisbon Strategy's tasks, namely: support for the manufacturing environment and competitiveness of companies, scientific research and technological progress, infrastructure investment, environmental protection, development of tourism and cultural investments as well as development of information society and cross-border cooperation. The second place in the structure was occupied by the European Social Fund (EFS), which was the tool to support employment in Member States and promote economic and social cohesion. EFS expenditure in the period analysed amounted to ca. 30% of all EU structural funds. At the same time, the EAGGF accounted for ca. 11% of structural funds, which was due to agricultural policy structural instruments being less developed. The largest part of expenditure was on direct aid for farmers, while less attention was given to structural measures in this respect. Meanwhile, of complementary importance was the Financial Instrument for Fisheries Guidance (FIFG), which received a stable share of structural funds.

When analysing the structure of the EU budget expenditure over the years, an increasingly clear diversification can be observed in the directions of allocation, though the amounts spent on agricultural purposes continue to be of the greatest economic importance. In 2000–2006, no other branch of economy saw the successful implementation of a common policy similar in scope to the agricultural policy. Otherwise the application of a similar solution, for example, in industry, education, transportation or scientific research would require – in addition to transferring national competencies to EU authorities – securing correspondingly higher funds in the budget. From 2000 onwards, a classification of expenditure by purposes was introduced as part of the Lisbon Strategy. All of the above measures were designated for implementation as part of the Lisbon Strategy. However, despite the gradually growing importance of the structural instruments in the CAP, they continued to represent only a minor percentage of the total EAGGF expenditure.

In 2006, the principles of the cohesion policy for 2007–2013 were adopted. Its three main objectives were as follows:

1) convergence – reducing the development differences between different EU regions (Barry, 2000; Maynou et al., 2016);
2) regional competitiveness and employment – increasing competitiveness and employment (Kutan and Yigit, 2007; Mohl and Hagen, 2010);
3) European territorial cooperation – implementing cross-border and transnational projects.

In the same year, major cohesion policy tools were also consolidated and integrated, limiting the EU budget expenditure categories in this respect to only three: EFS, ERDF and Cohesion Fund (Holgado et al., 2015).

To simplify the structural policy regulations, the previously existing so-called Community initiatives were scrapped. The contribution ceiling for investment projects was significantly raised from 75% to 85%. At the same time, which is of particular significance in the context of the analyses at hand, a strategic solution was adopted, providing for a close link between the cohesion policy in 2007–2013 and the implementation of the top European strategic document that was the Lisbon Strategy at that time.

As a consequence of these changes, the structure of EU budget expenditure also significantly changes from 2007 onwards. The European Commission applied a classification which divided EU budget expenditure into six headings relating to different areas of EU action. These areas changed not only in terms of thematic scope but also of the comparative scale. Sadly, this made it basically impossible to conduct comparisons with past periods as concerns the scale of allocation and of the impact on the sustainable development of the European Union. The autonomy of budget headings meant that respective budget items were financed as part of a given heading. The expenditure classification presented earlier was strictly linked to the EU's political priorities contained in the 2007–2013 programming period.

When analysing the EU budget expenditure structure, it can be concluded that expenditure items were mainly earmarked to Lisbon Strategy's chief goals, such as employment growth, research and development, climate change and energy, education and sustainable development. The EU's 2006 Sustainable Development Strategy and the Lisbon Strategy for growth and jobs complement each other (Dall'Erba and Fang, 2017). The Sustainable Development Strategy mostly referred to intra- and intergenerational equity and cohesion of all policy areas, including its external aspects. It recognised the role of economic development, seeing it as a factor that helps in the transition to a developed society. Meanwhile, the Lisbon Strategy fundamentally helped fulfil the ultimate goal of sustainable development as it chiefly related to measures and funds intended to enhance competitiveness, speed up economic growth and incentivise job creation.

Hence, the Sustainable Development Strategy laid down the general framework for the Lisbon Strategy, which – by placing the emphasis again on the economic growth and employment – provided a stimulus to make the economy more dynamic. The two strategies contained an assumption that economic, social and environmental goals may have a mutually stimulating effect and thus they should be implemented jointly. Therefore, both policy papers were meant to support the necessary structural changes to help Member States' economies better respond to problems linked to globalisation as these changes created a level playing field in which dynamism, innovation and creative entrepreneurship could flourish, while ensuring social equity and clean environment.

In this context, EU SDS recognised that investments in human, social and environmental capital as well as in technological innovations are the prerequisite for maintaining a long-term competitiveness and economic prosperity, social cohesion, quality employment and better environmental protection.

Thus, the change in the expenditure structure in 2007–2013 was related to the adopted division of expenditure into two main areas of EU action.

1. Sustainable development – expenditures supporting the goal of competitiveness and cohesion for growth and employment.

Expenditure in that area represented 38% of the total EU expenditure in 2007, going up to 48% in 2013. A trend analysis has revealed a stable growth in expenditure on that purpose in the period analysed, except in 2009. The highest growth was recorded in 2013, by ca. EUR 10 billion compared to 2012. The Lisbon Strategy provided for a sustainable and stable development, smart environment and higher employment rate (Mendez, 2013). The implementation of the Lisbon Strategy objectives caused expenditure as part of *Sustainable Development* to grow starting from 2012. The European Parliament and Council adopted in 2006 an integrated action programme in the field of lifelong learning 2007–2013 (Benedetto, 2013).

2. Conservation and management of natural resources – in 2007–2011, it represented the largest share of EU budget expenditure (down from 48% in 2007 to 40% in 2013). A trend analysis for the costs of measures related to Conservation and management of natural resources has revealed a stable level until 2011 (with a minor growth observable from 2011). In 2011, expenditure supporting the sustainable development goal exceeded the expenditure on Conservation and management of natural resources, precisely due to the implementation of the Sustainable Development Strategy (Wilkin, 2013, 2016).

Two sub-headings were identified as part of *Sustainable Development*: cohesion for growth and employment, representing a major share of expenditure as part of this heading, and competitiveness for growth and employment. In 2012–2013, a significant increase in the expenditure supporting cohesion for growth and employment could be observed in connection with the implementation of "Europe 2020" goals. Expenditures supporting competitiveness also increased year over year. As part of *Sustainable Development*, various programmes were implemented as part of expenditure oriented towards competitiveness – for example, Marco Polo programme to develop railway transport and to transfer freight from road to rail, Galileo programme providing funding for the satellite navigation system, and lifelong learning programme – which caused a visible rise in expenditure in 2013 compared to 2007. Cohesion for growth and employment was implemented, among others, with the structural funds available in the EU budget. Under that heading, the utmost emphasis was placed on convergence (in line with the Lisbon Strategy) and development of regions (Molina et al., 2015). Convergence expenditure represented a major share of expenditure on sustainable development.

The main part of the expenditure under *Conservation and management of natural resources* was expenditure related to the energy market and direct aid. Direct aid expenditure reached its peak in 2009, with a slight decrease recorded in the next two years (2010–2011), followed in 2013 by growth again (Hessami, 2010). Expenditure on the development of rural areas ranked second.

It should be emphasised that changes in the budget expenditure structure in 2007–2013 mainly concern the identification of six principal EU action areas and the allocation of expenditure among these areas. The decisions adopted in this field meant progress in the improvement of the EU expenditure allocative structure. The Lisbon Strategy implementation led to an unquestionable increase in sustainable development expenditure, with a still slight decrease in agriculture expenditure (European Commission, 2013, 2014b, 2014c, 2015a, 2015b).

The Lisbon Strategy was an obvious consequence of civilisational changes and its failure by no means suggests wrong assumptions were adopted; it simply shows that the challenges involved were too ambitious at a time where problems arose making its implementation difficult. These difficulties were related, among other things, to the global economic downturn, the accession of new EU members (for which the requirements formulated for old EU members turned out to be much too exacting), concern over the international situation (asymmetric threats to the stability of global peace and security) as well as the limitations of the EU countries' demographic situation. As a result, the vision of the EU successfully reaching an R&D expenditure of 3% of GDP (only ca. 1.9% of GDP was achieved) and catching up with the United States in that respect, has proven a still unattainable dream (with new contestants also entering the race – China and India). At the same time, demographic problems which generate social expenditure continue to be a hard-to-control challenge, as could have well been predicted back when the preparatory work on the Lisbon Strategy started. New challenges have also emerged, such as the vision of the fight for the Earth's limited natural resources further aggravating in the future and the need to mainstream the focus on countering climate threats.

Already in the early years of the implementation, it turned out that it was not possible to introduce changes on such a scale under the existing circumstances, with only superficial "systemic and legislative" modifications made; what was required was more in-depth human capital and quality-of-life reforms, and a breakthrough in the way the young generation is educated (the way it is done in the United States) to nurture minds that are open to innovation and have the courage to accept research challenges and implement solutions that foster economic growth (Dumciuviene et al., 2015). At the same time, there was an understanding that developing a modern social inclusion system would contribute to those changes.

Meanwhile, to present the Lisbon Strategy as evidence of total failure of the European integration concept would be an utterly unjustified overgeneralisation. In the context of problems with the strategy implementation, G.W. Kolodko rightly highlighted that in this case

> talking of fiasco is an exaggeration. Despite everything, the Union has proved to be an excellent idea on how to solve many social, structural,

institutional, and, last but not least or maybe first and foremost, economic problems on a transnational scale.

(*20 pytań do . . .*, 2008)

It is worth emphasising here that the revision, verification, update and realisation of the strategic assumptions for the EU by means of adopting another strategy, Europe 2020, to be discussed further in the Monograph, was based on the experience gained while its predecessor was effective.

4.4 Europe 2020 strategy

To carry on with extensive pro-development policies at the European Community level, drawing on the synergy of Member States' actions was the only rational alternative for the European Union, which was reflected in early 2010 by the finalisation of work on the EU's new strategy titled *Europe 2020. A strategy for smart, sustainable and inclusive growth* (European Commission, 2012a; Radulescu et al., 2018).

In the new – or renewed – strategy, the core, most general development philosophy was preserved, emphasising in the introduction that Europe may only be successful if it acts together as a Union. It announced that the EU economy should become smart, sustainable and inclusive "delivering high levels of employment, productivity and social cohesion" (European Commission, 2014a).

This strategy paper focuses its attention, to a greater extent than ever, on the social aspect of the economic policy. Significantly, the vision of the system to emerge as a result of making this strategy reality is called the "vision of Europe's social market economy".

Europe 2020 puts forward three mutually reinforcing priorities:

- Smart growth: developing an economy based on knowledge and innovation;
- Sustainable growth: promoting a more resource efficient, greener and more competitive economy;
- Inclusive growth: fostering a high-employment economy delivering social and territorial cohesion.

In quantifiable terms, the Commission proposed in this document a number of headline targets that should be pursued:

- 75% of the population aged 20–64 should be employed;
- 3% of the EU's GDP should be invested in R&D;
- The "20/20/20" climate/energy targets should be met (including an increase to 30% of emissions reduction if the conditions are right);
- The share of early school leavers should be under 10% and at least 40% of the younger generation should have a tertiary degree;
- 20 million fewer people should be at risk of poverty.

Europe 2020 adopted a more customised and thus, as it would appear, a more realistic approach to its implementation by respective countries. As a matter of fact, each Member State was allowed to tailor the Europe 2020 Strategy to its particular situation, meaning a possibility to translate the aforementioned EU goals into national targets and trajectories. Chapter 4 presents the outcomes of the implementation of these guidelines.

The above targets are representative of the three priorities of smart, sustainable and inclusive growth. At the same time, it was announced that the list of programme instruments available under this strategy is not exhaustive; the actions undertaken as part of its implementation should be more comprehensive, meaning they should not be limited to only domestic and EU level but should also involve the international one as these spheres interpenetrate.

Moreover, the Commission put forward seven flagship initiatives to catalyse progress under each priority theme:

1) "Innovation Union" to improve framework conditions and access to finance for research and innovation so as to ensure that innovative ideas can be turned into products and services that create growth and jobs;
2) "Youth on the move" to enhance the performance of education systems and to facilitate the entry of young people to the labour market;
3) "A digital agenda for Europe" to speed up the roll-out of high-speed internet and reap the benefits of a digital single market for households and firms;
4) "Resource efficient Europe" to help decouple economic growth from the use of resources, support the shift towards a low carbon economy, increase the use of renewable energy sources, modernise our transport sector and promote energy efficiency;
5) "An industrial policy for the globalisation era" to improve the business environment, notably for SMEs, and to support the development of a strong and sustainable industrial base able to compete globally;
6) "An agenda for new skills and jobs" to modernise labour markets and empower people by developing their skills throughout the lifecycle with a view to increasing labour participation and better match labour supply and demand, including through labour mobility;
7) "European platform against poverty" to ensure social and territorial cohesion such that the benefits of growth and jobs are widely shared and people experiencing poverty and social exclusion are enabled to live in dignity and take an active part in society.

It was assumed that the above seven flagship initiatives will commit both the EU and the Member States to solve major problems and deliver the Europe 2020 goals, using EU-level instruments available to the European Commission, notably the single market, financial levers and external policy tools. A decision was also made that at first the European Commission must determine what needs to be done to prepare a "credible [crisis] exit strategy", continue the financial system reform, carry out budget consolidation for long-term economic growth and improve coordination within the Economic and Monetary Union.

It was also pointed out that Europe 2020 will rely on two pillars: the thematic approach as presented earlier, which combines overall priorities and headline targets intended to fulfil them; and Member States' reports intended to help them develop their own strategies for returning to sustainable growth and stable public finance. Among the proposed measures to support this process, the so-called European semester was established in 2011 as part of the "Six Pack", which essentially covers six first months of each year, in which economic and budgetary policies should be coordinated within the EU. The key purpose of the European semester is to synchronise the processes of updating national reform programmes (prepared as part of the Europe 2020 strategy) and stability/convergence programmes.

Integrated guidelines were adopted at EU level, covering EU general priorities and headline targets as well as delegations to provide respective Member States with recommendations as to the implementation of their measures. In case of their inadequate response, policy warnings could be issued.

The reporting of Europe 2020 and the Stability and Growth Pact evaluation will be done simultaneously. Yet these instruments will function independently of each other, maintaining the integrity of the Pact. The European Council will be at the heart of the strategy, fully involved in its implementation while the Commission will oversee progress towards targets, facilitate the political exchange and present the legislative proposals necessary to give the right direction to and implement flagship initiatives. The task of the European Parliament will be to mobilise citizens and participate in adopting the key legislative initiatives. Such partnership approach should also extend to "EU committees, to national parliaments and national, local and regional authorities, to social partners and to stakeholders and civil society so that everyone is involved in delivering on the vision".

As announced in the introduction to the Europe 2020 strategy, general guidelines were also adopted with respect to economic policy in place at both Member States and EU levels. These guidelines seek to:

1) support policy actions for reaching the goals of the Europe 2020 strategy, based on investments, structural reforms and fiscal responsibility;
2) set the EU firmly on the path to growth, the goal of the Europe 2020 strategy, and allow it to maximise the potential to create new jobs;
3) contribute towards achieving the objectives of the European semester for economic policy coordination.

The implementation of all of the above programme provisions required, however, real adaptations consisting in providing an efficient supply of finance to support processes to achieve strategic EU goals, general and detailed alike (Hudrliková, 2013). Of course the principal mechanism to ensure effective achievement of those ambitions was the EU budget, with an allocation structure to enable considerable support for Member States' development processes, in both economic and social terms.

The EU budget in 2014–2016 was prepared on the basis of the 2014–2020 programming period. The Lisbon Strategy, as pointed out earlier, was replaced with the Europe 2020 strategy. Considering that the new strategy was an EU programme for employment and economic growth in the past decade, an emphasis was placed accordingly not only on smart, sustainable and inclusive economic growth as a way to overcome structural weaknesses in the European economy, improve its competitiveness and efficiency but also – which is no less relevant – the social aspect was given unprecedented importance, among other things by pointing to the need to strengthen sustainable social market economy (Bouthevillain and Dufrénot, 2016). The EU budget in the 2014–2020 programming period was, therefore, underpinned by the five fundamental goals defined in the Europe 2020 strategy, i.e.:

- 75% of the population aged 20–64 should be employed;
- funds representing at least 3% of the EU GDP should go to R&D;
- sustainable use of energy, greater share of energy from renewable sources, limiting greenhouse gas emissions;
- increasing the number of people aged 30–34 with tertiary education and decreasing the share of early school leavers;
- fight against poverty and social exclusion by reducing the number of people at risk of poverty by at least 20 million.

The expenditure structure, like in budgets from 2007 to 2013, was divided into six main areas and three additional ones (slightly different names in budgets from 2014 to 2016 compared to the period of 2007–2013).

An analysis of the budgetary expenditure structure has revealed that in 2014–2016, *Smart and inclusive economic growth* (formerly *Sustainable growth*) has the largest share of expenditure. This means the policy directions of the Lisbon Strategy were consistently continued and further developed in the Europe 2020 strategy and in the EU Sustainable Development Strategy, especially for agriculture (Milea et al., 2015). Hence, a stable increase in expenditure on smart economic growth can be observed in the period analysed as well as the continued predominant role of this allocation category. Expenditure on sustainable growth, similarly to the situation at the end of the previous period, represented as much as ca. 45% of EU budgetary expenditure and remained at this level throughout the period analysed. Other expenditure stood at a similar level to previous years, though now it had a lesser importance compared to the strategic expenditure on smart and sustainable growth.

An analysis of the expenditure structure for Heading 1: *EU Budget* indicates that expenditure on *Economic, social and territorial cohesion* had the largest share (80%) of the budget. In seeking to meet this goal, the highest amount of funds were invested in economic growth and employment (59%) in less developed regions (implementation of the Europe 2020 strategy, among others: fight against poverty, sustainable development of regions). Second place (though with a much lower amount than expenditure on the development of the less developed regions most in need of support) went to Cohesion Fund expenditure and to investment to boost competitiveness of developed regions. Measures promoting employment of young people, supporting technological progress and territorial cooperation between regions have also been observed.

Competitiveness for economic growth and employment was pursued using Common Strategic Framework instruments, and research and innovation – mainly with the Horizon 2020 framework programme for research and innovation. Common Strategic Framework was intended to translate the Europe 2020 strategy into the language of Community policies and the structural funds implementing them. The reason for linking these documents is the EU's negative experience with the so-called open coordination method adopted as an instrument to implement the Lisbon Strategy, which proved highly inefficient. The Horizon 2020 programme was introduced as part of Europe 2020 implementation. In aiming for greater competitiveness, expenditure to support educational and scholarship ("Erasmus") programmes was increased.

In the expenditure structure of Heading 2: *Sustainable growth: natural resources*, 78% represented financing from the European Agricultural Guarantee Fund (EAGF) while the European Agricultural Fund for Rural Development (EAFRD) accounted only for 20% of the expenditure on sustainable growth related to natural resources. A drop in the 2014–2016 CAP expenditure was also observed, though this category continued to hold a significant share of EU budget expenditure.

Relying on the above-presented strategic underpinnings, the European Parliament passed the MMF for 2014–2020 on 19 November 2013. It should be emphasised in this context that the budget for 2014–2016 provided for significant allocation supporting new job creation from the EFS and ERDF. As part of the reformed cohesion policy, further funds were made available for investments in European regions and cities as well as investment in the real economy. These were obviously the EU's key investment tools, which enabled the implementation of the principal goals of the Europe 2020 strategy such as ensuring economic growth and employment, tackling climate change and energy dependence, and reducing poverty and social exclusion. This was coupled with the ERDF adopting support for SMEs as a priority. With the support from the new EU programme "Erasmus+", more young people were able to plan their stay abroad. The European culture, cinema, television, music, literature, theatre, cultural heritage and other related areas received more money as part of the new programme "Creative Europe".

EU-financed R&D are making an increasing contribution to a quality-of-life improvement for Europeans and enhancing the EU competitiveness globally. The overall funding envelope of the new programme for research and innovation, Horizon 2020 in 2014–2016, stood at ca. EUR 28 million. The reformed CAP is the EU's response to the contemporary challenges including food security, climate change, sustainable economic growth and job creation in rural areas. Also small- and medium-sized enterprises can expect financial support with the new programme COSME.

To sum up the discussion so far, it is worth noting that the evolution of public funding allocations within the EU budget was, to a great extent, linked to the modifications in the direction of the EU's strategic development (Palová and Václavíková, 2018). However, one can observe a shortage of adequate tools to fulfil the defined goals, which would enable using the EU budget funds effectively and in good correlation with Member States' national budgets.

Before formulating the final assessment, though, it is worth checking to what degree the goals set have been successfully met and how the efficient use of EU funds is assessed, which is done by the ECA. When conducting such an analysis, one should bear in mind, however, that it will be incomplete unless the EU-level expenditure is considered jointly with the expenditure from national budgets, in line with the subsidiarity principle.

4.5 The new financial perspective 2021–2027 and anti-crisis measures in the fight against Covid-19 consequences

In 2020, the world underwent a supply and demand shock as a consequence of the Covid-19 pandemic which became not only a public health threat but also a harbinger of the possible onset of economic breakdown processes resulting in irreversible social changes. Judging by the past experiences, for example that of the Spanish flu of 1918–1919, it is in the nature of pandemics to not only reduce total demand, stimulate maintaining low interest rates and diminish consumption and investment opportunities (Jorda et al., 2020) but also to help accumulate capital only if sources of revenue can somehow be ensured that exceed the expenditure incurred. Of course a number of scenario-based studies were conducted before 2020 to investigate threats to the economic policy, also taking account of the emergence of a supply and demand shock (Berg and Kirschenmann, 2015) but never on such a scale. In this sense, such a major economic shock had been an unfamiliar phenomenon over the last couple of decades and caused a greater vulnerability to loss of health and to economic downturn than the past world wars or the so-called Great Depression of the 1930s did. Quoting the definition proposed by Raczkowski and Postula (2022), it can be said that "coronavirus is a respiratory deficiency syndrome ushering in a global-scale economic recession shock and social isolation, the antidote being an interventionist policy of subsidising the economy and the society at the expense of creating significant new public debt".

Certainly Covid-19 will forever change the EU's approach to the social and economic policy making and to introducing solutions to enable an immediate response, should a similar phenomenon occur again in the future. This can be already observed in the solutions put forward and approved with respect to the budget package for the coming years. As pointed out in Chapter 1, as a response to the corona crisis, the EU budget package was presented in 2021 for 2021–2027, including the EU recovery instrument Next Generation EU (EURI-NGEU), EU issuing joint debt instruments to finance EURI-NGEU programmes and a greater focus on climate and digitisation. Efforts to work out this solution and to find a compromise were extremely challenging as they were undertaken against the backdrop of the difficult fight against the pandemic and the debate on the future of the European Union. Work on the budget package for 2021–2027 was also complicated in that it was necessary to reach an agreement on a regulation proposed by the European Commission already back in 2018 on how to deal with EU funds in case of an infringement of the rule of law in Member States. Moreover, budget proposals undoubtedly should have accounted for the implications of the fight against the consequences of Covid-19 by elaborating on the existing MFF and the recovery fund. In this context, of particular importance was the new source of finance for post-corona crisis development activities proposed by the European Commission in May 2020: the "European Union Recovery Instrument" (EURI) called Next Generation EU (EURI-NGEU). A significant element of this solution is that 60% of the EURI-NGEU funds must be used until the end of 2022, and the rest, by the end of 2023 so that all payments as part of these measures are made by the end of 2026. The European Union, in proposing this solution, demonstrated for the first time such a clear and concrete instrument to respond to the crisis which also affected the Community Member States. As indicated by the European Commission, the creation of this additional instrument is motivated by:

- a desire to put in place an instrument of additional support for Member States' national measures to counter the consequences of the Covid-19 pandemic;
- a desire to develop mechanisms to accelerate Member States' capacity growth and cohesion when it comes to environmental protection and digital transformation actions;
- a will to create an instrument that is founded on the principles of solidarity, subsidiarity and conscious self-interest;
- reluctance to burden EU Member States with further levies, hence measures undertaken as part of this instrument will be financed from public debt contracted on behalf of the European Union, keeping the national public debt level from rising and increasing real EU budget expenditure on investment in structural changes.

Moving on to the instrument known as MFF for 2021–2027, it was adopted and approved by Member States in the amount of EUR 1,074 billion, which should represent ca. 1.1% of the GNI in 2021–2027. This should be viewed in the context of the information contained in the previous subchapter that the ceiling for these payment appropriations is lower than:

- the actual MFF expenditure of EUR 1,083 billion (1.19% of GNI in 2014–2020) in MFF 2014–2020;
- the original level of EUR 1,100 billion (1.13% of GNI 2021–2027) proposed by the Commission in May 2020.

The reduction of the MFF funding envelope for the following years is due to Brexit, among other things. In addition, an overall *ex ante* margin created as part of MFF (space between recover fund ceilings and MFF ceilings) was set at 0.36% of GNI 2021–2027 compared to 0.26% for EU28 in 2014–2020. To further enhance flexibility, the European Union thought it necessary to introduce non-thematic special instruments: the Single Margin Instrument and the Flexibility Instrument. The Single Margin Instrument should enable shifting margins available as part of relevant funds below the ceilings for commitment and payment appropriations, respectively, between financial years and, for commitment appropriations, between MFF headings, without exceeding the total amounts of the MFF ceilings for commitment and payment appropriations for the entire period of the MFF. The Flexibility Instrument should allow financing of specific unforeseen expenditure in a given budget year. Moreover, the approved cohesion policy for 2021–2027 is to rely on the following funds, the way it did in the previous MFF for 2014–2020:

- European Regional Development Fund (ERDF), which aims to strengthen economic, social and territorial cohesion in the European Union countries; in particular, financial resources allocated through the Fund should correct development imbalances between European regions and address the challenges of the disadvantaged regions;
- Cohesion Fund (CF), which, similarly to ERDF, aims to reduce economic and social disparities as well as to promote sustainable development. It supports strategic environmental protection and transport projects, including trans-European transport networks (TEN-T);
- European Marine and Fisheries Fund (EMFF), supporting the EU's marine and fisheries policy, whose role is to provide broadly defined support to coastal communities, for example helping fishers transition to sustainable fishing or financing projects that create new jobs and improve quality of life of coastal communities in Europe.

ESF+, which is to be the EU's main instrument for increasing social cohesion; in particular, projects implemented through it should address labour market challenges and social challenges as well as stimulate sustainable economic development by investing in human capital. ESF+ will involve instruments which were fragmented in the previous programming period: EF, Young

Employment Initiative (YEI), Fund for European Aid to the Most Deprived (FEAD) and the Employment and Social Innovation programme (EaSI).

The proposed Cohesion Policy funds are complemented as part of MFF for 2021–2027 by the Just Transition Fund (JTF), which is part of the European Green Deal and an element (first pillar) of the Just Transition Mechanism. The purpose of JTF is to alleviate the social and economic consequences of the energy transition.

Moreover, as part of the MFF for 2021–2027, expenditure is divided into a number of impact areas:

- Single Market, Innovation and Digital (12.36% of the total MFF 2021–2027),
- Cohesion, Resilience and Values (35.16% of the total MFF 2021–2027),
- Natural Resources and Environment (33.17% of the total MFF 2021–2027),
- Migration and Border Management (2.11% of the total MFF 2021–2027),
- Security and Defence (1.23% of the total MFF 2021–2027),
- Neighbourhood and the World (9.16% of the total MFF 2021–2027),
- European Public Administration (6.8% of the total MFF 2021–2027).

The European Union expects to spend EUR 132.8 billion on Single Market, Innovation and Digital measures, and EUR 377.8 billion on cohesion and strengthening EU Member States' economies. These amounts will go up to EUR 143.4 billion and EUR 1,099.7 billion, respectively, taking account of the additional financing from NGEU, including loans to Member States. Further EUR 356.4 billion will be earmarked to natural resources and environment (together with the NGEU instrument, this will amount to EUR 373.9 billion).

Expenditure on Migration and Border Management will total EUR 22.7 billion over the next seven years while EUR 13.2 billion will be allocated to Security and Defence. The funding for the EU neighbourhood instrument and for aid to other countries in the world will reach EUR 98.4 billion.

To support digital transformation, new financing programme, Digital Europe, was established to promote diffusion and large-scale use of key digital technologies, such as artificial intelligence and cutting-edge cyber security tools. The digital component of the "Connecting Europe" instrument will also receive sizeable financial support. Programmes targeting young people, such as Erasmus+ and European Solidarity Corps, will also be strengthened, with Erasmus+ expected to triple the number of participants in the new MFF.

To support the most vulnerable high-emission regions in their transition to a climate-neutral economy, the new JTF was established. It will obtain funding both from the next long-term budget and from the EU recovery instrument (as part of NGEU).

The goal of earmarking 30% of the total expenditure for climate objectives, set in the EU's final budget package for 2021–2027, is less consistent than the lower goal proposed by the European Commission as part of the original draft and, despite strong determination there is a high risk the environmental targets assumed as part of it will not be met, as further discussed in Section 4.6. On the one hand, the European Council made budgetary cuts to the climate-focused programmes proposed by the Commission. In particular, the proposed total MFF+NGEU 2021–2027 expenditure on the JTF (within Heading H.3.9 Environment and Climate Action), aimed to ensure social support to speeding up the from climate-damaging production, was cut by EUR 22.5 billion down to EUR 17.5 billion. On the other hand, the European Council increased the overall climate spending target from 25% to 30% of the total MFF+NGEU envelope excluding loans, coupled with introducing the "no-harm" principle. Despite the combined MFF+NGEU expenditure being lower in the final package than in the Commission's proposal, the higher target requires higher climate expenditure also in absolute terms (EUR 439 billion compared to EUR 400 billion).

4.6 The process of evaluating the effectiveness of EU expenditure and selected examples of its performance

The ECA, as already mentioned in the introduction, is an audit authority which performs its tasks at EU level, undertaking cyclical and ad hoc audits of EU level public policy implementation. The audit results are presented in publications such as annual reports, special reports, opinions, specific annual reports regarding various EU bodies and agencies, reviews and annual activity reports. ECA work programming is based on several elements, the first one being a strategic document: ECA's multiannual strategy. The current strategy covers 2021–2025 and contains three strategic goals that need to be reflected in every annual work programme. The first strategic goal defined is "Improving accountability, transparency and audit arrangements across all types of EU action" (The 2021–25 strategy of the European Court of Auditors, 2021b), which aims for the Statement of Assurance to provide higher value-added.

The second strategic goal is to place greater emphasis on the outcomes achieved thanks to EU action, which seems more important to this publication and requires highlighting a number of elements that should address this strategic goal. The ECA should focus first and foremost on audits that can demonstrate the value added of EU action. This is why, in addition to standard publications that are special reports and annual performance reports, the ECA plans to prepare and publish more landscape reviews where it will focus not only on revealing irregularities and shortcomings but also on indicating the so-called good practices. As part of this strategic goal, the ECA will also look into the risk of corruption and fraud involving EU funds.

The third strategic goal contained in the strategy for 2021–2025 is to ensure clear and accurate information on ECA's work results and strong audit assurance in a challenging and ever-changing external environment, meaning that if something is not working, the institution is tasked to identify such a phenomenon. It can be observed that the Strategy is a document with quite a short time horizon, more planning-oriented than strategic in nature, but it is where the main operative goals of the ECA for this period are set.

Another element taken into account when programming the ongoing ECA work is the annual work programme which contains information on the special reports, annual reports and all other reviews and opinions planned for publication in a given year. Additionally, ECA's partners are consulted when preparing the programme, mainly the European Commission and the European Parliament. The ECA, before starting work on programming work for the year ahead, formally consults its plans with the European Parliament, requesting respective thematic committees to indicate issues or areas of special importance to MEPs. ECA's work programme is annually presented at a European Parliament session where audit requests from the Parliament are discussed and ECA justifies its decisions on whether to accept or reject the proposed audit topics.

Here it is worth making some remarks on how respective post-crisis challenges facing the European Union translate into specific topics of special reports. For example, in connection with the challenge of sustainable management of natural resources, the ECA published three special reports in 2018 which address this issue to a certain degree. These are matters related to food safety in the European Union and the future of the CAP. So where do the ideas for planned audit topics come from? Does the ECA check only what serves to prove the positive effects of the European Community? Nothing could be further from the truth. In second half of each calendar year preceding the preparation of a new work programme, all ECA employees – auditors and members of their Cabinets alike – are requested to prepare brief (half a page long) audit topic proposals called policy scans. Then, all these ideas are collected by respective thematic audit chambers. First, members belonging to a given chamber carry out an initial review of the ideas submitted whose topics fall within the chamber's competence, and then the proposals shortlisted by chambers are sent to the Directorate of the Presidency – to the President of ECA – where they undergo another selection and review to ensure there are no overlapping topics. After this selection, topics identified as qualifying to be included in the work programme return to their authors with a request for more details. As the next step, authors of the selected proposals prepare several-page long audit ideas (prepared on the basis of a specific template) discussing the reasons why a given topic should be included in the Annual Work Programme, how it should be audited as well as what could be the principal questions, assessment criteria and timescales for conducting a given audit. This document should also indicate whether any legislative changes are planned in the nearest future, providing a potential for such a publication to feed into the legislative process, etc. Once those materials are prepared, they are selected again at the level of Directorate of the Presidency to be expanded into Proposed Audit Tasks. Next, several dozen are chosen to be presented at a session attended by all ECA members, where they are discussed and a set of high priority tasks is selected to be included in the work programme for the following year.

Relying on the strategy and work programme, the ECA aims to reflect in its activities the main challenges facing the European Union at a given time. Hence, in its audits and reports, the ECA is tasked with checking the effectiveness and efficiency of the EU and its action, which is its core competence and the reason why it was established. A current example of such activities would be ECA's preparations to a future audit of National Recovery Programmes. The expenditure items contained therein will, in many Member States, eat up funding that could otherwise go to reforms, and, furthermore, it is extremely difficult to build metrics to measure their efficiency or effectiveness.

As part of its mandate, ECA carries out both financial audits and audits to measure performance against relevant targets. This duty is imposed on it by the *Treaty on the Functioning of the European Union*, which in Article 287 indicates that

> The Court of Auditors shall examine whether all revenue has been received and all expenditure incurred in a lawful and regular manner and whether the financial management has been sound. In doing so, it shall report in particular on any cases of irregularity.

This provision – quite modest in its substance and form – is reinforced by the provisions of the Financial Regulation applicable to the general budget of the European Union (EU), the implementation of which is audited by the ECA on a yearly basis. The Regulation explicitly emphasises that "Budget appropriations shall be used in accordance with the principles of sound financial management, namely in accordance with the principles of economy, efficiency and effectiveness". In response to such a definition of its tasks, the ECA integrated them in its mission, considering them as the basis for assessing how EU institutions deliver on their duties. Such an assessment is – in other words – performance auditing, to which ECA devotes a major part of its work. At the same time it is a field whose methodology is dynamically evolving at ECA. Due to its heterogeneous nature and the necessary flexibility of approach, performance audits are a constant challenge to the employees responsible for laying down the audit procedure and to auditors who conduct the audits.

ECA defines the performance audit as an "audit of sound financial management, that is of economy, efficiency and effectiveness with which the Commission [European Commission, the principal auditee – Author's note] and/or other auditees have used the Community funding in performing their tasks" (Radecka-Moroz, 2015). Information revealed by such an audit should focus on the outcomes achieved and contain an assessment of the implications of the findings for economy, efficiency and effectiveness (Cepiku et al., 2017). This is of particular significance to the main recipients of ECA reports, namely to the European Parliament, Council and Commission as well as other auditees (including Member States).

When it comes to a performance audit, the audit approach combines two main components, i.e. auditing performance directly and auditing the control systems involved in conducting the audit.

The proportion in which these components are present in a given audit depends on relevant circumstances. Direct performance auditing focuses on analysing inputs, outputs, results and impacts. This assessment is conducted on the basis of relevant measurement criteria for quantity, quality and costs of all of the aforementioned elements. If the findings about the results obtained are unsatisfactory, auditing control systems should help find the causes of incomplete performance. Meanwhile, if the results are satisfactory, the risk that the systems in place are badly designed or implemented is quite minor.

When auditing control systems, auditors' work mainly consists in assessing whether the auditee has designed and implemented a management and monitoring system so as to optimise economy, efficiency and effectiveness (Muratbekova et al., 2017). Another important aspect of this audit is to check if the system produces reliable information on the implementation of a given measure and whether, where any problem arose, relevant remedial action was taken.

From the organisational point of view, the ECA employs different approaches to performance auditing. Some thematic Audit Chambers have separate sections dedicated to performing this very type of audits, while in others financial and performance audits are mixed within one section concentrating its efforts on one thematic area. Each solution has both pros and cons, which is why this issue is left to the discretion of individual Audit Chambers.

It is also worth mentioning the broad methodological support provided to auditors in planning and conducting the performance audits. A very important stage of performance audit preparations is to properly define the concepts of economy, efficiency and effectiveness and to identify in the highest possible detail the various risks involved in the audited public intervention. Here is how the ECA, drawing inspiration from the EU legislation, defines these elementary principles underpinning sound financial management (Moullin, 2017):

- the principle of economy requires that the resources used by the auditee in the pursuit of its activities shall be made available in due time, in appropriate quantity and quality and at the best price;
- the principle of efficiency concerns the best relationship between resources employed and results achieved;
- the principle of effectiveness concerns the attainment of the specific objectives set and the achievement of the intended results.

These principles are commonly abbreviated to 3E. For some time now, a fourth E, for (natural) environment, has been added to this group. This is in response to the changing control environment, with environmental commitment lately becoming one of the top priorities of all public action. For the ECA, this audit element is related to the European Commission's interventions and commitments on issues such as climate change, environmental pollution, waste management and sustainable energy use. Performance audits which take account of that aspect include an audit of the implementation of environmental programmes, an environmental impact assessment of other actions or monitoring of environmental compliance (Radecka-Moroz, 2015; Laman et al., 2018).

In this context, a performance audit should allow for an assessment of the degree of achievement of various objectives. As a first step, the achievement of the so-called operational objectives is analysed, regarding the expected outputs (e.g. whether a planned training programme has been held, whether a road has been built). Next, verification of the achievement of immediate objectives will enable checking if a given measure has brought positive results for direct addressees (e.g. whether completing the training programme has helped its participant find a job or whether a new road provides its users with a better access to a given area). Checking the achievement of intermediate and global objectives means conducting an audit outside the auditee and assessing the impact of the public intervention. This kind of assessment is difficult to perform as the actual impact of a given programme's implementation can be analysed only once as substantial time has passed since its completion. Difficulties also arise when intermediate objectives are defined too loosely or when the collection and analysis of audit evidence would require a disproportionate workload. What can prove a simpler solution in this case is analysing the achievement of outputs (operational objectives) and results (immediate objectives) of a given intervention. If its underlying objectives are specific, measurable, achievable, relevant and timely (SMART), their achievement can be relatively easily measured to enable a clear effectiveness assessment. The European Commission has a similar outlook, being of the opinion that assessing performance of a given task requires a specific framework including tools and procedures for setting objectives as well as measuring and monitoring progress.

Performance audit explains how the information produced helps achieve EU's policy goals, improve its capacity for flexible response to unforeseen emergencies, ensure accountability and enable the EU to effectively communicate with the interested parties and the public on the EU budget and on how it adds value to the life of Member States' citizens. The EU budget outcomes are divided into two main sections: policy documents and Annual Management and Performance Reports. The former, i.e. policy documents, are part of the draft budget, based on which the Commission allocates financial resources. Meanwhile, an Annual Management and Performance Report serves to discharge authorities as a document providing an overall summary of information on how the EU budget has contributed to the achievement of the European Union's policy goals and to the outcomes achieved thanks to the EU budget. Moreover, this information also represents the Commission's budget management report.

Over the recent years, in order to meet the expectations of the society, the European Commission has introduced a number of changes in planning and reporting. Performance reporting is at the heart of this initiative, which aims to find ways to enhance the openness, timeliness and efficiency of communication about the results of the EU budget.

Information presented by the Community clearly reveals that the European Commission's reporting system is very complex and comprehensive, which undoubtedly affects its transparency. Another issue is the quantity and quality of the indicators used – especially those measuring the result. Firstly, the European Commission has itself admitted that one-fourth of the indicators prepared have turned out to be of no use. Secondly, there are cases where what is referred to as a result indicator is in fact an indicator that measures the output or even assesses the expenditure incurred on a given intervention. However, the issue of qualitative assessment of the indicators prepared was only raised in ECA's annual report for 2015. It was also mentioned in a number of special reports of the ECA taking a close look at the indicators prepared by the Commission and the same conclusion – the doubtful quality of result indicators – can be found in all those publications. Accordingly, the ECA – both in its annual report and in special reports – recommends, on the one hand, limiting the number of indicators prepared, and, on the other, preparing proper high-quality result indicators and avoiding the trap of calling an output or input indicator a result indicator.

Another challenge of reporting is how to measure objectives and their achievement. Also in this case, ECA publications mention the too broad definition of objectives, which obviously makes it easier to achieve the so-called formal consistency between the objectives set out in strategy documents and targets contained in programme documents, allocated to specific funds but fails to translate into making a given intervention outcome-oriented. This is especially visible in a "cascade" assessment of how the strategic objectives enshrined in "Europe 2020" translated into the 11 thematic objectives, how they were next reflected in national partnership agreements and, finally, in a given fund's detailed targets (Jääskeläinen and Laihonen, 2014). When evaluating the achievement of these objectives and the outcomes obtained, the Court concluded, on many occasions, that it is hard to demonstrate how measures undertaken as part of a given fund translate into the achievement of strategic objectives.

Another problem, very strongly linked to the implementation of individual interventions and to the outcome orientation, is the so-called vicious circle or the cyclically recurring problem, which is typical and probably unavoidable also in future negotiations regarding the next programming period. This is a problem of excessively long negotiations at the European Parliament and Council regarding the preparation of the new financial perspective. As a reminder, for the current financial perspective for 2014–2020, the Commission's motion was submitted in October 2011 while the last element of the legislative process, i.e. the executive regulation, was not published until July 2014, meaning that these negotiations actually went on for nearly three years. Such a long process of preparing the final version of the document has negative implications for the achievement of outcomes as part of the EU budget implementation. Most of all, the late adoption of the necessary financial framework causes natural delays in the process of working out and adopting national progress. In the perspective of 2014–2020, this was true of partnership agreements, operational programmes for cohesion and rural development programmes for agriculture. These delays, in turn, translate into late release of funds, which, obviously, results in their low absorption. This situation means that European expenditure will cumulate at the end of the programming period, which, on the one hand, will increase the likelihood of error and, on the other hand, will result in poorer quality projects being accepted for implementation "at the last minute" (meaning that a project that would have been quite negatively assessed at the beginning of the programming period may get a positive assessment due to the need to avert the risk of losing the funding). Another undesirable consequence is that funds may be reallocated to other measures, not necessarily where they are most needed.

The delay in the legislative process has another negative result. At the time of mid-term evaluation, due to the low uptake of appropriations, it will be challenging to evaluate respective measures against the objectives in place. Consequently, once the European Commission embarks on preparing new financial framework proposal, it will not be in possession of a reliable assessment indicating which measures have passed muster and which have not. This is the case of the present financial perspective. During the mid-term evaluation, it turned out that there was still not enough performance information to conduct a reliable assessment of what needs changing, strengthening or improving in the next perspective for 2021–2027. The European Commission, as required by the legislative agenda, already had to prepare its proposal, even though it did not have the information on good practices, lessons learnt and experiences from the previous financing period. ECA's annual report includes a mention that the College of the Commissioners do not take responsibility for the performance information they provide. This means that this information is prepared and discussed, and, in a way, has an impact on the discharge procedure, but the College of the Commissioners takes no formal responsibility for it. EMPs are not entirely enthusiastic about ECA audits relying on the so-called evidence-based assumptions. We have many such examples where evaluation and even the mid-term assessment has already demonstrated that a given form of intervention does not entirely work as it does not bring the expected outcomes and yet the European Parliament and Council decided to carry on with it in the form criticised by the audit authorities which may compound the inefficient trends in European allocations.

Policy documents by the European Commission are intended to justify the financing for EU programmes requested in the draft budget. For each programme, these documents contain current information on their implementation progress as well as key financial and performance information using indicators that will apply throughout the seven-year duration of the MFF. This approach enables the budget authorities to take account of the ongoing performance in the course of budget procedure.

One of ECA's fundamental goals contained in the previous audit strategy for 2009–2012 was to maximise their overall impact (the current strategy being in effect for only a year in 2022, it would be difficult to evaluate it at this point). This means that ECA should provide the Parliament and the Council with top quality, useful and up-to-date outputs. This requires the Court to adopt a flexible approach to the changing control environment and to continuously improve its own strategy and its auditors' skills. To perform this task effectively, ECA must obtain feedback on the actual impact of its own reports and of the findings and recommendations contained there. To that end, the Court published a specific report for the first time in 2012 (which contained selected special reports published in 2011), where it presented the real impact of its reports and their contents on the changes undertaken most of all by the European Commission. This report gives an insight into the number of recommendations formulated by the Court in various areas of the European policy, which led to concrete legislative changes. This is a useful tool both to the Court as it helps check the effectiveness of its own work and to the public, which can use this material to assess the usability of this audit institution (Radecka-Moroz, 2015).

Special reports drafted by the ECA are intended to check the correct application of the principles of sound financial management in the EU budget implementation. It follows from the published replies to the Court's reports that nearly three-fourths of the recommendations (74%) were fully accepted by the auditee, which was, in most of the cases, the European Commission. This is a very satisfactory result, considering that points of disagreements in which recommendations were not accepted in the end represent less than 10% (see Figure 4.1).

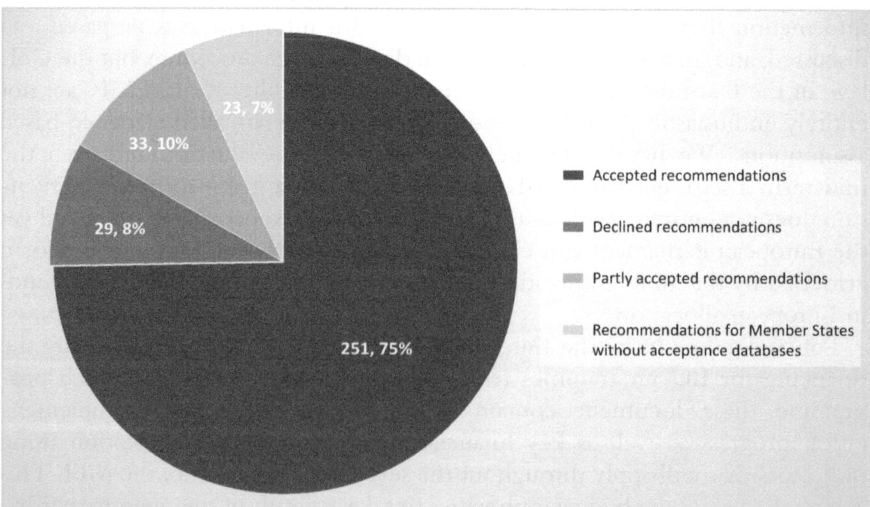

Figure 4.1 How strong is the Court's power of persuasion?

Source: based on the European Court of Auditors' data.

Information on the audit results is provided to the discharge authority, auditee and the public. Effective communication is of paramount importance to the good quality of a report: the main findings and conclusions regarding audit questions must be clearly and objectively presented in the report allowing the reader to easily understand what was done, why and how. The report must also contain practical recommendations.

The expenditure evaluation system complements the performance-based approach to accountability for the efficiency of expenditure on projects financed with European funds. Performance-based approach means that it is possible, also at the executive level, to refer the information on the scale of respective projects' financing to measurable outcomes (effects) of their implementation. This mechanism closely resembles the assumptions of performance budgeting which informs the allocation, the difference being that its cognitive and summative aspects involve mostly the functionality of the *ex post* evaluation. This Monograph presents to what degree these evaluation mechanisms are consistently applied to the main elements of the structure intended for financing pro-development measures in the EU.

The objectivity of the way those evaluations are conducted is manifested by the critical approach to the effects being evaluated. In the years analysed, 7 and 12 projects, respectively, were deemed to have partly achieved their objective. The evaluation of these projects focused only on indicators of the outputs, overlooking the impact indicators. Meanwhile, where it was required to measure intermediate effects by evaluating a given measure's results (rather than evaluating only outputs intended to ensure their achievement), then partial failure to achieve the objective was has been found more frequently, in as many as 38 and 45 cases, respectively, for the years analysed. At the same time, it has been found that as a consequence of using the performance-based approach, it was only in exceptional cases that programmes could not be evaluated (which was, incidentally, the case of non-implemented projects); it was tantamount to the inability to assess projects, either. This indirectly points to a desire to ensure adequate methodological quality of the measurement applied. Where metrics are indeed defined by reference to the projects implemented in practice – whether or not they represent a result or an output – it is possible to use them as a basis for evaluation of the phenomena taking place in this area. The system has, admittedly, a number of shortcomings, and the evaluation of efficiency and effectiveness may often serve as merely a reference point for formulating conclusions on whether it is advisable to implement the accepted undertakings (thereby building the knowledge and experience base for the future), but it should be borne in mind that all public financing systems worldwide using the performance budgeting methodology show significant dysfunction in many aspects of their operation. The prevailing opinion, though, is that even imperfect but consistent and systematic measuring of public service tasks brings more benefits than abandoning performance analyses altogether and, consequently, relying exclusively on financial analyses devoid of the performance context. The scope and modus operandi of ECA fit squarely into the pro-efficiency outlook on the public management methods, in this case with respect to Community funds.

To illustrate in practice whether ECA is an institution whose knowledge and assessments should be used by the European Commission, the Author has decided to present, in a nutshell, the results of a number of ECA audits. An excellent example of a special report relating to one of the European Union's priorities would be the *Special report 16/2021: Common Agricultural Policy and climate. Half of EU climate spending but farm emissions are not decreasing* (June, 2021). It shows the effective impact of one of the European public policies, for which the European Commission earmarked more than EUR 100 billion in 2014–2020 from CAP funds, i.e. mitigating climate change. In accordance with the rules in force, Member States were able to decide on the greenhouse gas emission reduction to be achieved in the agricultural sector. In the example of audit results presented here, ECA audited whether the 2014–2020 CAP supported climate mitigation practices with a potential to reduce greenhouse gas emissions from three key sources: livestock, fertilisers and manure, and land use (cropland and grassland). It also analysed whether CAP better incentivised the uptake of effective mitigation practices in the programming period 2014–2020 than in the 2007–2013 period.

However, the results obtained can be hardly considered satisfactory, for example livestock emissions accounting for half of the greenhouse gas emissions from agriculture, including land use emissions and removals from cropland and grassland, did not decrease between 2010 and 2018. The ECA identified four potentially effective mitigating measures for emissions from manure management, but the CAP rarely incentivised their uptake because the CAP does not intend to limit livestock numbers, nor does it provide incentives to do so. The CAP market measures include promotion of animal products, the consumption of which has remained unchanged since 2014. This contributes to keeping greenhouse gas emissions at the same level rather than reducing them. Greenhouse gas emissions from the use of chemical fertilisers and manure, which account for one-third of the EU emissions from agriculture, increased between 2010 and 2018. The CAP supported an expansion of organic farming and grain legumes, but the impact of such practices on greenhouse gas emissions is unclear, according to ECA. The CAP provided little or no support to effective mitigation practices such as nitrification inhibitors or variable rate nitrogen technology. In ECA's opinion, the 2014–2020 CAP did not increase its support of carbon sequestration measures such as afforestation and the conversion of arable land to grassland compared to the 2007–2013 period. Though there was an increase in areas covered with catch/cover crops between 2010 and 2016, the estimated impact on climate mitigation is low. Another problem indicated by ECA is that the European Commission had reported 26% of CAP funding as earmarked to climate action, but failed to set a specific mitigation target for these funds. The Commission's monitoring system does not provide data that would allow a proper monitoring of the impact of CAP climate funding on greenhouse gas emissions. Though the greening scheme was meant to boost the environmental and climate impact of direct payments, the resulting climate benefits were negligible. With cross-compliance rules and rural development measures barely changed compared to the 2007–2013 period, farmers were not encouraged to adopt new effective climate mitigation practices.

The above example of the findings of one report by the ECA (at least a dozen or so of which are published every year) reveals many problems that are laid bare by such audits and clearly demonstrates the important role of this institution in efficient spending of Community funds and how much there is still to be done in this field at EU level.

Summary

The conclusions of the analyses conducted in this chapter help understand if participation in the supranational undertaking that is the European Union indeed gives Member States a real opportunity to use Community mechanisms as an efficient and effective support for their own development, obviously coupled with synergised development of Member States. What needs to be emphasised here is that formulating even the most ambitious strategic plans and approaching those challenges without first securing proper funding and their coordinated management, and then using an outcome evaluation system leaves such undertakings with slim chance of succeeding. This is why strategies that are well designed in terms of methodology either themselves contain integral provisions (sections) on how to finance their implementation or come with other dedicated documents which stipulate the ways to secure the funding, the ways to implement them and the responsibility of those managing them, which will contribute to the achievement of strategic goals. However, the number and thematic variety of development goals indicated in the last subchapter of this Monograph seems too vast and gives rise to the question of whether it is possible to effectively manage their implementation to maximise the public utility of the EU budget expenditure.

As pointed out in the introduction, one of the economic growth drivers in some countries narrowing the gap with more developed regions are transfers of structural funds from the EU budget, which also contribute to a social development. However, a question arises whether the effects achieved warrant the conclusion that EU funds are efficiently used. This chapter has pointed to some imperfections of the existing solutions, which, nevertheless, evolve and seek improvement.

Between 1995 and 2020, the years representing the chronological scope of this chapter, five periods have been identified where funds were allocated from the EU budget to different expenditure classifications, especially those intended to support measures set out in two main strategy documents, i.e. in Lisbon Strategy and "Europe 2020" strategy. The varying approaches and different ways to assess the effects in the long-term perspective make it impossible to compare these values and directly calculate the effect of a given category. As a matter of fact, these categories often interpenetrated one another, with some measures moved between them. Such an approach by the European Commission to the classification issues raises concerns and blurs the clarity of the assessment of the measures undertaken.

An analysis has revealed that these funds were usually grouped in six vast spending categories (called headings) and according to 31 different policy areas. EU budget funded measures and projects in those policy areas in which all Member States agreed to undertake action at Union level.

As the foundations of strategic planning evolve in the EU, more traction is being gained by the approach that increasingly emphasises the equal importance and synergy between economic and social development, which is fully reflected by the improved successor of Lisbon Strategy that is "Europe 2020".

That is why any future actions towards the EU development policy goals should increasingly commit funds not only to economic development, including an improvement of the global economic competitiveness, but also to EU social cohesion. Some areas should be integrated and coordinated at EU level at the expense of national autonomies, but, on the other hand, it turns out that certain supranational measures do not bring any value-added and therefore should fall under the competence of national authorities.

A systematic increase in the amount of funds committed by the European Union generates a growing risk of inefficient use of some of them. To ensure development expenditure contributes to development at the optimum level, efficiently and purposefully, bringing the results and outputs expected as part of relevant interventions, an effective audit and evaluation of this expenditure is necessary. This function is performed, with an increasing focus on performance audit, by the ECA, whose role is continuously growing in proportion to the increasing intensity and scale of tasks such as evaluations of reports and recommendations. ECA results presented, for some time now, in the form of impact indicators clearly demonstrate that there is room for reform and change in the approach to the allocation and accounting of EU funds, while not discrediting their immense role for the sustainable development of European countries.

5 Identification of domestic, European and global-level tasks as a process that improves their efficiency

Introduction

The ongoing process of globalisation of social and economic phenomena as well as the crises occurring at increasingly short intervals show that only joint international action can bring results that are unachievable by one country acting alone, as perfectly exemplified by the Covid-19 pandemic. The survey conducted in 2021 (Eurobarometer, 2021) reveals clearly observable support for the role of the EU in crisis management, with 84% of the Europeans concurring that intensified EU action and coordination is needed to respond more effectively to future disasters and crises. More than nine in ten Europeans agree that their country should offer help to another country if it is too large to tackle the crisis alone – there is a clear sign of support for EU solidarity. This is also reflected in the European Commission's documents, for example the new MFF contains an increasing number of temporary as well as permanent instruments intended for quick crisis response (the classical: rescUE; the Union Civil Protection Mechanism as well as a number of so-called special instruments) and ever more funds are being earmarked for such measures.

In a global world, it is necessary to establish a sort of global public finance guided by the principles of the contemporary economic trends; to put in place a web of flows between countries, regions and continents modelled on the web of national flows and to divide tasks among them (in the same way that within a single country various tasks can be identified that can be performed by both a given local and central government, here they could be performed both by a given country and by the whole European Union or globally, by the whole world) (Arze del Granado et al., 2018). One of the factors in deciding at which level a given task should be performed could be an assessment as to which level will help achieve better outcomes, ensuring higher efficiency and effectiveness (Adam et al., 2014). This should be the key consideration in taking such decisions. The world could not have tackled the Covid-19 pandemic without joint action and financial support for the poorest countries so that this life-taking and economy-crippling crisis could be overcome in the fastest possible way. The discussions presented in Chapter 1 have demonstrated that public sector is

DOI: 10.4324/9781003222033-6

strongly committed to alleviating the consequences of the successive crises, but it would be best to do that as effectively and efficiently as possible.

5.1 Classification into domestic, EU and global tasks

The analyses of public spending level and structure in EU Member States, presented in the previous chapters, as well as the analysis of EU budgets in respective periods have unequivocally demonstrated that many joint tasks are performed as part of those budgets. The European Union supports projects that fit squarely into the strictly defined goals which are implemented in individual countries by means of specific strategies formulated at the level of the European Commission or, since 2021, in National Recovery Plans. The analyses conducted have also revealed that the expenditure structures in respective Member States are based on varied classifications developed for the purposes of a given Member State. Even though EU countries are obliged to apply in their reporting a single classification of the functions of government (COFOG) – as already mentioned in Chapter 4 – when evaluating, at the allocation stage, i.e. *ex ante* rather than *ex post*, the effectiveness with which these funds are spent, it is not fully possible to consolidate this information with data on allocation from EU funds. In turn, the European Commission, when discussing budget issues, creates the financial framework containing respective priorities identified in strategic documents, relying on its own classification. The analysis has demonstrated, though, that in the entire period analysed, i.e. between 1995 and 2020, the expenditure classifications used at the EU level differed greatly from COFOG and were modified six times. It was therefore difficult (or sometimes even impossible) to compare their presentation with that of domestic expenditure in order to indicate, at the stage of making spending decisions, the full source of financing for a given area. As a rule, comparing domestic budgets with the general EU budget is not entirely justified – if for no other reason than due to the subsidiarity principle. Such an approach seems quite deficient as spending decisions should be made on the basis of the outcomes they can or should help achieve, which has been emphasised, on many occasions, by the European Commission and other international organisations alike, for example OECD, WB, IMF. Therefore, one should have access to data that are classified in a manner to include all sources of financing for a given area, comparing the effectiveness and efficiency indicators at several levels at which the task is performed.

The public finance allocation and reporting system in place in Europe (and worldwide) cannot be deemed transparent as it does not provide data in a form that would enable a clear allocation of public funds to the policies being implemented – neither in the European, nor in the global context. As revealed by the analyses, both allocation of public funds and the reports submitted later with respect to the implementation of policies and programmes and to domestic budget execution were incoherent and non-transparent. That is why the public finance data published are difficult to interpret and can lead to opposite conclusions, which are presented in Chapters 3 and 4. A lot of data of great significance to the assessment of the financial situation and of the implementation of the social and economic policy in place has not been published at all, for example some special reports by the ECA referred to in Chapter 4. Such an approach has failed to meet the principal requirements laid down in the *Code of Fiscal Transparency* whereby reports should be reliable and internally consistent.

All of these factors also warrant an analysis of how to ensure a uniform presentation of the classification of funds earmarked for specific tasks at all levels of their implementation, both domestic and European. A question presents itself: What classification should be relied on when implementing public tasks to ensure proper expenditure planning, payment and reporting, and a correct evaluation of the outcomes obtained for maximised efficiency of the allocated resources (Abramov et al., 2016). Taking this assumption as a point of departure, one of the three solutions can be opted for, i.e. when spending public funds one needs to rely on the COFOG classification, apply the European Commission's methodology or try and create a new classification.

At first one feels inclined to develop a new classification that would reflect contemporarily significant issues and indicate the scale and scope of impact of the spending policy on the global challenges. One should, however, bear in mind the key purpose of the discussions presented in this Monograph, i.e. to improve the efficiency of public expenditure at every level and to enhance the effective impact of the public institutions that perform a given task. With the ultimate goal defined this way, developing a new classification would be problematic for many reasons, the most important being: lack of comparable *ex post* data, very high costs of implementation, impossibility to reflect in a supranational classification all spheres of impact existing in respective countries and, last but not least, the implementation process being lengthy and fraught with the risk of failure. When maintaining the countries' budget autonomy and using the supranational budgets of the European Union and World Bank, such a solution could be implemented approximately 8–10 years from now, judging by earlier experience with the implementation of much simpler changes, such as, for example, the adaptation of cash basis accounting to the accrual basis principles of public expenditure or the implementation of the International Public Sector Accounting Standards (IPSAS), and the outcomes would not be observable before ca. 15 years (Normansyah et al., 2015). It seems, therefore, that this solution is too distant in time while the world and the European Union need tools for the coordination and effective financial support for respective areas of public policies to be available much sooner.

The second potential solution is to rely in public expenditure on six areas of the EU policy making. Major difficulties of such a solution include the frequent changes in the expenditure classification. Moreover, adding to the difficulties similar to those mentioned for the first scenario are further concerns – how to manage domestic budgets based on a couple of categories only, what would be the structure of national governments and how would they be made accountable? Is the world ready for governments composed of six to seven ministers? The recent decades show it probably is not. Moreover, the fluidity of the European classification and the frequent changes introduced to it, on the one hand, suggest flexibility of the public spending, and on the other – makes it impossible to conclude whether it is indeed adequate and enables efficiency measurement. Researchers' analyses demonstrate that there can be serious doubts about that.

Consequently, COFOG classification seems like the best choice when addressing the implementation of public tasks at the supra- and domestic level. Currently, it is used to classify individual and collective consumption in the general government sector and also serves to analyse expenditure in that sector. It is especially useful for international comparisons. This presentation includes 10 main categories and 68 subcategories. European as well as OECD countries use this presentation to show their expenditure and often use it to prepare strategic documents. It should be pointed out that they rarely use this presentation in the day-to-day budget management as this classification is rather presentational in nature. However, it is worth using for a better management of public funds, if for no other reason than because it provides breakdowns of expenditure data for a long period for many countries and we can use them for comparative purposes. Moreover, this solution seems capable of implementation in the shortest time and with relatively low costs of the entire process. It obviously requires approval and cooperation of Member States and supranational organisations alike, but if the ultimate goal is an effective implementation of a common policy, then this is a necessary process.

With such an assumption in place, it is proposed to adopt the COFOG classification and divide its subcategories into three types of tasks: global, European and domestic. As the criterion by which the division into the proposed three categories will be made can influence the subsequent social and economic development, its choice requires adopting a comprehensive approach, inclusive of all the domestic, European and global expenditure and comparing their outcomes with quality indicators.

Of greatest significance is the way funds are spent on respective categories of the COFOG classification and the identification of collective tasks at the European and also global level which cannot be performed by each country individually. It should be borne in mind, however, that not all collective tasks are global in nature. Some of these should be classified at the lower, European level related to the European policy, Europe's competitive edge and European priorities, which will not necessarily match the priorities of the world as a whole. There is also a category of tasks which are significant only from the point of view of a given country: these are related to the political situation and to the prevalent school of economic thought as well as to demographic and social elements for which global action is of relatively little significance. Admittedly, the European Union has an impact on these in general through the European finance system, as presented in Chapter 3 but without directly targeting a specific task at domestic level.

Such an approach has led to defining three categories of areas (tasks, government action), which should be financed as part of the existing solutions but in a varied manner, depending on whether their nature is global, European or domestic (see Figure 5.1).

As mentioned before, the basis for the division proposed by the Author is the COFOG classification consisting of 10 areas, with 68 subcategories defined as part of them. The proposed division has been introduced at the subcategory level rather than at that of main areas as this would represent an excessive simplification and would not meet the objectives it is intended to fulfil. The presentation includes not only a quantitative division but also the degree of a given task's implementation at the three proposed levels. The criterion for the attribution to respective levels is the degree of responsibility for monitoring, ensuring accountability and decision-making with respect to an efficient performance of tasks, which gives the assurance that if a task is global in nature, the resources planned will be employed at domestic, European and global level alike to boost the chances of an improved efficiency of their use. It must be emphasised here that the idea is not to have one common budget and one ministry of finance. This issue should be approached differently, finding a solution that would enable maintaining a sort of autonomy in the actions undertaken by a given country, the European Union and other global organisations. Indeed, it is hard to concur with the proposition that introducing a single budget would be the best solution. This is also an overly idealistic view of the reality, furthermore, one that is strictly linked to the debate on the functioning model of the

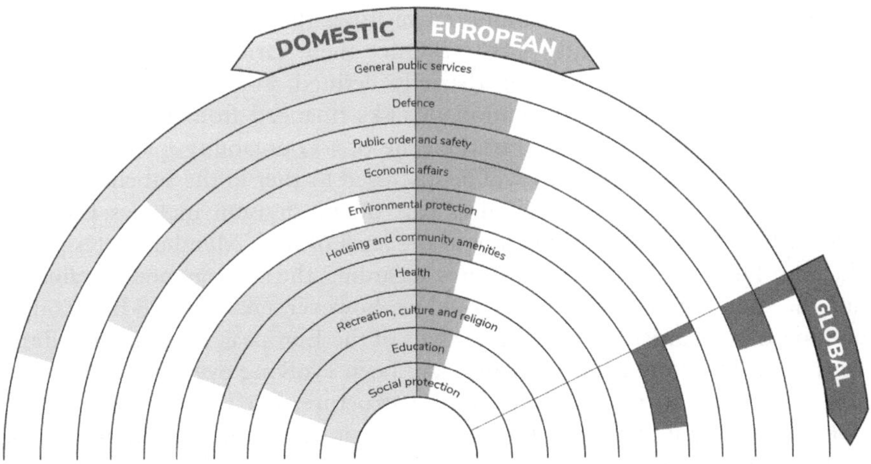

Figure 5.1 Implementation of public policy in accordance with the COFOG classification broken down into domestic, European and global tasks

Source: own elaboration.

European Union, and thus certainly impossible to implement in a short time or even in the foreseeable future. Global finance is currently facing a specific challenge. Global tasks are being implemented whose objectives cannot be achieved only at the level of a relevant country, of the European Union or as part of another community. Actions need to be undertaken at each of these levels, and their coordination and accountability for their outcomes – at the level corresponding to each public service task category. As commented by M. Gorynia in one of his publications:

> The threat of the tragedy of the commons with respect to the specific category of resources that are common pool resources is an objective and real threat to raising the economic welfare and to the ecological continuity of our civilisation.
>
> (Gorynia, 2017)

A good example of such an area of common, global impact is the aforementioned environmental protection activity (fourth category in the COFOG classification). This is a typical impact area, along with respective categories, where expenditure at one level alone (that of a given country or of the EU) will not be efficient (such reasoning being confirmed by the related findings of the Paris consensus). Only coordinated action at the global level, undertaken by both individual countries and regional organisations/communities such as the EU, will help achieve the expected outcomes so they are justified. If no accounting principles are in place or a specific procedure governing the flows, especially the financial ones, these funds will serve as no more than a window dressing, with some of them (which is currently the butt of the criticism of global tasks) spent to a larger extent on administrative issues than on specific measures to solve a given environmental problem. Once these varied origins of resources are centralised and managed in a strictly defined, coordinated manner, the effectiveness of the implementation of tasks financed from these funds will be certainly higher. By all means, the issue of accountability for the decisions taken must be solved, but this will be discussed further in the subchapter.

The second category proposed as part of the division includes European tasks, which need to be carried out at the level of both Member States and by the EU. Decisions on these measures regarding the management, evaluation and the scale of funds employed should be, however, taken by the EU Council and the European Parliament. An analysis of the European budget expenditure has revealed that the main priorities have been evolving over the last 20 years, when it comes to the EU expenditure structure, but the key elements are constantly present in the EU budget, with their significance beginning to rise.

This leads to the question: What is then a European task, which – according to the COFOG classification – could be identified as particularly important and requiring coordination at the supranational level? It seems economic matters or digitisation would qualify as this type of tasks. It also includes the whole EU financial envelope for measures to ensure competitiveness, further increased in each subsequent Financial Perspective, which generally speaking has an impact on all common market participants. These COFOG categories are mostly European in nature; some of them can be obviously seen as a sphere of state action, but in fact, within the EU, these interests should be treated as supranational to ensure a greater scale of intervention and prevention, and some measures, for example those related to agriculture, forestry, hunting or general economic matters should be addressed at the European level.

Not all the categories identified in the COFOG classification can be assigned to one type of tasks without hesitation. For example, the issues related to security, cybersecurity and public order have been predominantly assigned to domestic measures but their remaining part is European in nature as some security measures would be much less efficient without the EU's internal territory being protected as part of military and security cooperation. One typically domestic task, as demonstrated by international research, is housing and community amenities (Nath and Sharma, 2014). It can be said, of course, that the European Union, as part of its supranational measures to improve the quality of life, among others, also handles some housing-related aspects, but in this case, it is the country itself that decides whether and to what extent it wishes to develop and pursue a housing policy or to leave it up to the market. Except for strategic intervention, it is difficult to find here any trends of supranational action or common allocative decisions as it is a function, as will be discussed in further detail in Section 5.4, where not only the diversity of a country's impact but (it should not be forgotten) also its wealth can be well demonstrated. Another group that should be classified as domestic issues (ca. 20% of these tasks could also be coordinated at the European level) involves healthcare matters: even though health is significant from both the European and global perspectives (a solitary fight against diseases, especially the infectious ones, is doomed to failure, as we have learnt the hard way during the Covid-19 pandemic), tasks related to the medicines policy, hospital network and voluntary service network, all of which are part of the healthcare policy, are largely financed and implemented at domestic level.

The following subchapters discuss the general issues related to the categories identified and an attempt will be made to prove, in the efficiency context, the validity of the division proposed, based on selected examples from various public policy spheres of influence.

5.2 Global tasks

Global tasks can be said to include 10 subcategories defined as part of the COFOG classification, the largest number of which refers to the already mentioned area of environmental protection. The necessity of global financing of environmental protection is beyond discussion. This matter will be discussed in further detail when going over the global problems that need solving. These include, without limitation: sewerage management, waste management, water management, pollution abatement, etc., i.e. problems that no country will solve on its own. As is the case of the nationwide policy, where various tasks can be identified that can be performed both by a given local government and by the central government, here they can be performed either by a given country or by the European Union as a whole or even at the global level, by the entire world (Rambarran, 2015; Davidson, 2017; Arze del Granado et al., 2018). In this situation, it should be borne in mind that the challenges posed by the new, more complex reality may call for new, more complex formulas to address the circumstances around us and to implement public policies.

When discussing the matters related to the climate policy as a global task, one cannot start otherwise than from issues related to air quality, and particularly the CO_2 emissions, which have been widely discussed for a long time now. A report by the ECA published in September 2018 and 2021 reveals that the measures undertaken by the EU to protect human health from air pollution did not yield the expected results. Each year ca. 400,000 people die prematurely as a consequence of air pollution and the related external health costs run into hundreds of billions euros. The scale of the phenomenon makes it advisable to undertake coordinated global tasks. Recently, however, another very important problem has emerged, sadly, also present in the Polish realities: the lack of global governance of the waste management policy, which not only translates into inefficient expenditure of funds earmarked to waste mitigation but also has a major impact on a number of other expenditure categories, for example those related to healthcare, security, fire safety, etc. It is worth reflecting on whether if there was a global waste management policy in place, the current trade in waste situation worldwide would look different now. Another major issue to tackle is that China has ceased to accept waste in the context of the new regulations that have banned the imports of waste plastics since 1 January 2018, with some other countries like the United Kingdom refusing to accept waste as well. Hence, there is a new problem that needs to be solved at the global level.

Environmental protection is not the only area of intervention that should be classified to the global category. Military defence is another such element. This category comes second in the COFOG classification. The situation in this case is, however, less clear and some measures taken as part of it should remain at the European level while others, at domestic level. States that brought NATO into being concluded that these tasks are supranational in nature, though at times it is very difficult to reach a common position within this association. Unfortunately, history has proved on many occasions that individual countries have much lower chances of defending their territory when acting alone, with these chances increasing in the event of community action. (Florén et al., 2017). All areas of influence that should be classified as global are presented in Figure 5.2.

It would be worth, however, confirming that such a division of global tasks, rather than merely creating additional burdens and organisational structures, will also contribute a measurable effect of greater efficiency of the resources used. Such an analysis is conducted further in this subchapter, focusing on the

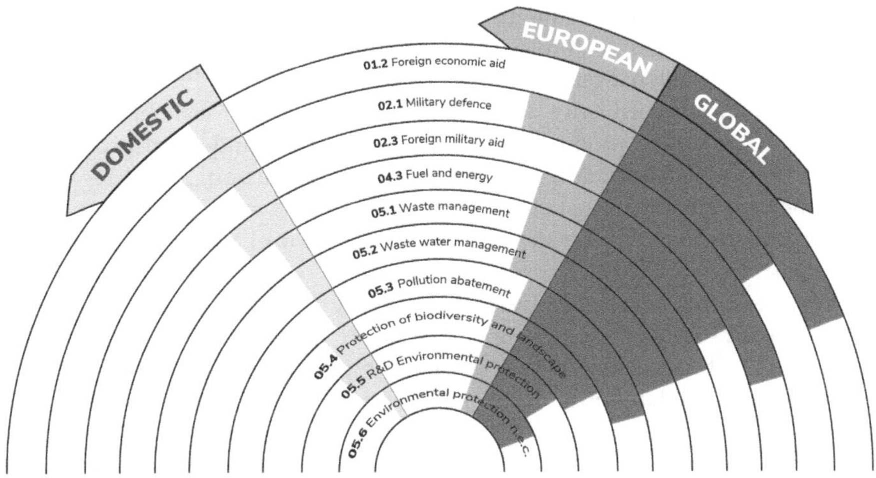

Figure 5.2 Global tasks – scale and scope at respective levels of public policy implementation

Source: own elaboration.

environmental policy, which is the most broadly represented among global tasks.

K. Amartya Sen, as a winner of the Nobel Prize in Economics, wrote in his book *Development as Freedom* that the path to improving human prosperity will be paved by expanding choices and opportunities. While a policy that promotes sustainable development can lead to (some but not unlimited) economic growth, the reverse is certainly not guaranteed. Achieving sustainability, presented in more detail in Chapter 4, will require strengthening the government action, which should "explicitly embrace environmental and social goals as a core self-standing dimension of development" (Sen, 1999).

The area of rational environmental policy requires support from all participants of the ongoing economic processes (state, market, world and financial markets) as environmental protection calls for reconciling the interests of the economic activity, social welfare and future generations' needs, as presented by Donella H. Meadows, Dennis L. Meadows, Jørgen Randers and William W. Behrens III in their book *Limits to Growth* (1972). The book demonstrates, based on a dynamic simulation model, that with businesses and households taking short-sighted decisions without concern for long-term consequences of short-term production and consumption, there is a possibility that natural resources depletion and environmental degradation will lead to an irreversible collapse of the global economy in the 21st century.

The phenomenon of climate crisis has exposed the imperfection of the existing economic theories and consequently of the way they are reflected in the economic and social policy in place. It turned out that the political and social expectations focusing on sustainable development, financial stability and on mitigating the economic and social vulnerability require new economic paradigms and efficient national and international institutions. Preventive legislation which sets the effective course of action for the government and helps avert crises, as well as modified economic propositions and social expectations as to how government and public services should function, have become the substance and organisational characteristics of political sciences, and to find the way to make science reflect the processes taking place has become one of the key challenges of our time.

An interesting perspective was presented by J. Ravetz and S. Funtowicz (2006) in their concept of post-normal science, which argues that a positivist, linear approach to science is part of the problem that is present-day environmental crisis, and demonstrates the ineffectiveness of the "puzzle-solving" suggestions offered to date (Kuhn, 1996) which fail to take account of the system complexity in solving our top challenges of today. Post-normal science accepts the existence of the inherent contradictions and inconsistencies. A good example of such a seemingly unsolvable conflict would be our constant pursuit of development and enrichment while the planet's limited resources necessary to achieve this ambition are running out (Rockström et al., 2009). There is no single scientific method to solve this antagonism and that is why the role of science in this perspective is defined as the initiator of the mutual learning process rather than an objective supplier of final solutions.

Irrespective of the research aimed to resolve the dispute within economic theory, it is desirable to focus attention on the economic policy actually implemented and on its outcomes for stable development, and thus to approach the problem relying on basic fiscal policy parameters related to the scale of GDP redistribution and to the growth rate achieved, while taking account of the policy's underlying qualitative factors related to social customs, procedures, legal regulations and their application. The choice of the adequate scale of redistribution, measured with the revenue- and expenditure-to-GDP ratio, and the achievement of the desirable growth rate represent a fundamental problem for policymakers responsible for a given country's medium-term social and economic development, irrespective of the political option they represent. The contemporary economic policy implemented in different countries should also take account of the changing internal and external determinants (read more Postula and Radecka-Moroz, 2020).

An analysis of EU Member States' 1995–2020, expenditure indicates non-uniform approach to environmental protection across countries (Dumciuviene et al., 2015). It reveals that in as many as eight cases, there is a negative correlation between environmental expenditure to GDP and an increase in HDI. In further three cases, there is a positive correlation but its coefficient stands below 0.25. This means that in as many as 16 out of 28 cases analysed, the priority attributed by a Member State to environmental tasks and the actual commitment to implementing them are not correlated (or they are correlated to a minor extent) with HDI, which describes the life expectancy, education and income per capita.

The analysis results reveal that the implementation of environmental tasks at domestic level is contingent on a number of factors and on many occasions it does not allow for achieving common goals at the same level in all the countries. This is due, among other things, to the varied priorities assigned by countries' governments to respective segments of these measures. For example, the correlation between expenditure on water pollution measures and HDI is very negative in Italy (–0.75), while in Denmark a very high negative correlation coefficient has been observed for expenditure on air pollution abatement.

As a next step, to confirm that only global action can be effective in the climate policy implementation, the efficiency of public expenditure earmarked for this purpose by the Community as a whole and in respective countries has been analysed. An attempt has been made to determine whether it has an impact on the CO_2 emissions. Consequently, country-level analyses have been first conducted using a linear regression model with CO_2 emissions in a given country as the response variable and a given country's environmental expenditure as the explanatory variable. Sadly, the results obtained have shown a low efficiency of domestic policies in the area under analysis, i.e. the impact of public spending on the important goal of CO_2 emissions reduction (see Table 5.1). In only five EU countries can we find some correlations between

Table 5.1 Impact of environmental expenditure on CO_2 emissions in EU Member States.

Country	*Impact of total general government expenditure: environmental protection on CO_2 emissions*	*Country*	*Impact of total general government expenditure: environmental protection on CO_2 emissions*
Belgium	–2242.03	Luxembourg	662.884
Bulgaria	–50488.56	Hungary	–4.374601
Czech Republic	105.6802*	Malta	4860.948
Denmark	588.7945	The Netherlands	–4681.265*
Germany	–22134.87***	Austria	9566.254
Estonia	–12106.58	Poland	49.80605
Ireland	–2549.74	Portugal	3108.326
Greece	–13301.39**	Romania	–2331.153
Spain	3513.696	Slovenia	–8843.736**
France	–8454.415***	Slovakia	–11121.49*
Croatia	–2978.82	Finland	121992.4
Italy	–47924.08***	Sweden	255.5788
Cyprus	–6414.916	Iceland	–12134.73
Latvia	–5776.755	Norway	–3190.979
Lithuania	–6120.844	Luxembourg	662.884

***Significant parameter at a significance level of 0.01; **significant parameter at a significance level of 0.05; *significant parameter at a significance level of 0.1.

Source: own elaboration.

these variables, their impact being minor even taking account of the time shift in the analyses.

In the European context, the environmental policy narrative is anchored on the EU measures, for example those defined in July 2021 in the Fit for 55 package and its ambitious plans to become a climate-neutral continent by 2050. These assumptions translate into actions required of Member States, which are reflected in the 10-year National Energy and Climate Plans. Combined with the planned changes resulting from the adoption of the European Green Deal and the Just Transition Fund, this means that Member States must rise up to the urgent challenges and expectations of profound changes without which it will be simply impossible to achieve the climate goals. Hence, this vision presents how the EU environmental policy is to function and what its intended outcomes are for 2050. The programme spells out 10 top-priority environmental goals. Identification and a proper analysis of the links between the environment, the economy and the society are necessary to take effective systemic decisions aimed to build sustainable solutions. A correct interpretation and evaluation of the environment's contribution to how human beings function in various dimensions is among the most important tasks to be performed in the context of sustainability policy. The condition of the environment, its sustainability defined as the existence of the suitable conditions for natural regeneration and its capacity to provide environmental services in the long term – all of this is of key importance to the future of humankind. Environment is present in each of the Sustainable Development Goals. For example, goals directly related to the quality of the environment are as follows: Goal 6 (water), Goal 13 (climate), Goal 14 (oceans) and Goal 15 (land and biodiversity); meanwhile, others are indirectly linked to the environment, for example Goal 2 (zero hunger), Goal 1 (no poverty) and Goal 11 (sustainable cities and communities).

In addition, each of the strategy documents highlights the significant role of cooperation between the European Union and international partners, especially with reference to the sustainable development goals adopted in connection with the "Rio +20" conference. The utmost goal is to ensure that all environmental protection measures should take account of the global nature of these challenges rather than focus only on the EU area. Such an approach by the European Commission is a further confirmation that environmental protection issues should be viewed in the global rather than domestic or European context.

Following this reasoning and excluding a significant impact of domestic-only policies on the air quality improvement (measured with CO_2 emissions), a random-effects GLS regression panel model has been developed, which the analyses have shown to be the best suited and best reflecting the size of impact of the entire European Union on this indicator. Sadly, also this time, no significant correlation has been found between the environmental expenditure within the Community as a whole and the CO_2 emissions within its territory (see Table 5.2).

Table 5.2 Impact of environmental expenditure on the CO_2 emissions at EU level.

Carbon emission	*Coef.*	*Std.*	*z*	*p > z*	*95%*	*Conf.*	*Interval*
Total general government expenditure: environmental protection in million euros	–6.453198	32.73716	–0.20	0.844	–70.61685	57.71045	
_cons	9.94e+07	2.63e+07	28185,00	0.000	4.78e+07	1.51e+08	
sigma_u	1.443e+08						
sigma_e	14019037,00						
rho	.99065294	(fraction of variance due to u_i)					

Source: own elaboration.

Own observations and research results as well as those presented by other researchers confirm the need to plan and implement environmental policy along the horizontal dimension at EU level and in cooperation with other world regions. This is extremely important due to the global nature of the environmental pollution, and, consequently, due to the fact that actual environmental outcomes can only be achieved with coordinated action in this respect. An effective change in the scope of public policy financing must link funding streams and the authorities ensuring them at the global level with the accountability for the results obtained. Such situation can be achieved at the global level using several instruments, creating institutions intended for that purpose, for example by creating a global fund that would pursue its tasks as part of multiannual financial and operational planning.

The data demonstrating low efficiency of domestic expenditure and the position of the EU authorities, which, ever since the first programme adopted by the Community in 1973, have emphasised the international nature of environmental pollution, point to the need to undertake action not only at the international level but also at the intercontinental one for environmental protection. Obviously such proposals are questioned by sceptics who only believe in the domestic dimension of such measures, but it is worth confronting them with a couple of examples which have strongly demonstrated in the recent years how little effect such approach brings in the long-term horizon. To illustrate this point, it is worth quoting the example of a global problem (notorious in 2018 also across Europe) due to a large number of landfill fire incidents caused by spontaneous combustion. According to estimates, less than 30% of plastic waste in the EU is recycled, with ca. 31% stored in landfills and 39% burnt at incinerators. Both landfilling and burning involve the risk of generating additional pollution – with landfills contaminating water and incineration releasing toxic chemical compounds into the atmosphere. Though the attempts to increase the share of recycled and reused waste undertaken by respective countries may bring measurable results, the lack of common action in that respect will not allow for actual outcomes to be achieved globally. The circular economy discussion is all about creating a common market in the EU, in the same way we attempt to do that with respect to the "traditional" economy. Once we get there, it will make economic sense and the stimulus can also translate into real change in the environment. Even the highest reduction of emissions, for example from burning waste in one country, while others have no similar measures, will bring positive results only to a very limited extent. With regard to the air pollution level, the effect generated by a single country will not translate into a major improvement of air quality in a given region.

In this context, it is worth emphasising that the EU exports most of its plastic waste to third countries. China's ban on imports of plastic waste, in place since January 2018, means that the country will no longer receive this type of waste from abroad. This may have a significant impact on Europe as in the past China used to import most of European waste – for example, the United Kingdom would send two-thirds of its plastic waste there. Plastic pollution is a global problem so the role of the EU in combating it is significant. In January 2018, the EU Strategy for Plastics in a Circular Economy was adopted. The strategy sets out a goal whereby 2030, all plastic packaging placed on the EU market should be either reusable or recyclable in a cost-effective manner. At the same time, recycling of plastic packaging waste should reach a comparable level to that of other packaging materials, i.e. approximately 65%. Support from private sector as well as from national and regional authorities has a vital importance to the fulfilment of these goals. The costs of measures meant to achieve them will be high, and an efficient use of the means available requires an integrated and consistent approach worldwide.

Another good example of the global dimension of environmental issues is biodiversity. For instance, to preserve biodiversity in the seas and oceans, an adequate marine management policy is paramount. In June 2021, the European Parliament adopted a biodiversity strategy, mainly addressing the problems of a mass extinction of further and further species, which is generally consistent with the concept of the European Green Deal and the announcement of the fight to contain climate change on multiple fronts. Decisions taken in this regard by each Member State individually will not have a significant impact on preserving biodiversity. Only a common approach, one integrated with the common marine management policy, can positively contribute to preserving biodiversity in respective waters (Newman and Perl, 2014).

Another thing that needs to be highlighted is the international dimension of the environmental policy with respect to ensuring competitive equilibrium. It is only by adopting uniform principles and goals at the global level that we may avert competitive imbalance caused by an economy not bound by environmental goals or fees gaining an upper hand. The best example of that would be limiting the atmospheric emissions. Should there be no harmonised approach to that issue, major inequalities in competitiveness among economies would be generated, resulting, among other things, from higher electricity or production prices. A common approach to that matter – both at EU level and globally – is the only way to ensure that individual economies will not build their competitive advantage on increased emissions (not bound by any standards, etc.) compared to other countries. Likewise for production, respective entities required to comply with norms, standards and goals with respect to limiting emissions are obliged to bear the costs of implementing cutting edge solutions and technologies to meet specific requirements. Competition between such entities and businesses not bound by such restrictions and requirements would not ensure equal treatment and would result in the former losing out on the market due to higher business costs.

To emphasise the horizontal dimension of the environmental policy and the need to place it in a global context, it is also worth quoting here the results of EU opinion polls. According to the latest survey (Special Eurobarometer, 468) conducted in 2020, 78% of the respondents believed environmental decisions should be taken jointly at EU level, while environmental decision-making at Member State level was favoured by 36% of those polled. Even though this result means that most of the respondents consider the EU level to be the only competent one for solving environmental problems, a decline in this indicator compared to 2008 should be noted. According to the survey conducted back then (Special Eurobarometer 295), the share of those indicating the EU as the competent level of environmental decision-making was 74%, meaning it had fallen by 14% in nine years. This situation may stem from either the lack of social awareness of the measures taken at EU level or from new challenges being identified which are perceived by the public opinion as local problems. The latter case can be illustrated by urban pollution, where the society considers local or national authorities competent to take action. Nevertheless, as pointed out before, with no global goals or standards defined also with respect to problems occurring locally (noise, urban pollution), adequate outcomes may not be achieved. This means that it is vital to take measures to promote the social awareness of the scope and principles of the common environmental policy.

The above measures take on a special significance in the light of other results as regards the social perception of environmental issues. The survey conducted in 1976 (The Perception of Poverty in Europe, March 1977) revealed that for 94% of people, environmental protection and limiting air pollution was significant (63% very significant, 31% significant). The latest survey in this respect conducted in 2017 (Special Eurobarometer 469) shows that this result is still at a similar level, i.e. 95% of those polled believe environmental protection to be a significant issue (53% very significant, 42% significant). Also when asked if it would be advisable to develop EU regulations intended for environmental protection in respective Member States, a great majority (77%) replied in the affirmative.

The above-presented survey results indicate that, despite a slight drop in the support for environmental decision-making at EU level, a great majority of the Community's residents still consider environmental issues to be significant (Pereira, Pereira, 2017). At the same time, most of the respondents believe the EU should introduce Community-level regulations that would include environmental protection issues in individual countries. This means that the environmental policy dimension is naturally understood and identified as horizontal.

5.3 European tasks

European tasks are a category comprising 24 subcategories of the COFOG classification which involve actions from many public policy areas. The decision to include such a large number of subcategories in it stems from the fact that the benefits of joint actions co-financed from the EU budget (as discussed in Chapter 3) are clearly observable already today. At the same time, though, there is a noticeable shortage of well-defined rules for checking the synergy brought by implementing this action jointly with Member States. In conclusion, a number of areas can be found that require cooperation supervised at European level, not only when it comes to allocating European funds to specific measures but also in terms of authorising the European Court of Auditors to audit their implementation by Member States (see Figure 5.3).

The category of European tasks comprises, for example transport expenditure, where European impact and some joint decisions by EU countries, including the co-financing of those tasks from EU funds, contribute to efficiency.

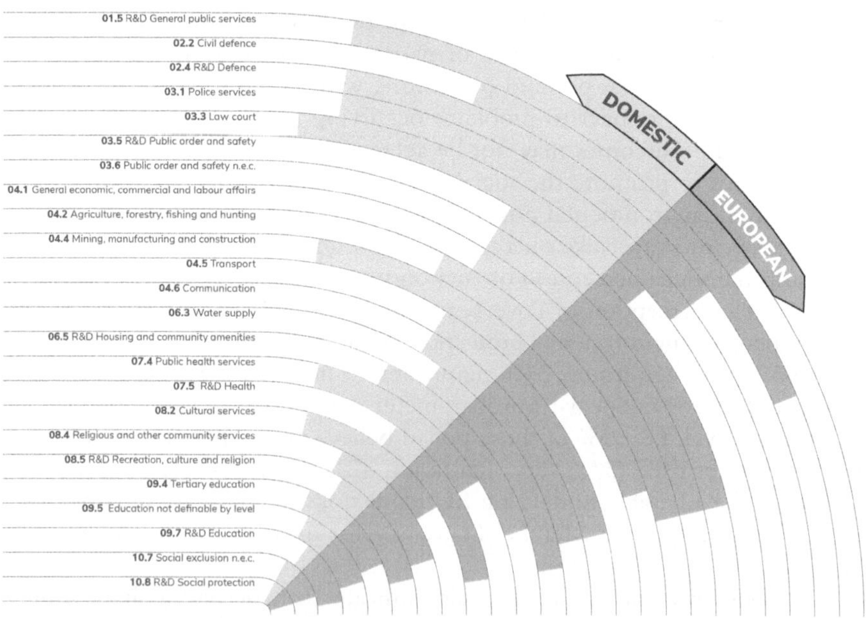

Figure 5.3 European tasks – scope and scale of implementation at selected levels

Source: own elaboration.

A good example of such cooperation would be the development of the TEN-T network intended to connect Europe. This example will be discussed further in this chapter.

Another area that could be mentioned here is the issues related to education, improving the efficiency of education as well as exchange of experience and educational expertise including student exchanges between countries. The role of the state in this process is obviously of utmost importance, but the European Union can undoubtedly play a major role, too, in increasing the value of human capital.

Some of the COFOG subcategories classified as European tasks are these days often implemented and co-financed from the EU budget, offering additional benefits of applying the new proposed methodology for this process. The advantages of the proposed division and of identifying European tasks as well as the proposed way to manage them will be presented further in this subchapter, taking as an example the TEN-T network, which is presently being developed.

One of the principal goals of the European Economic Community was to ensure free movement of goods and persons, as discussed in Chapter 3 of this Monograph. Of greatest importance to achieving this goal, i.e. to creating a single market, is to provide a cohesive transport system in the economic area acting as its necessary bloodstream (Kegalj, 2013). The technical and formal limitations in transport have a direct negative impact on the progress on the path towards that goal. Actions in that respect obviously can and are taken at the level of respective countries. The question, however, is how efficient these actions will be in the context of achieving the main goal that is the competitiveness of Europe as a whole vis-à-vis other continents and free trade to support this process. In the proposed division of tasks financed from public funds, a great majority of subcategories in this area are classified as European tasks.

The transport sector is an interesting case that deserves attention in the context of reflections on the division of public tasks suggested in Section 5.1. As a matter of fact, tasks implemented as part of the infrastructure policy have both local and European dimensions. This is why they should be pursued in a different manner, depending on whether they emanate from the common economic policy or from a local transport policy managed by the national authorities, which should complement the European policy (see Figure 5.3). Infrastructural European tasks serve to achieve the latter goal and should be implemented and managed as part of a concerted EU policy and accounted for based on the outcomes obtained by it (Ferrara et al., 2017). Performance of such a task, and of respective projects as part of it, has an impact not only on the economic development of regions but also that of all Europe. Why these outcomes are greater than if these were domestic tasks – a number of arguments and historical facts have already been presented in this subchapter. Another important thing is to look chronologically at the instruments used for managing European tasks in the context of the goals achieved, which will make it possible to propose a new way to manage European tasks in future, using the existing practices. The European infrastructure policy experience of recent decades validates such an approach. The example of a task defined as European, analysed in this subchapter, the trans-European transport network, has been selected on purpose as it perfectly illustrates the change in the approach of the European Commission to the implementation of European tasks, showing the evolution of this approach (European Parliament, 2013a, 2013b). Hence, one cannot negate the concept of implementing tasks at a supranational level merely because some errors once occurred that diminished their effectiveness. Instead, it is worth placing greater emphasis on the tools used in implementing them and not giving up on the benefits of the European approach.

These problems lead to obstacles in the operation of the single market, i.e. to free movement of goods and persons. Moreover, their effect is that the funds earmarked from the EU budget for these goals do not ensure their achievement. In addition, a risk of excessive volume of traffic has been identified for respective network sections, which, in the absence of support from other transport sectors, may lead to the quality and timeliness of transport services deteriorating even further.

In addition to the above-presented aspects, the *White Paper on the Future of Europe* (2017) discusses the EU's current role in the efforts to create TEN-T in the context of financing infrastructure projects with the Community budget funds. It indicates efforts to integrate transport systems as the main goal of TEN-T, helping to close gaps between countries and contributing to the development of Member States (Love et al., 2017). An operational objective is also defined, i.e. to create the legal framework defining the rules of development and creation of TEN-T along with a description of how to achieve it.

The first TEN-T guidelines were passed in 1996 by decision of European authorities (Decision No. 1692/96. . .). This decision held that TEN-T networks should be created in stages until 2010. No technical requirements were set out for respective transport sectors, only general requirements were indicated for the network as a whole, i.e.:

- ensure the sustainable mobility of persons and goods under the best possible social and safety conditions, while helping to achieve the Community's objectives, particularly in regard to the environment and competition, and contribute to strengthening economic and social cohesion;
- offer users high-quality infrastructure on acceptable economic terms;
- include all modes of transport;
- allow the optimal use of existing capacities;
- achieve interoperability and encourage intermodality;
- achieve economic viability;
- cover the whole territory of the Member States so as to facilitate access (link island, landlocked and peripheral regions to the central regions and interlink the major conurbations and regions of the Community);
- ensure connectability with EFTA countries, CEE and Mediterranean countries.

Even though these were quite general requirements, they constituted an important step towards creating a true, Community-wide transport system and, ultimately, harmonising the standards offered across the entire TEN-T.

At the same time, the Decision created a new category of a "project of common interest". The ability to classify a project to this category was of significant importance to the possibility of obtaining dedicated financial support under Council Regulation (EC) No 2236/95 of 18 September 1995 laying down general rules for the granting of Community financial aid in the field of trans-European networks (1995). The regulation allocated ECU 2.25 billion for the implementation of projects related to transport networks, communications networks (eTEN) and energy networks (TEN-E) between 1995 and 1999 (European Commission, 1997, 1999, 2001).

Moreover, the European Commission indicated 14 priority projects (PPs), which the Council of the European Union, at its meeting in Essen, identified as particularly important. Further to the Council's decisions, work on the projects indicated in the Decision was to start before the end of 1996. In the original version, no parameters or indicators for the target infrastructure were set for project of common interest and for PPs, which could be viewed as a major oversight. Only general objectives were identified for respective sectors, for example for the road network – "The network shall guarantee users a high, uniform and continuous level of services, comfort and safety" and for the rail network – "The network shall offer users a high level of quality and safety, owing to its continuity and to gradual implementation of its interoperability, brought about in particular by technical harmonization and a harmonized command and control system". Nevertheless, it should be borne in mind that this was merely a point of departure. Working out common technical parameters has never been a simple task, especially in strongly "national" transport sectors such as railway, where each of the countries has its own technical regulations regarding infrastructure and traffic management (Jabri et al., 2010).

Changes in regulations are reflected, among others, by the funds earmarked to this purpose as described in the *White Paper – European Transport Policy for 2010: time to decide*. It emphasises the need for further modernisation measures in the road and rail sectors and for Community action (Laryea and Watermeyer, 2018). It also points to the necessity of promoting maritime transport and inland navigation and to ensure sustainable development of the air transport, taking account of the environmental conditions and intermodal transport development.

What should be viewed as the most important changes, in addition to extending the time limit for network creation until 2020, is the introduction of new solutions for project implementation coordination: establishing the function of European coordinators and extending the list of PPs to 30 and describing them in greater detail. This is the very significant element in the context of the division of tasks proposed in Section 5.1 which includes European tasks. It turns out that already back then there was an awareness that such projects cannot be implemented without a proper coordination and a mere allocation of funds will not suffice to fully achieve the goal. The progress of those tasks and the outcomes of the European coordination have shown that this kind of projects may not be implemented and managed at domestic level.

European coordinators who were back then introduced in the process of the TEN-T management are appointed by the Commission in concert with the interested Member States and act for and on behalf of the Commission. A coordinator's tasks include, without limitation:

- encouraging the use of common project assessment methods and giving advice on how to finance the projects;
- preparing annual reports on the project progress;
- participating, at the Commission's request, in the assessment of grant applications.

In 2005, six coordinators were appointed for the following projects: PP1 Berlin – Palermo, PP3 High-speed axis of southwest Europe, PP6 Lyon – Budapest, PP17 Paris – Bratislava, PP27 Rail Baltica and ERTMS horizontal priority. EUR 4.17 billion out of the available EUR 4.6 billion were earmarked as part of trans-European Network for transport. These funds were allocated on the basis of the *Multiannual Indicative Programme* 2001–2006.

According to the report from the Commission on the implementation of TEN-T guidelines 2004–2005 (data as of the end of the period 2000–2006 were not published), in 2005, the length of the TEN-T road network was 98.500 km, of which 28.300 km classified as ordinary roads in need of an upgrade to meet TEN-T standards. This means that the project progress for the TEN-T road network stood at 71%. This ratio had grown by ca. 6% compared to 1999, but it should be borne in mind that the network in 2005 also included new EU Member States whose infrastructure largely did not meet TEN-T requirements. With respect to railway lines, no detailed data were provided except for high-speed lines, whose length in 2005 was 10.700 km, i.e. 36% of the 29.600 km planned for 2020.

The report also presents the implementation progress of the 28 PPs (no data were presented for motorways of the sea and the Galileo project). By the end of 2005, EUR 3.5 billion was earmarked for the implementation of these projects, i.e. 85% of the allocation for 2001–2006. The average PP progress was 27%, and the number of projects completed compared to 1999 was the same (three tasks had been completed).

The opinion on the implementation progress of the TEN-T projects in that period is divided. As pointed out, the implementation progress of the PPs was quite low as it stood at merely 27%. Nevertheless, half of those projects were among tasks introduced only in 2004. The analysis of the 14 "old" PPs defined in 1996 suggests that their average progress is close to 50% (not including the completed projects). When it comes to the TEN-T road network, quite a significant progress had been made until 2020, even though in relative terms, the ratio of roads meeting the standards has increased by only 6% since 1999.

Nevertheless, this increase is significant, considering the EU's 2004 enlargement to include as many as 10 new Member States.

The understanding of the importance of the TEN-T manifested itself in the regulations being adopted, which were systematically clarified and worded in a manner to enhance the efficiency of the tasks to be implemented. By 2006, the TEN-T programme was monitored in material and financial terms by the Commission itself. Due to its significance and the future development plans, a special Agency was established (TEN-T Executive Agency) which took over these tasks from the Commission. As already mentioned, European coordinators were appointed in 2005 for five PPs and the ERTMS horizontal priority. Later on, further six coordinators were appointed. As at the end of the period under discussion, their efforts had not been significant as only a year had passed since their appointment. In addition, some Member States challenged the advisability of appointing coordinators and called into question the actual value added by such a function to projects. Following major changes and an evolution in the principles of both TEN-T network itself and those relating to the financing of infrastructure projects as part of TEN-T, the period of 2007–2013 was characterised by a greater stability.

Project financing as part of TEN-T is regulated by the Regulation 680/2007 of 20 June 2007 (Regulation (EC) No 680/2007. . .). In accordance with that regulation, a total of EUR 8.01 billion was allocated to finance projects of common interest from 2007 to 2013. Support is prioritised for PPs, i.e. 30 tasks listed in the Decision on Community guidelines for the development of TENT-T (Decision No 1692/96. . .).

According to the statistics published by the Executive Agency for Innovation and Networks, EUR 6.95 billion was allocated to 662 projects from TEN-T funds from 2007 to 2013. More than half of these funds (56%) were allocated to railway projects and the additional 7% of funds were allocated to ERTMS development projects. EUR 5.04 billion was granted for PPs, EUR 1.27 billion for horizontal priorities (ERTMS, ATM, ITS, RIS) and merely EUR 0.65 billion for the remaining projects of common interest. In addition to TEN-T funding, which is dedicated exclusively to projects defined in the regulations related to the TEN-T guidelines, support for projects involving trans-European network sections was also provided from the cohesion policy funds. EUR 40.8 billion (49%) was allocated this way to TEN-T projects (European Commission, 2016). These funds helped rebuild more than 1.8 thousand kilometres of roads and 1.7 thousand kilometres of railway lines belonging to the TEN-T network.

Between 2007 and 2013, the role of European coordinators gradually increased. The description of their responsibilities and competencies being quite general, the efficiency of their efforts depended on respective coordinators' skills. The *ex post* evaluation report prepared for the European Commission in June 2014 pointed out that the role of coordinators contributed a lot to the Member States and the Commission achieving the TEN-T goals. As reputable experts with extensive experience are most often selected to serve as coordinators, they are able to influence decisions at both EU level and that of respective countries to support processes intended to fulfil TEN-T assumptions. The fundamental questions in this respect are: What is the scope of such influence? And: Is it advisable to promote and suggest solutions that are not fully justified at the level of respective countries? Such situations may lead to unreasonable investment projects, which take no account of national transport systems' needs. In this context, it is vital to shape the rules governing the functioning of coordinators so as to avoid infringing on the countries' rights to develop their transport systems in a manner to ensure that domestic priorities are complied with as well. The greatest challenge here is to strike the right balance between the EU's needs and priorities, and the domestic needs and priorities. Such a detailed presentation of the European Commission's efforts in this part of the Monograph is aimed to demonstrate the complexity of the issue and the existence of conflicting, at times, interests between individual countries and the EU as a Community.

Still in the period 2007–2013, work commenced on further development of the TEN-T assumptions and regulations. A major element of this process was the adoption, in 2011, of another *White Paper on Transport* (European Commission, 2011). It pointed to the still serious challenges and investment needs involved in the creation of a complete TEN-T network. The financial needs until 2020 were estimated at ca. EUR 550 billion. The document emphasised the need to build a new TEN-T network structure to include core network corridors (CNCs) as well as the core network itself and comprehensive network.

The lines of action set out in this *White Paper* were reflected in the new TEN-T regulations. The key goals remained largely unchanged since the creation of the TEN-T, though obviously they are naturally developed further to changes in the EU's policies and priorities. One of the most significant changes was the introduction of a dual-layer TEN-T network composed of:

- comprehensive network – a European-wide network to ensure accessibility of regions;
- core network – consisting of those parts of the comprehensive network which are of the highest strategic importance for achieving the objectives for the development of the trans-European transport network.

In addition, a core network overlay was identified in the form of CNCs consisting of the most important routes of the core network, their major task being to optimise cross-border connections in the EU. In this context, a decision was made to further develop the role of the coordinators, anticipating the appointment of European coordinators for all nine CNCs.

The regulation sets out, for all sectors included in the document, parameters to be met by the infrastructure allocated to both core and comprehensive network. Previously, these parameters were definitely missing in the management of these investment projects. The year 2030 was set for the core network and

2050 for the comprehensive network as the deadline for ensuring compliance with all the conditions defined by those parameters.

Unlike in the previous periods, in 2013, complete framework for TEN-T project implementation and development was adopted together with the new TEN-T guidelines. The CEF Regulation (*Connecting Europe Facility*) laid down rules for providing project support, replacing the budget line principles (of the TEN-T programme). As pointed out in the preamble:

> Experience with the MFF (2007–2013) shows that some Member States which are eligible for financing from the Cohesion Fund are facing significant obstacles in delivering on time complex cross-border transport infrastructure projects with a high European added value, as well as allowing efficient use of Union funds.

Based on that conclusion, a decision was made to include in the CEF budget some of the funds (EUR 11.31 billion) allocated from the Cohesion Fund. The rules for granting these funds are a combination of the TEN-T/CEF principles (i.e. competitive selection process) and those of the Cohesion Policy, especially with respect to the beneficiary's eligibility and the funding level. The total amount of CEF allocation for the 2014–2020 period for transport sector was set at EUR 26.25 billion.

The European Commission analysed the progress of the implementation of the TEN-T guidelines and the CEF Regulation. The results and findings were published in late 2018. In addition, work continues on the provisions for the following financial perspective post-2020, in which – as announced by the European Commission – CEF, the European tool to support investment projects in transport, will be strengthened even further.

Efforts to develop the regulations and describe the network itself started from providing a brief overview of sectors and general objectives as well as identifying PPs (Helm and Mayer, 2016). The first regulations did not specify any concrete parameters to be met by the TEN-T network. Implementation of further transport network projects led to an increasingly detailed description of TEN-T and the final definition of the actual parameters to be met by infrastructure. The present solution based on core and comprehensive network and CNC was implemented 17 years since adopting the first decision on TEN-T and 21 years since the *White Paper on the common transport policy* (1992) indicated the need to build a trans-European transport network. It is worth emphasising here that each subsequent step of the development was based on the original assumptions and CNC are largely based on PPs set out in 1996 (and in 2004–2006 for new Member States).

The development of regulations has increasingly recognised cross-border and priority connections as having special significance and thus requiring special treatment (Zdražil and Kozuń-Cieślak, 2017). This is manifested by both creating new solutions (European coordinators, CNC) and dedicating increasing resources to the implementation of these projects. The CEF allocation agreed in 2013 is 10 times higher than the TEN budget line agreed in 1995 (EUR 26.25 billion and ECU 2.25 billion, respectively). Another important thing was moving some of the Cohesion Fund resources to CEF, which was motivated, among others, by the desire for greater influence over the prioritisation of tasks selected for support from the EU funds. For projects financed from mechanisms managed at domestic level (Cohesion Fund, ERDF), funds can be allocated also to tasks that are not necessarily of special significance to the needs of the EU transport system and to the achievement of common transport policy objectives. Meanwhile, for tools centrally managed at the EU level (CEF), the funding decision is taken by the European Commission services (with Member States approving the list of CEF projects) and it reflects, to a greater degree, the Community objectives, giving less importance to strictly domestic decisions.

An analysis of indicators, despite varied perspectives on the TEN-T network development, warrants the conclusion that measures taken in this respect over the years bring measurable effects. It should be emphasised that the evolutionary development of regulations and conditions represents a major added value, which has enabled a progressive decision-making integration at EU level. This is of particular importance in view of the greater emphasis naturally placed on domestic needs when allocating the funding managed on domestic level rather than on projects characterised by added value and significance to the transport system at EU level. One should reflect, however, on how European tasks should be managed and learn lessons from the experience to date to continue striving for greater efficiency in the achievement of the goals identified in the EU strategic documents.

There should be a multiaspect and multidimensional management of European tasks in place – such is the message clearly emanating from the example of infrastructure project implementations presented here. The current management processes focus on the European dimension, i.e. they refer exclusively to funds earmarked from the EU budget, with the domestic dimension of their implementation not verified in much detail. The report from the ECA of September 2018 reveals that in the 2007–2013 programming period, the Commission did not monitor the funding absorption, i.e. the EU spending level in Member States. It was not until late 2014 that it appointed a working group to support Member States struggling with EU spending in some programmes. The same is confirmed by the analyses presented in Chapter 4, where one can easily observe domestic spending being crowded out by EU spending, which can generate problems with regard to overall goals set out in the EU Treaty. Moreover, the example of the TEN-T implementation points to one more important aspect related to EU project management: the EU's inability to directly influence domestic-level decisions when implementing European tasks may lead to much poorer performance. "Absorption capacity refers to a Member State's ability to efficiently and effectively spend the financial resources it has been allocated. . . . Thus, while absorption is important to achieve policy objectives, it is not an end in itself" (European Court of Auditors, 2018). As such, it is suggested to develop a new formula for implementing European tasks in the form of multiannual programmes containing overall resources (not only co-funding) – both domestic and the EU budget – allocated to a given task.

The current multiannual programmes function at two levels: domestic and European. However, as presented in previous chapters, their goals are not compatible. Moreover, they differ in terms of management method, time horizon and entities responsible for their implementation. When developing this sort of multiannual programme for the implementation of a European task, one needs to take account of the policy underlying the EU budget making and implementation as well as of Member States' financial documents (budget acts). This proposal does not entail the idea of common budget for all EU countries; instead, it is essentially based on a division of tasks into categories, the relevant criterion being the decision-making element intended to enhance the efficiency of the implementation.

In this context, it should be emphasised that a great majority of the multiannual governmental programmes currently in place (especially those passed over the recent years) are innovatively designed programmes which also take account of additional specific goals and operational metrics (Hovik and Hanssen, 2015). Hence, these programmes include (based on their provisions), in addition to the goals and metrics related to the programme as whole, also goals and metrics with respect to their respective structural parts. Consequently, such an approach allows for monitoring and assessing of a given programme's efficiency not only in general but also with reference to its individual components. This helps assess how and to what extent individual types of measures undertaken as part of programmes, which are oftentimes of high complexity, actually contribute to the achievement of the general goal of the programme. As a result, it is possible, still at the time of programme implementation, to optimise the selection of means and methods of such implementation and to verify the accuracy with which they were planned.

The form of multiannual programmes is used with varying intensity, on a different scale and for measures of different nature in respective public policies, which partly stems from the specificity of activities of the state. Looking collectively at objects of those programmes, they cover fragments (though often very fundamental ones) rather than all of the EU and Member States' activities. These are innovative tools for managing the implementation of public service tasks, which comprise solutions such as: an advanced diagnosis – an *ex ante* evaluation (also based on a SWOT analysis), well-ordered internal "subprogramme" structure, a set of goals (main and detailed), a set of metrics to measure the achievement of those goals (measuring both general results for the programme as a whole and detailed results), a predefined monitoring, reporting and evaluation system as well as precise physical and financial implementation schedules and financing schedules with detailed definition of sources of finance.

As a first step, it would be appropriate to create multiannual programmes for the implementation of European tasks, to be adopted by Member States together with budgetary frameworks for the coming seven years (see Figure 5.4).

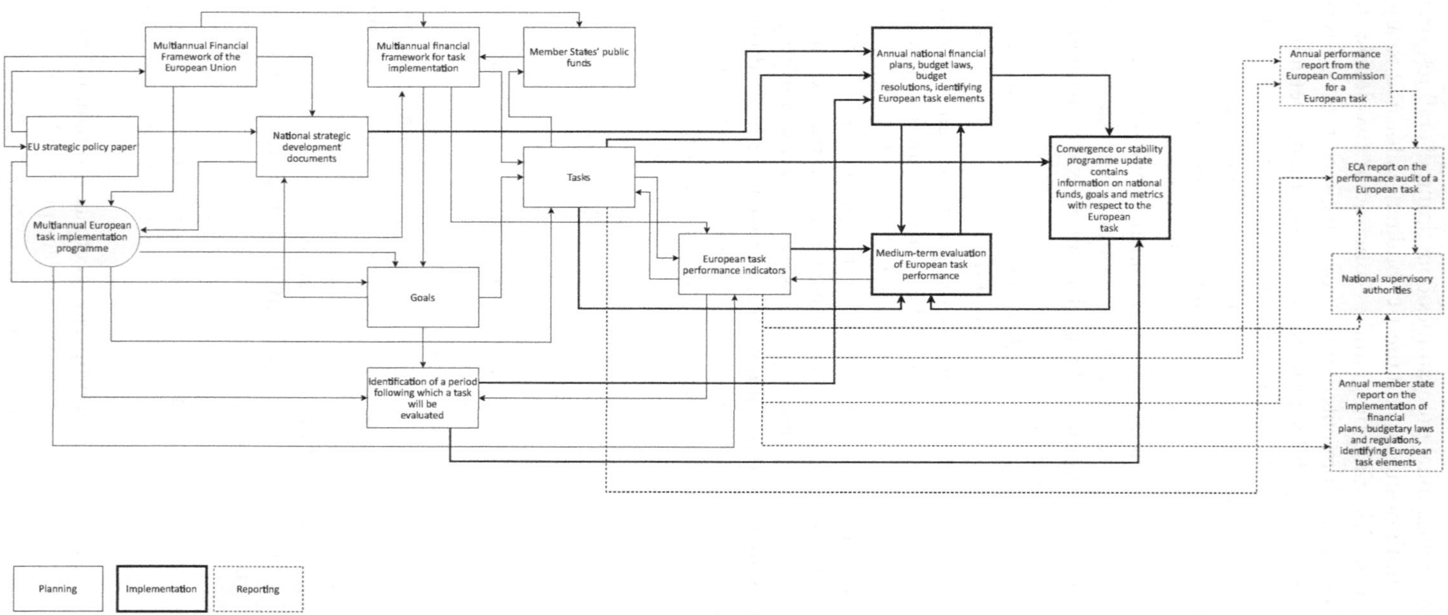

Figure 5.4 Identification and management of the multiannual programme for the implementation of the European task

A multiannual programme for a European task implementation would specify tasks to be implemented by respective countries with an indication of financial resources to be earmarked by them both from the domestic budget, which is already dedicated to them, and from the funds allocated under the corresponding European financial perspective, and, in addition, from the funds of third sector organisations, should the implementation of a given task fall within their field of interest. As a result, the European Union and Member States, by opting to adopt budgetary frameworks, would also adopt multiannual programmes containing specific information on all sources of their funding (domestic and European) as well as performance metrics for respective tasks broken down into domestic and European levels. This way, on the one hand, respective Member States would not be deprived of control over the allocation of funds, and on the other, this would enable an *ex ante* verification of the allocation of funds earmarked for European tasks, with a direct indication of outcomes to be achieved. This would help prevent the current situation, where areas and priorities are, indeed, well defined but the European financial sources are not sufficient to implement them, and Member States have different approaches to their implementation, oftentimes allocating the funds obtained to efforts that are not strictly consistent with those planned by the European Union and there is no possibility to clearly measure their efficiency. Should there be a multiannual programme adopted at the European level, all Member States would be obliged to implement it.

Further elements that could serve as a sort of progress reports for such a multiannual programme adopted on the European level would be reports incorporated in the updates to convergence programmes and stability pacts. Then all countries submitting those documents would present domestic expenditure on European tasks, specifying their outcomes. This way the European Commission, in its assessment of medium-term documents, could use the tools at its disposal to monitor whether a Member State complies with the obligation imposed on it by the multiannual programme. Moreover, those documents would also define medium-term outcomes which, if necessary, could be modified at EU level. This would give rise to a multiannual programme comprising goals and metrics defined for all European countries and for all of Europe as an association, and tasks assigned to respective countries, specifying their sources of financing. Thus, there would be no need to create a single budget. Individual countries would implement tasks from their own budgets, whose effects would serve predefined goals. The auditing and reporting effect is present in the annual reports submitted to the European Commission and Eurostat as part of COFOG statistics; the planning control and any correction required would take place in the framework of the assessment and update of convergence programmes. Moreover, the proposed solution allows for ECA to fully audit the implementation of a European task in collaboration with national authorities. Currently, ECA may audit a given task only with respect to funds from the EU budget, which is presented in more detail in Chapter 3, while national audit authorities – only with respect to domestic funds. Such a solution makes it virtually impossible to conduct a comprehensive assessment of the effects of a given public service task. Hence, the proposed new approach to this process which would enable a uniform implementation and audit of European programmes and tasks.

5.4 Public service tasks at domestic level

Domestic tasks represent a major part of COFOG subcategories, where, I believe, national authorities should retain their full competence with respect to public policy making and to driving the process of financing and implementing tasks from a defined catalogue. European authorities could have a significant impact – in line with the competence vested in them, as described in Chapters 2 and 3 – on the European policy in specific areas and shape the relevant coordination and audit methods. However, domestic policy is of great significance, which is why one cannot outline the Community's direct impact on how domestic tasks are implemented. Figure 5.1 in Chapter 5 clearly illustrates the extensive scale of national government action in shaping the domestic social and economic development policy. COFOG qualifies 34 subcategories as domestic tasks, mainly those related to housing, social, health and internal security policy. It is believed that the efficiency of their implementation and management results from a given country's development model (economic school of thought followed by those in power) adopted by the democratically elected authorities, and research confirms that it is possible to obtain good results even when implementing these tasks at domestic level (Wildman et al., 2016). This is perfectly illustrated by analyses of how social policy is implemented, providing a great example of how specific local conditions, the existence of different forms of dedicated aid and significantly varying levels of prosperity across EU Member States make it impossible to create a single blueprint for government action: local or central. Social policy also means different history that has informed its current shape and the role of the state in this respect. Originally, providing support for the needy who have found themselves in difficult living conditions was a charitable activity inspired by compassion, solidarity and a desire to help the vulnerable and disadvantaged. It was therefore a philanthropic activity of landowners or municipal authorities. It is not until the 19th century that the linkage between social security and national government tasks becomes visible. The first legal regulation of government intervention in the form of social assistance can be found in England. In 1536, a ban on beggary and giving alms was introduced, with a general duty of poor relief imposed on parishes. In 1598, the Poor Law was first passed, which was fundamentally amended in 1601. It imposed on communes a duty to provide help to those not cared for by their family. This help consisted in placing them in shelters called almshouses (orphans, the elderly, the sick, the handicapped), workhouses (the active unemployed) or in houses of correction (those refusing to work). The evolution of social assistance shows a decrease in philanthropic activity replaced by public activity, and then by the emerging state assistance institutions.

Political transformations, the development of administration, the growing importance of legal instruments and the emergence of human rights – these are the key determinants of the state's social assistance. The development of industry and waves of protest resulting from the increasingly worsening living conditions were the main reasons for establishing public social security system including social work. Upon recognition of the state's duty to safeguard existential conditions of individuals relevant legal regulations were formulated and public institutions providing support to citizens began to emerge.

The literature on the subject points to the existence of several stages of social assistance development. The first stage is individual care focused on a human being shaping their fate themselves. The second stage is taking care of larger groups, for example children, old people or the handicapped, which indicates the awareness of the interdependence between a group and an individual and of the situation of respective individuals being dependent on the conditions in which they live. The third stage of development is integral care which combines the two previous forms of care. History demonstrates that with an increase in state's involvement in social assistance, the array of actions undertaken as part of it is expanded. Such a correlation can be observed for example in the ever-expanding range of social benefits and material and financial assistance.

Social assistance is an indispensable social policy instrument. The contemporary social policy is understood as a purposeful action by the state intended to correct market mechanisms, achieving a general prosperity of the whole population and to directly satisfy important social needs, taking account of the existing social and economic inequalities and power inequalities. The state pursues economic goals related to the increase in the general living standards and social goals meant to ensure a widespread prosperity and its equal distribution among the population as well as to empower the most vulnerable groups. Social policy defined this way is implemented through social assistance, healthcare, employment policy, education policy, family policy and housing policy, among others.

The perception of social assistance as an element of social policy points to the role played by the state in organising and providing this assistance. Moreover, it also expresses the state's responsibility for the fate of members of a society. A state's welfarism is measured with funds earmarked for social purposes. In a way, they represent the level of the state's commitment to the social policy. Social assistance being a peculiar domain and a delicate matter shaped by the political system and the ideology and policy prevailing in a given country, it seems advisable to pursue this task at domestic level. Social assistance delivered at the global or even European level by default seems pointless and doomed to fail, if for no other reason than the specificity of respective countries and societies. Governments of specific countries are best positioned to understand the needs of their citizens as they know better than anyone which aspects of social assistance require greater or lower cash transfers. Such reasoning is confirmed by the results of the correlation between general expenditure on social assistance and the social benefits granted, as presented further in this chapter.

Public spending and the management tools used as part of that process should serve to enhance the efficiency of providing public services to citizens (Zaheer and Rashid, 2017). Based on comparative analyses and practical experiences, the most universal and widespread paradigm observed is that of performance budgeting. This method combines the basic principles of good, reasonable and transparent planning and spending of public funds, which should be supported by adequate institutional solutions.

Research for this chapter has been conducted in two steps, i.e. first analysing the correlation between public expenditure on a given social policy area and the COFOG subcategory and then building panel models to test how a state's involvement impacts the poverty level and quality of life. The first step has been to analyse *r* Pearson correlation to identify whether the quantitative variables being measured are linearly correlated. The study has been conducted on a sample of EU Member States based on data for 1996–2020. Respective variables' values have been retrieved from the database available on the European Commission's web pages, and the results are presented in Table 5.3.

An analysis of the correlation reveals that social assistance expenditure was strongly correlated with most of the strictly targeted benefits granted to citizens in respective countries included in the study. Of all expenditure groups, expenditure on fighting poverty and social exclusion is the least correlated with general social assistance expenditure at domestic level, which is why analyses reveal that some subcategories from this area should be addressed at EU level.

All of the EU countries demonstrate care and willingness to help people with disabilities whose health prevents them from working. Community members are obliged to provide this social group with dignified living conditions (De Simone et al., 2012). The scope of the state's obligations towards people with disabilities is governed by internal laws on social assistance and rehabilitation. They set out the form and amount of benefits as well as disability and old-age pensions. The results of the correlation between general social assistance expenditure and sickness and disability benefits contained in Table 5.4 point to a high efficiency of the funds spent in that area. In 16 countries, the results reveal a very strong correlation between those two variables. The only country showing a moderate correlation in this analysis is Portugal, though the result obtained is not bad, it simply lags behind compared to other countries' results.

Demographic changes, both those already happening and those forecast, are among the most important topics discussed in European countries. According to UN projections, by 2030, the share of the population aged 65 and above in Europe will stand at 23.8%. It should be added that this is twice the number from 1990. Currently, countries with the largest number of people aged 65 and over as a share of total population are Italy, Germany and Greece. Sustainable social development is linked to economic development, which in highly developed countries has ensured social and economic order and helped shape and develop the *welfare state* social policy (Di Gioacchino, Sabani, 2009). From the point of view of social expenditure, population ageing changes the structure of the latter as an increasing portion of the expenditure is dedicated to

Table 5.3 Results of the correlation analysis for given categories of social assistance benefits and R&D expenditure on social protection in EU countries in 1996–2020.

Country	*Social assistance expenditure (in EUR million)*									
	Sickness and disability	*Old age*	*Survivor's benefits*	*Family and children*	*Unemployment*	*Housing*	*Social exclusion n.e.c.*	*R&D Social protection*	*Social protection n.e.c.*	*Fighting poverty and social exclusion*
Austria	0.98	1.00	1.00	0.92	0.98	0.80	0.95	0.01	0.72	0.45
Belgium	0.97	1.00	0.99	0.98	0.72	0.92	0.98	–0.10	0.68	–0.63
Czech Republic	0.75	0.99	0.99	0.88	0.70	0.56	0.83	–0.20	0.93	–0.91
Denmark	0.98	0.98	–0.50	0.96	0.21	0.99	0.87	0.51	0.89	0.66
Estonia	0.99	1.00	0.48	0.99	0.94	–0.29	–0.12	0.88	0.76	–0.09
Finland	0.80	0.99	0.98	0.98	0.84	0.89	0.98	–0.48	0.01	–0.43
France	0.99	1.00	1.00	0.99	0.95	0.99	0.88	0.08	0.93	–0.63
Germany	0.97	0.99	0.83	0.98	–0.32	0.60	0.00	0.85	0.84	0.10
Greece	0.82	0.98	0.88	0.74	0.53	0.29	0.30	0.84	–0.61	–0.25
Hungary	0.99	0.98	1.00	0.99	0.78	0.56	0.50	0.64	0.46	–0.22
Ireland	0.95	0.98	0.97	0.97	0.95	0.95	0.99	0.63	0.46	0.45
Italy	0.98	0.99	1.00	0.87	0.96	0.96	0.93	–0.85	–0.24	0.71
Latvia	0.75	0.96	0.17	–0.24	0.45	0.07	0.73	–0.66	–0.75	–0.73
Lithuania	0.99	0.98	0.93	0.88	0.92	–0.09	0.72	–0.78	–0.42	–0.76
Luxembourg	0.99	1.00	0.43	1.00	0.77	0.69	0.99	–	0.79	0.86
The Netherlands	0.89	1.00	–0.91	0.92	0.80	0.91	0.97	0.99	–0.80	0.07
Poland	0.98	0.99	0.98	0.86	0.22	–0.57	0.95	–0.50	0.81	–0.91
Portugal	0.44	0.99	0.98	0.67	0.92	–0.76	0.73	–0.22	0.62	–0.02
Slovakia	0.78	0.98	0.98	0.98	0.87	0.88	0.98	0.53	0.58	–0.80
Slovenia	0.95	0.99	0.92	0.98	0.65	0.91	0.93	–0.86	0.68	0.62
Spain	0.97	0.98	0.99	0.93	0.90	0.50	0.86	0.68	0.67	0.76
Sweden	0.75	0.97	–0.51	0.99	0.32	–0.11	0.90	–0.65	0.92	0.71
United Kingdom	0.98	1.00	–0.32	0.63	0.12	0.95	0.96	–0.63	0.63	–0.08

Source: own elaboration.

the economically inactive group. It is hard not to note that population ageing affects both the revenues of the broadly defined social policy system (reduced number of those financing it) and its expenditure structure (growing group of those benefiting from services and cash transfers) (Kuitto, 2016). Old-age pension expenditure represents one of the largest items in the social expenditure budgets. Therefore, any financial imbalance manifesting itself in pension system deficit may have an impact on the overall public finance situation (Gerrish, 2017). This is why an increase in pensionable age is an element of reforms in many countries. Based on the results of the correlation between expenditure on old-age benefits, it can be concluded that in all countries this expenditure is nearly perfectly planned and properly distributed. Such results confirm that this category of tasks is well implemented at domestic level. An ideal and very strong correlation can be observed between social assistance expenditure and old-age benefits. The results of the correlation in this expenditure category have shown an ideal result for seven of the countries analysed with $r = 1$. The other countries analysed have obtained very similar results between 0.96 and 0.99, with the lowest result recorded in Lithuania. This means that a given country's pension system, of course combined with the demographic situation, is the top determinant of changes in the level of funds allocated to these benefits. Family members as well as non-relatives are entitled to financial assistance as part of survivor's benefits, which they receive upon meeting certain conditions. In the countries analysed, the beneficiaries may, following death of a close one, apply for a funeral allowance, death gratuity or survivor's pension. The results of the correlation between social assistance expenditure and survivor's benefits point to a generally ideal or very strong correlation between these variables.

As revealed by data, an ideal correlation of $r = 1$ can be observed in four countries, i.e. in Austria, France, Italy and Hungary. In four other countries, there is a negative correlation, which is due to a decrease in survivor's benefit expenditure amount coupled with an increase in the general social assistance expenditure. Countries with the negative correlation between these variables are Denmark ($r = -0.50$), the Netherlands ($r = -0.91$), Sweden ($r = -0.51$) and the United Kingdom ($r = -0.32$). A weak correlation is observed in Lithuania ($r = 0.17$), and a moderate one, in Luxembourg ($r = 0.43$). For other countries, the correlation results point to a very strong correlation between the variables analysed.

Family support systems vary across EU Member States. Citizens of the countries analysed can count on direct financial assistance in the form of family allowances or benefit from child tax credits or the possibility to deduct expenses (e.g. babysitting, education, etc.) from taxes. There are systems where pro-family policy solutions are mirrored by pension systems. Each EU Member State's legislation provides for help for a family, should it find itself in an emergency situation. In the EU, it is a given person's economic status and place of residence rather than their nationality that determines which country is responsible for the disbursement of social benefits, including family benefits (family and child-raising allowances). The terms on which parents receive family benefits are stipulated in national regulations.

The results obtained from quantitative research unequivocally point to a very strong correlation between the variables analysed. Most countries have achieved a correlation of $r < 0.90$. The only country showing a weak negative correlation between family and child benefits and general social assistance expenditure is Latvia with a result of $r = -0.24$. The correlation results presented indicate that the most important problems and challenges relating to the situation of children and families in respective countries are relatively well identified and adequate measures are undertaken to improve the situation of those in need (Viscusi and Batini, 2016).

Unemployment benefits mostly include unemployment allowance. Social security systems vary greatly in this respect across EU countries, each of them having full freedom to shape its system and its own rules of granting unemployment allowances. Periods in which such benefits are disbursed differ as well – in one country it can be disbursed for 24 months while in another (e.g. in Poland) only for 6–12 months.

Like in the previous case, the results of the correlation point, in a great majority, to a very strong link between the variables analysed. Only in Germany, a moderate negative correlation is found between these expenditure categories, but this should be seen as resulting from the continuously falling unemployment rate (Pfeifer, 2012). In addition, it is worth mentioning that the amount of unemployment benefit in Germany is very high, second only to the allowance paid out in Sweden. The poor correlation between the two variables analysed can be observed in Denmark ($r = 0.21$), Poland ($r = 0.22$) and in the United Kingdom ($r = 0.12$). In 15 countries analysed, the correlation is very strong, with the correlation coefficient of more than $r = 0.7$. In the other cases we can observe a moderate positive correlation.

Housing benefits differ among countries most of all in terms of their amount and the system through which these are granted. As a rule, the eligibility and the benefit amount depend on the family's income and the number of children. In some countries, another condition is imposed whereby the housing benefit is granted to families that rent an apartment or pay mortgage loans. Of all the countries analysed, 12 have demonstrated a very strong correlation between social assistance expenditure and housing benefit expenditure. Most often such a correlation can be found in highly developed countries known for considerable social welfare provided to citizens. Four countries have had a strong correlation of 0.50–0.60 between the variables analysed, while five others have demonstrated a negative correlation (Estonia, Lithuania, Poland, Portugal and Sweden). A very high correlation between the social assistance expenditure and social exclusion n.e.c. benefits can be observed in nearly all countries included in the analysis. Among all of the countries analysed, 19 have shown a very strong positive correlation between the variables analysed. Greece and Hungary have had a moderate correlation between the expenditure categories analysed, $r = 0.30$ and $r = 0.50$, respectively. The only country where a weak negative correlation is observed is Estonia. The results of the correlation between social assistance expenditure and social protection n.e.c. show a positive correlation between the variables in most countries analysed.

The positive correlations existing in Hungary and Ireland have reached a moderate level of $r = 0.46$. All the other countries with a positive correlation recorded reveal a strong or very strong relationship between the variables analysed. Five of the countries analysed have shown a negative correlation. These countries, except for the Netherlands, do not belong to the group of highly developed countries, were hard hit by the world financial crisis and continue to tackle its consequences.

The above-discussed high results of the correlation between social assistance expenditure and respective expenditure categories as part of the social support provided by the EU countries analysed to their citizens point to the countries managing these funds adequately. Such results confirm the advisability of having these benefits provided at domestic level.

The correlation values between last two variables differ much from the relationships presented earlier; these are social assistance expenditure and expenditure on support for people at risk of poverty and social exclusion. Half of the countries included in the analysis show a negative correlation between the ratios analysed. This means that despite the increase in the general social assistance expenditure, the funds spent in respective countries on fighting poverty and social exclusion are decreasing. Positive relationships between the variables analysed are most often observed in highly developed and wealthy countries.

A similar situation can be seen for the value of the correlation between social assistance expenditure and social protection R&D expenditure. In this case, too, half of the countries analysed show a negative correlation between the variables analysed. Such a high percentage of negative correlations may point to the need to implement these tasks at a supranational level.

As a next step, econometric models have been built for each Member State and for the European Union as a whole presenting how the size of social assistance expenditure impacts the Gini coefficient and the poverty level measured with People at risk of poverty or social exclusion by income quintile and household type. To achieve the goal, analyses have been conducted on panel data (balanced panel) and the following panel models have been built: generalised least squares method, fixed effects and random effects (experience has shown that this model is not appropriate for the data in question, but a decision has been made to attempt using it). Statistics such as R2, residual standard error and residual sum of squares, *F*-test, Doornik–Hansen test (1994), chi-square test and Hausman test have been used to verify the models. Data from Eurostat databases have been used for analyses, in particular a decision has been made to use two perspectives on the social assistance expenditure in respective countries, i.e. expenditure in nominal values in million euros and per capita expenditure. Meanwhile, when it comes to the explained variables, two synthetic indices have been chosen at this point, not going into details of specific benefits but reflecting the overall effect of the social policy in place. The first one, the Gini coefficient, is the most prevalent metric of income inequalities at the international level. This coefficient is used to measure the income distribution, comparing every household's income situation to the situation of all other households. The second explained variable is the index People at risk of poverty or social exclusion by income quintile and household type. It corresponds to the sum of persons who are either at risk of poverty or severely materially deprived or living in a household with a very low work intensity. Eurostat points out that persons are only counted once even if they are present in several sub-indicators. At risk-of-poverty are persons with an equivalised disposable income below the risk-of-poverty threshold, which is set at 60% of the national median equivalised disposable income (after social transfers).

The results obtained are very interesting and vary across countries (see Table 5.4), indicating that the undoubtedly comprehensive outlook on the social policy in place points to its varied efficiency in respective countries. As a rule, though, a positive correlation between the expenditure indicators analysed and the explained variables can be observed in most Member States.

In view of the adopted hypothesis that having a domestic policy helps achieve better social policy effects than looking at the matter from a "bird's eye view", i.e. EU level (even though the situation is not perfect everywhere), a decision has been taken to conduct, for the Community as a whole, research mirroring the one conducted for Member States. The results obtained have revealed that the aggregate social policy expenditure in all of the EU causes no major change in the coefficients selected for the analysis (see Table 5.5).

Research results have demonstrated that no correlation is recorded between the aggregate public expenditure and the Gini coefficient/poverty rate in the European Union, thus validating the argument that this sort of tasks can be implemented with a greater effectiveness and efficiency when using domestic tools addressing local needs of respective countries' citizens.

Population ageing, low number of births and income stratification are only some of the challenges facing those in power, not only in EU countries. Currently, social policy financing is not a topic that attracts much attention of the academic community, though it seems it should play a greater role among topics of scientific research: firstly, due to the scale of social expenditure and, secondly, considering the welfare function of the state as an entity that organizes life for its citizens and whose apparatus is at their service.

Summary

The issue of rationality of tasks financed from public funds, even though described and analysed ever since the beginning of the history of economic thought, never loses its attractiveness and in the period we are living now is gaining even greater significance. The development of civilisation contributes to changes in the functioning conditions of state organisms, followed by an

Table 5.4 The impact of public transfers on the Gini coefficient and People at risk of poverty or social exclusion by income quintile and household type in 2005–2020 in EU Member States.

Country	*People at risk of poverty or social exclusion by income quintile and household type*			*Gini coefficient*		
	Total expenditure million euros	*Total expenditure Euro per inhabitant*	*Coefficient x*	*Total expenditure, million euros*	*Total expenditure Euro per inhabitant*	*Coefficient x*
Belgium		–0.0000631779**			–0.00032904**	
Bulgaria		– 0.00486945***			0.0137092 ***	
Czech Republic	–0.0000178812**			–0.00011688***		
Denmark					0.0000740888***	
Germany				0.000480982*		
Estonia			92.5803			254.315**
Ireland						
Greece						
Spain						
France	–0.00000171546**			–0.0000108858**		
Croatia		–0.0008656***			–0.00254785***	
Italy	0.0000139223***				0.00189761***	
Cyprus						
Latvia			–13.7809**			–37.1090**
Lithuania						
Luxembourg		–0.000191843***			0.000554793**	
Hungary			309.421***			1411.08***
Malta					0.000781625*	
The Netherlands			–116.51*			
Austria						

Poland	−0.0000183986***			−0.000093192***		
Portugal				−0.00049471***		
Romania						
Slovenia						
Slovakia	−0.000111665*			−0.000866425***		
Finland		−0.0000372053**				
Sweden				0.000035427**		
Iceland	− 0.00000706773**					
Norway			−21.1901*			−100.775*
Switzerland						
United Kingdom						
Serbia	−0.00260823**				−0.0288991***	
Turkey	−0.0000479			−0.0000499849**		

***Significant parameter at the significance level of 0.01; ** significant parameter at the significance level of 0.05; * significant parameter at the significance level of 0.1.
Source: own elaboration.

Table 5.5 The impact of public transfers on the Gini coefficient and People at risk of poverty or social exclusion by income quintile and household type in 2005–2020 in the Community as a whole.

	Coefficient	*Standard error*	*z*	*p value*
Dependent variable Gini				
Const	30.3765	0.543241	55.92	<0.0001***
Total expenditure Euro per inhabitant	−5.53661e-05	8.02415e-05	−0.6900	0.4907
Total expenditure in million euros	1.27766e-06	3.37658e-06	0.3784	0.7054
People at risk of poverty or social exclusion by income quintile and household type				
Const	5.28000	0.281578	18.75	<0.0001***
Total expenditure Euro per inhabitant	−3.92454e-05	2.25802e-05	−1.738	0.0822*
Total expenditure in million euros	4.88495e-07	8.06520e-07	0.6057	0.5447

***Significant parameter at the significance level of 0.01; **significant parameter at the significance level of 0.05; *significant parameter at the significance level of 0.1.
Source: own elaboration.

evolution of the ways in which public service tasks are performed and financed. In this context, G.W. Kolodko observes that

> The government is not supposed to be "big" or "small", but rather "efficient". Political slogans promising a "cheap government" are similarly naïve. Talk is cheap, not government. The job of the government is to supply the population with the public goods, at the requisite level of quality, needed to function and develop. That costs money.
>
> (Kołodko, 2008)

For decades now, practitioners and theoreticians alike have engaged in a discussion on the need to introduce reforms at both European and global levels to enable a more efficient implementation of a long-term sustainable development policy. As a matter of fact, the emerging new problems, related to the spread of terrorism, migration or environmental pollution require a perspective that is not just domestic or even regional but strictly global as handling them without coordinated action at all levels simultaneously will cause them not only to grow but also never to be solved. The financial aspect also plays a considerable role here – who and why should pay for this sort of policy? In a long-term perspective, the consequences of the lack of action in this respect will be suffered by all countries. It should be borne in mind that the migration problem, which is so widely debated today, started much earlier and now is the consequence of uneven development and of the failure by the countries of origin of today's migrants to take appropriate measures. The proposed division of COFOG subcategories into three main groups of public service tasks is quite a bold and innovative move, which will be surely debated and not everybody will agree with it. The most important thing, however, is to engage in the discussion on the effective allocation of public funds, talk about the effects that can be achieved and about the ways to integrate these measures to prevent waste and a situation where global or European policy could lead to domestic expenditure on specific purpose being crowded out by Community funds. Indeed, irrespective of the problems, directions and findings outlined in this chapter, undoubtedly ground-breaking and paramount for the development of programming and managing public services tasks, should come with methodological solutions that make it possible to assess the outcomes obtained at the time they are implemented as part of a mid-term and final evaluation. Regardless of what is decided in future with respect to the system of development management at domestic, regional and global level, the optimum use of the resources available should be the supreme goal, while the scale of resources ultimately allocated for the implementation of respective tasks should remain the competence of respective levels represented by authorities elected in accordance with democratic principles.

Conclusion

The last decades have increasingly seen the social and economic policy in place falling short of addressing the challenges of the ongoing transition in global civilisation. Another phenomenon manifesting itself is the failure of the existing institutional order or actually a disorder caused by the "shifts in economic tectonic plates" jeopardising the harmonious development or – as described by L.C. Thurow (2000) – a state of globally punctuated equilibrium. One could go as far as to venture a conclusion that the recent years have shown that we are living at the time of a revolution that brings with it drastic changes in the social and economic life, translating into a different approach to the management of public resources. Indeed, the scale and type of changes – mainly those linked to globalisation – undoubtedly require analysing on which level a given type of public intervention will be the most effective. It is worth looking for answers to questions such as: Are individual countries, even the largest ones, able to cope with climate change or pandemic on their own?

In the contemporary debate, there is no shortage of those claiming that the crisis of 2007–2008 and the crisis caused by the Covid-19 pandemic – with its subsequent phases from a sharp downturn on economic markets to an overall slowdown of economic processes – have also led to a crisis in economics which needs to have its main tenets substantially redefined, with a revision of the formerly predominant paradigms and concepts. All this goes to show that the neoliberal policy is failing to address the mounting contradictions, both in respective world regions and globally, that reality is increasingly diverging from models (Galar et al., 2012) and that the whole edifice of economics needs to be thoroughly rebuilt. This new situation is a challenge to science and to the social and economic policy, both of which have been dealt a blow by financialisation introducing uncertainty to the real economy, which is increasingly dependent on unstable financial markets. Some researchers believe the world of two extremes – growing financial capital on one end and indigence and unemployment on the other – must be reformed. New concepts emerge in response to the need for change, such as new nationalism, new pragmatism, new capitalism and other proposed changes to this bipolar system. State plays a significant role in each of these new concepts, but it relies on different instruments in pursuing its aims. The proponents of new nationalism see benefits of respective

DOI: 10.4324/9781003222033-7

countries acting in a sort of "isolation" and focusing on a domestic approach to fiscal policy. Meanwhile, opponents of such an approach, for example G.W. Kolodko, proposes new pragmatism as its antithesis emphasising global, joint measures because these are the only ones that can ensure positive long-term development rather than passing problems on to other countries. The discussion presented in the Monograph is more inclined towards the latter concept and towards EU level measures as it points to the benefits of joint action at supranational level, while highlighting the shortcomings of the instruments used to date in that respect.

It is worth citing the 2009 Nobel Prize winner, E. Ostrom, who demonstrates the effectiveness and efficiency of community-based resource management systems, thus disproving the claim that privatisation is the only efficient way, and maintains that the much richer and pro-development institutional regulatory framework should be preferred. She argues that the institution of local community cooperation may quite often be a perfect solution to many problems. The beneficial impact of actions by a local community may be well extrapolated to actions of a bigger local community that is the European Union, bearing in mind, however, that some problems cannot be solved at its level. Some need to be tackled at domestic, and others, at global level. At times, this Community is inefficient in its operations, which is proven in the Monograph, but, according to the Author, it is worth drawing conclusions from the errors committed, providing constructive criticism and suggesting new solutions.

Currently, we are witnessing a lively debate on the future of the European Union and on the need to change its organisational shape and the scope of tasks performed with the use of its budget expenditure as well as to implement instruments that enable an automatic response to the inescapable crises to come. Part of this debate is a discussion of the need to introduce changes at both EU and global levels to ensure a more efficient implementation of a long-term sustainable development policy, measured not only with GDP but also with social welfare and quality-of-life indicators, which are increasingly popular with researchers. These discussions still have not provided an unequivocal answer to the most important questions, let alone result in developing a vision for optimum strategic solutions and operational mechanisms that could remedy the challenges of integration and civilisation alike. The Author is of the opinion that a full assessment of the allocation of EU budget funds and of their impact on the social and economic development requires adopting an all-round approach, which she proposes in respective parts of her book – taking account of all expenditures (both domestic and European) and referring their outcomes to quality indicators. One should also always bear in mind the supreme principle of subsidiarity applicable in the European Union.

The Monograph discusses the challenges related exclusively to European integration due to the vastness and complex scope of the issue at hand. Its analysis from a global perspective would be undoubtedly interesting and remains to be further explored in the Author's next publications.

The idea of integration, as a universal management formula and, at the same time, a guarantee of safety from all global challenges, has failed to meet all the hopes staked on it. Meanwhile, the emerging new global challenges, for example pandemic phenomena, make it necessary to undertake joint and coordinated action at both domestic and global level. The question arising in this context is: Who should pay for such policy making? The answer is of particular importance as the willingness among EU societies to carry the burden together for the common good is largely declining year over year, as revealed by the surveys presented in the Monograph. The idea of fraternity and community identity, still resounding in the lines of the EU anthem, is undoubtedly experiencing a crisis, making way for selfish, separatist nationalist motives – for now mainly as part of nationalist political doctrines. In a long run, the consequences of the lack of concerted, integrated action will fall on all countries, their costs becoming disproportionately high, especially for selected public policy categories identified in the Monograph as European and global tasks, if the funds earmarked for them are spent by each of these countries autonomously.

Addressing the goal of the Monograph defined in the *Introduction*, its respective sections present the results of the analyses conducted that prove its hypothesis, point to the need to introduce changes in the solutions currently in use and show non-standard interventions in response to crises. The Multiannual Financial Framework passed in 2021 is the quintessence of the changes taking place, with the Resilience and Reform Fund being its flagship programme (and a response to the corona crisis). As the name suggests, the goal of spending is obvious, but there is also another aspect that is the innovative financing method – de facto by means of incurring common public debt. This is a good example illustrating how quickly and unconventionally the EU has responded to another crisis, that of Covid-19.

The quest to redefine the European identity, forging one that would give a chance for social and economic development not only to the EU itself but also (through efficient cooperation) to the neighbouring regions, requires a bold defiance of the current trends in doctrine and of the institutional weaknesses as well as looking for new, optimal fundamental tenets in the currently professed political and economic doctrines.

Some civilisational experiences are universal in nature. Contrary to the common conviction that nothing happens the same way twice, history is in a way turning a full circle, bringing back the vices of those before us. What is most difficult to understand is that new generations find it increasingly hard to appreciate the unquestionable accomplishment of integration, begin to doubt the opportunities and the potential of the European cooperation, looking for the mythical Eden in the stale- and short-sighted ideas of economic nationalism that were only recently consigned to the dustbin of history. There is hope, however, in the forward-thinking doctrines that offer constructive input to the idea of European integration in its current shape. An example indicated in Chapter 1 of the Monograph is the concept of new pragmatism, which gives a chance to fulfil social goals in the spirit of solidarism while maintaining equilibrium in the sphere of economic development. A correlation of that sort should also work in the opposite direction – for economic growth to be equitable, its effects should translate into the quality of life of all European Union citizens.

The commitment to maintaining and saving the goals that were self-evident not so long ago requires at present more and more courage, prudence and self-criticism in choosing and perfecting working methods and tools as well as in ensuring transparency, rationality and efficiency of the way they are financed. Such conditions are of substantial importance considering that, in the context of the global trends, ideas that do not go hand in hand with fashionable concepts with separatist undertones on the subject of nation-states' economic policy are fiercely criticised.

This Monography is intended to identify, assess and propose solutions, at Community and domestic level alike, which could efficiently support the implementation of goals in a manner that is pro-development, solidarity-based and also pragmatic in medium term. It also aims to show the great variety of responses by those in power to the crisis phenomena of the past several decades at the level of not only EU but also Member States' governments. An analysis has also been conducted of the shift in the expenditure structure in respective countries under the effect of EU membership and strategic management adopted at Community level. Moreover, an attempt has been made to identify the scope and scale of public service tasks implemented by the state. A new division of public service tasks is proposed, its criterion being the level of responsibility for managing domestic- and supranational-level tasks and for the achievement of the goals planned. An assessment of the effectiveness of the proposed solution is also presented for selected areas of public policy implementation.

Having regard to the final considerations of the first part of the Monograph, the Author points to one of the absolutely fundamental dilemmas for the future of the European Union, for all of us, especially the new generation of Europeans, which should enter adulthood in a climate of constructive optimism and hope for development in the integrating European Community rather than that of determinism which destroys these hopes. There is presently no magic formula to solve the integration difficulties in the same way as there is no cure for the flourishing Euroscepticism which calls for abandoning this integration in favour of nationalism. The answer to the question about the future should be found in our own choices, which will often require sacrifice and compromise; these should be guided by a mature long-term development vision rather than the immediate but illusory comfort of tomorrow.

The quest for theories, means and methods that could help strengthen and cement the crumbling foundations of the European unity is no simple task and requires overcoming the ideological constraints and finding unprecedented, daring and innovative solutions. As such, the main challenges of the search for the optimum and most forward-looking path for the European Commission's future economic and social policy include reflecting on the extent to which these policies should be implemented at domestic level or using EU community instruments. In this context, the Monograph presents practical tools contributing to the efficiency of public policy implementation at EU level (management based on strategy documents, definition of the scope of economic policy coordination for respective countries, use of EU budget expenditure evaluation method) and at domestic one (aligning the expenditure structure with the Community's strategic goals, leveraging EU membership to increase the quality and sometimes also the scale of implementation of public service tasks).

One should hope that all these problems are successfully solved. The pandemic crisis and the migration crisis before that are not the greatest threat in the history of Europe which has overcome, throughout many centuries of its existence, much more difficult and complex challenges. The problem in this case may lie rather in the mentality of Member States' societies and in the need to comply with the elementary characteristic (and requirement) of the Christian civilisation which is the principal source of this continent's culture. I am talking of course about the ability and willingness to share with those in need.

The following parts of the publication outline the framework, background and rational room for manoeuvre with respect to measures to coordinate the European macroeconomic policy. They also highlight the important part played by public finance stability at both community and domestic levels in the continued development of the European Union. Then a discussion follows of the impact of the institutional and legislative choices adopted in the budget policy system, mainly in the public expenditure subsystem, on the implementation of the sustainable development concept, especially in the context of aspects such as budget stability and public finance stability. In this part of the Monograph, the Author proves that the EU macroeconomic policy coordination tools have no significant effect on improving fiscal performance. Both the actual and the desirable comprehensive impact of respective budget policy instruments on budget policy coordination is shown for instruments such as legislative solutions, medium-term planning documents, i.e. development strategies and programmes (as instruments of fiscal condition assessment of EU countries, among other things). Consideration is given here to the quality and reliability of the macroeconomic content of these documents that is Member States' forecasts. Another thing discussed is the performance of the European fiscal rule system. Having regard to the criterion of an existence of debt and excessive deficit, the analyses conducted here have the advantage of testing correlations between variables such as: growth, GDP and HDI. Of great significance among the findings is the conclusion that generating a high GDP and HDI growth does not require exceeding the debt criterion but, as a rule, does involve incurring an excessive deficit. This part of the publication highlights the relatively minor relationship between the solutions designed in the area of economic policy coordination and the quality-of-life indicator. Thus, a need is emphasised for institutional reforms that take greater account of the social aspect, which is the key focus of discussions of new economic paradigms in the context of the global processes currently taking place. The findings of the analyses are also confirmed by measures adopted by the European Commission, sending a message that it will strive for a profound reform of the Stability and Growth Pact.

The aforementioned discussions serve as an introduction to further issues, such as an overview of new developments in the impact of the EU allocations, taking account of the evolving strategic priorities contained in the principal strategy documents by the European Commission, with a special focus on the assessment of the impact of the two main documents that lay out the directions for EU development in the medium term (meaning the Lisbon Strategy and its successor and follower, "Europe 2020" strategy). The conclusion from these analyses is optimistic when it comes to aggregate, most generally defined consequences of the efforts to implement policy directions outlined in the aforementioned EU strategy documents. The expenditure increase aimed to finance the expansion of structural measures in 1995–1999 had an impressive scale, with an ever-widening range of new mechanisms such as funds playing a major role in the structural policy. The growth of this sort of expenditure, undeniably the most valuable from the perspective of strengthening the EU's global competitiveness in the second period analysed in this part of the Monograph (1995–1999), significantly surpassed the agricultural policy expenditure, which also experienced massive growth, and led to a reduction of the EU's strictly administrative expenditure. This came hand in hand with the finding, representing a breakthrough for the quality of the EU strategic planning, that global competitiveness cannot be generated without strengthening more than ever the Community's social capital understood as the need to raise the EU citizens' quality of life. Importantly, such measures were to be characterised now by a significant scale and versatility and involve public intervention areas such as education for living and working in a knowledge-based society, developing an active employment policy, modernising social policy, promoting social involvement and even positive impact on the natural environment of human beings (environmental aspects). An analysis of the EU budget expenditure data has also revealed a significant methodological weakness with respect to testing the ability to assess the scale of its overall impact on respective public policies. This weakness stems, among other things, from the often modified presentation of the EU budget expenditure classifications and from the inability to match them not only with domestic classifications but also with COFOG, which can be due to the principle of subsidiarity applicable to European funds.

These discussions are complemented by demonstrating the institutional significance of the ECA as a body that enforces (through monitoring efforts) the achievement of optimum cost-saving, efficiency and effectiveness or even transparency (as regards generating information on the execution process) of the implementation of tasks financed from the EU budget. The Monograph shows the evolution of this process, mainly involving attempts to keep pace with changes and irregularities committed by the beneficiaries, Member States or even entire European regions. In this context, of particular importance to this assessment is the performance aspect and ensuring that the European budget is allocated and spent in such a manner that it can be said that it is a "performance-based budget". Such initiatives are of great significance considering the audit results obtained by ECA, which point to a low achievement of goals.

With such an approach to promoting rationalisation of public finance allocation and management, there naturally comes another phenomenon: a strengthened position of the philosophy of governance that is evidence-based policy. It involves managing the state (including its public finance) based on evidence and knowledge (understood in this case as performance information produced, as indicated in the Monograph, as a result of ever more extensive and comprehensive and methodologically advanced evaluation research). The expansion of the evaluation culture is of particular importance as it should further intensify the effect (through rational and efficient allocation of resources) of the dynamically growing expenditure intended to ensure the achievement of the EU's structural goals. At the same time, ECA activity aims to limit the inefficiency in Community finance management, which is why it is assumed that the role and scope of tasks of this institution should grow in the future. To enable ECA to effectively control the efficiency, the practice of formulating and applying performance information needs strengthening and enhancing both for EU programmes and for respective projects implemented as part of them.

The penultimate part of the Monograph focuses, among other things, on Member States' domestic expenditure policies, generally painting a positive (in a multiannual perspective, except the crisis of 2008) picture of the economic and structural circumstances for this side of public finance functioning throughout the period analysed. A number of deficiencies are indicated, which are due to the change in the domestic expenditure policy related to the EU membership. Analyses and discussions provided in Chapters 3 and 4 of the Monograph confirm that being part of the European Union does not significantly contribute to increasing Member States' expenditure on priority goals related to EU level strategy documents. Of course, there are also unquestionable benefits that the integration with the Community has brought to nation-states, such as raising the quality of the public finance management system in those countries, though, unfortunately, this has not been coupled with positive effects in the domestic expenditure structure. Research has revealed that expenditure on public policies co-financed from the EU budget partially replaced, rather than add to, domestic expenditure. Such analyses results have caused the Author to propose developing new solutions that will help mitigate this problem.

To mitigate the scale of shortcomings emerging in the currently functioning solutions, it is proposed to:

- develop a new classification or use the existing one, COFOG – a uniform classification to enable planning, spending and reporting public funds earmarked from domestic budgets and from the EU budget alike;
- assess the efficiency of public policy implementation taking account of the committed resources, both domestic and European, not only during the

implementation of respective projects or programmes but also with respect to their outcomes measured with impact indicators in selected areas;
- provide domestic audit authorities (e.g. Poland's Supreme Audit Office) and the European ones (ECA) with relevant powers and tools to enable an assessment of the resource allocation not only partially but also on a comprehensive basis, which will enhance the performance of these authorities. Obviously the accession as well as the benefits of the structural aid (especially that oriented to improving competitiveness) also generated significant advantages to Member States' economies in the form of GDP growth, which translated into higher incomes (in PPP) of EU societies, and thus into raising their standard and quality of life (HDI). In this context, it would be good, however, to consider implementing changes, for example those proposed in this Monograph. One should also welcome the fact that EU authorities, in addition to solutions applied to date, are also opening up to new institutional solutions, i.e. the new MFF has more crisis response instruments (classic ones such as: rescEU and Union Civil Protection Mechanism as well as a number of so-called special instruments) and more funds are earmarked for it. So this is not just about NGEU, which is supposed to be a one-off initiative, but about instruments included in the budget "proper", i.e. permanent ones.

The Monograph closes with the Author's proposed concept of a new division of public service tasks into domestic, European and global ones to boost the efficiency of their implementation, and a concept of them being managed at the European Union level. Examples of such systematisation are identified and described by indicating tasks at global, European and domestic levels. The results of this analysis show that respective expenditures' efficiency is determined by the choice of an adequate implementation method and location of tasks for which they are earmarked. Quoted as particularly characteristic examples, which demonstrate the correctness of this logic, are selected domestic social policy tasks. The efficient funding of these tasks largely depends on matching in the best possible way the beneficiaries' needs and thus it requires a perfect and all-round understanding of the local circumstances and competences resulting from experience and good practice acquired in this area.

The proposal is based on the COFOG classification and helps divide its subcategories into three groups of public service tasks:

- domestic – where decisions are taken at domestic level as government interventionism is something obvious and linked to the political process; these tasks are financed from respective countries' budgets and result from the directions of development adopted by democratically elected public authorities;
- European – where decisions on their adoption are taken at Community level, their implementation is part of a multiannual programme adopted separately for each of them and they will be financed from both domestic

and European funds; definition of such tasks will also strengthen the fiscal policy coordination and ensure tighter fiscal discipline throughout the entire integration grouping;

- global – where decisions are taken as part of international agreements such as, for example, Paris Agreement, which provided for the notifying countries earmarking, until 2020, USD 100 million for environmental protection goals. Undoubtedly, such globally coordinated measures are one of the challenges of the contemporary world.

The proposed division is – in the Author's opinion – a forward-looking and constructive solution, which could, also through ECA's action in all significant planes of this analysis, integrate the domestic and Community evaluation process, thus achieving a more versatile and in-depth information base to formulate more universal and comprehensive and hence useful conclusions and recommendations warranted by such research.

A new model for the management of planning, implementation and evaluation is also suggested for the group of European tasks. The Author has correlated her proposal with the decisions taken at the time of establishing new financial perspectives and then coordinated and reflecting the implementation level in a manner integrated with the yearly updates of convergence and stability programmes. A direct implementation of those tasks would be supervised by authorities at domestic and European level.

In summary, the Author wishes to share her optimism and hope with the readers of this Monograph, especially those belonging to the young generation of Polish Europeans to inspire them to believe that the EU has a future ahead and also to understand that our European affairs need to be solved not only by debating but mostly by implementing concrete and effective solutions (also when it comes to the system for financing and evaluating European tasks) and by making daily choices not only in the spirit of community, fraternity and integration, but also tolerance and openness to global challenges and problems. It is indisputable that the battle for victory of our European Community and its identity should be waged first and foremost in the public finance "arena". It needs, however, to be waged now, without procrastinating and counting on additional time as there might be none.

References

Abdel-Maksoud, Ahmed, Said Elbanna, Habib Mahama and Raili Pollanen. 2015. "The Use of Performance Information in Strategic Decision Making in Public Organizations." *International Journal of Public Sector Management* vol. 28(7): 528–549. doi: 10.1108/IJPSM-06-2015-0114

Abramov, Victor, Robert T. Mukhaev and Maxim S. Sokolov. 2016. "To a Question about the Criteria and Parameters of the Effectiveness of the Government in Democratic Countries." *Journal of Advanced Research in Law and Economics* vol. 7(6): 1248–1262.

Acemoglu, Daron and Carlos Molina. 2021. "Converging to Converge? A Comment." *NBER Macroeconomics Annual* vol. 36.

Adam, Antonis, Manthos D. Delis, Pantelis Kammas. 2014. "Fiscal decentralization and public sector efficiency: Evidence from OECD countries." *Economics of Governance* vol. 15(1): 17–49.

Alcidi, Cinzia and Daniel Gros. 2019. "Public Debt and the Risk Premium: A Dangerous Doom Loop." *CEPS Policy Inside* No. 2019–06/2.

Alegre, Juan Gonzalez. 2012. "An Evaluation of EU Regional Policy. Do Structural Actions Crowd Out Public Spending?" *Public Choice* vol. 151(1): 1–21.

Alvaredo, Francudo, Lucas Chancel, Tomas Piketty, Emmanuel Saez and Gabriel Zucman. 2018. "World Inequality Report 2018. Executive Summary." *World Inequality Lab.* https://wir2018.wid.world/

Annoni, Paola and Angel Catalina Rubianes. 2016. "Tree-Based Approaches for Understanding Growth Pat-Terns in the European Regions." *REGION* vol. 3(2): 23–45.

Arbatli, Cemal Eren, Quamrul H. Ashraf, Oded Galor and Marc Klemp. 2020. "Diversity and Conflict." *Econometrica. Journal of the Econometric Society* vol. 88(2): 727–797.

Archick, Kristin and Derek E. Mix. 2012. "The European Union's Reform Process: The Lisbon Treaty." *Congressional Research Service* 7–5700.

Ardanaz, Martín, Eduardo Cavallo, Alejandro Izquierdo and Jorge Puig. 2021. "Growth-friendly Fiscal Rules? Safeguarding Public Investment from Budget Cuts Through Fiscal Rule Design." *Journal of International Money and Finance* vol. 111(C).

Athanassio, Ersi. 2009. "Fiscal Policy and the Recession: The Case of Greece." *Intereconomics* vol. 44: 364–372. doi: 10.1007/s10272-009-0318-7

Baldacci, Emanuele, Sanjeev Gupta and Carlos Mulas-Granados. 2009. "How Effective Is Fiscal Policy Response in Systematic Banking Crises." *IMF Working Paper* vol. 160.

Baran, Bernadeta. 2013. "The Medium-Term Budgetary Objective in the European Union." *Gospodarka Narodowa. The Polish Journal of Economics* vol. 268(11–12): 23–47. doi: 10.33119/GN/100932

Barbier-Gauchard Amelie, Kea Baret and Alexandru Minea. 2021. "National fiscal rules and fiscal discipline in the European Union." *Applied Economics* vol. 53(20): 2337–2359. doi: 10.1080/00036846.2020.1859453

Barry, Frank. 2000. "Convergence Is Not Automatic: Lessons from Ireland for Central and Eastern Europe." *World Economy* vol. 23(10): 1379–1394.

Benedetto, Giacomo. 2013. "The EU Budget after Lisbon: Rigidity and Reduced Spending?" *Journal of Public Policy* vol. 33(3).

Berezin, Mabel. 2009. *Liberal Politics in Neoliberal Times: Culture, Security and Populism in the New Europe*. New York: Cambridge University Press.

Berg, G. and Kirschenmann Karolin. 2015. "Funding Versus Real Economy Shock: The Impact of the 2007–09 Crisis on Small Firms' Credit Availability." *Review of Finance* vol. 19(3): 951–990.

Bergman, Michael, Michael Hutchison and Svend Jensen. 2016. "Measurement and Effectiveness of National Fiscal Rules and Governance in the European Union." in *Makropolitik i kris,* edited by Lars Jonung, 127–143. Media-Tryck. https://www.researchgate.net/publication/313658879_Measurement_and_Effectiveness_of_National_Fiscal_Rules_and_Governance_in_the_European_Union

Bernanke, B. 2010. "Fiscal Sustainability and Fiscal Rules, Board of Governors of the Federal Reserve System." https://www.federalreserve.gov/newsevents/speech/bernanke20101004a.htm

Bhattarai, Keshab. 2016. "Growth and Income Distributions in Four EU Economies." *International Advances in Economic Research* vol. 22(3).

Białek, Jacek and Adam Oleksiuk. 2009. *Gospodarka i geopolityka. Dokąd zmierza świat?* [Economy and Geopolitics. Where is the World Going?]. Warsaw: Difin.

Biraschi, Paolo, Marco Cacciotti, Davide Iacovoni and Juan Pradelli. 2010. "The New Medium-Term Budgetary Objectives and the Problem of Fiscal Sustainability after the Crisis." *SSRN Electronic Journal*. doi: 10.2139/ssrn.1985247

Blanchard, Olivier. 2019. "Public Debt and Low Interest Rates." *American Economic Review* vol. 109(4): 1197–1229. doi: 10.1257/aer.109.4.1197

Blanchard, Olivier, Álvaro Leandro and Jeromin Zettelmeyer. 2021. "Redesigning EU Fiscal Rules: From Rules to Standards." *PIIE Working Paper* No. 21–1. doi: 10.1093/epolic/eiab003

Blanchard, Olivier, Álvaro Leandro, Silvia Merler and Jeromin Zettelmeyer. 2018. "Impact of Italy's Draft Budget on Growth and Fiscal Solvency." *PIIE Policy Brief* No. 18–24.

Boboc, D., G. R. Lădaru and F. Marin. 2016. "Effectiveness of EU Funded Interventions in the Rural Labour Market." *Quality – Access to Success* vol. 17.

Borrás, Susana. 2009. "The Politics of the Lisbon Strategy: The Changing Role of the Commission." *West European Politics* vol. 32(1): 97–118.

Bouthevillain, Carine and Gilles Dufrénot. 2016. "Fiscal Policies Enhancing Growth in Europe: Does One Size Fit All?" *Oxford Economic Papers* vol. 68(4): 1146–1165.

Bova, Eva, Nathali Carcenac and Martine Guerguil. 2014. "Fiscal Rules and the Procyclality of Fiscal Policy in the Developing World." IMF-World Bank Conference on Fiscal Policy, Equity and Long-Term Growth in Developing Countries, Washington, DC.

Bova, Eva, Tidiane Kinda, Priscilla Muthoora and Frederik Toscani. 2015. *Fiscal Rules at Glance*. Washington, DC: IMF.

Bowles, Samuel and Wendy Carlin. 2020. "Shrinking Capitalism." *AEA Papers and Proceedings* vol. 110: 372–377.

Brander, James A. and Barbara J. Spencer. 1984. "Export Subsidies and International Market Share Rivalry." *Journal of International Economics* vol. 18(1–2).

Bregman, Rutger. 2020. "Free Money Work." www.bigissue.com/latest/rutger-bregman-free-money-works/

Bremmer, Ian. 2010. *The End of the Free Market: Who Wins the War Between States and Corporations?* New York: Portfolio.

Brown, Wendy. 2018. "Neoliberalism's Frankenstein: Authoritarian Freedom in Twenty-First Century "Democracies." *Critical Times* vol. 1(1): 60–79. doi: 10.1215/26410478-1.1.60

Brunila, Anne, Marco Buti and Daniele Franco. 2001. *The Stability and Growth Pact the Architecture of Fiscal Policy in EMU.* London: Palgrave Macmillan.

Budimir, Kristina. 2017. "Debt Crisis in the EU Member States and Fiscal Rules." *CESifo DICE Report* No. 15: 53–57.

Burriel, Pablo, Cristina Checherita-Westphal, Pascal Jacquinot, Nikolai Stähler and Matthias Schön. 2020. "Economic Consequences of High Public Debt: Evidence from Three Large Scale DSGE Models." *Working Paper Series* 2450, European Central Bank.

Burriel, Pablo, Panagiotis Chronis, Maximilian Freier, Sebastian Hauptmeier, Lukas Reiss, Dan Stegarescu and Stefan Van Parys. 2020. "A Fiscal Capacity for the Euro Area: Lessons from Existing Fiscal-federal Systems." *Paper Occasional* No. 2009 from Banco de España.

Buti, Marco, Daniele Franco and Hudwig Ongena. 1997. "Budgetary Policies during Recession: Retrospective Application of the Stability and Growth Pact to the Post-War Period." *Recherches Economiques de Louvain* No. 63.

Buti, Marco and Gabriele Giudice. 2002a. "EMU's Fiscal Rules: What Can and Cannot Be Exported?" *Paper prepared for the Conference on "Rules-Based Macroeconomic Policies in Emerging Market Economies"*, Mexico, February 14–16.

Buti, Marco and Gabriele Giudice. 2002b. *EMU Fiscal Rules: What Can and Cannot Be Exported?* Brussels: European Commission.

Buti, Marco, Sylvester C. W. Eijffinger and Daniele Franco. 2005. "The Stability Pact Pains: A Forward-Looking Assessment of the Reform Debate." *CentER Discussion Paper* No. 2005–101.

Caselli, Francesca and Julien Reynaud. 2020. "Do Fiscal Rules Cause Better Fiscal Balances? A New Instrumental Variable Strategy." *European Journal of Political Economy. Elsevier* vol. 63(C).

Cavallo, A. M. E., A. Izquierdo and J. Puig. 2020. "Growth friendly fiscal rules? safeguarding public investment from budget cuts through fiscal rule design." *Inter-American Development Bank, IDB Working* Paper No. IDB-WP-1083.

Cebotari Aliona, Jeffrey Davis, Lusine Lusinyan, Amine Mati, Paolo Mauro, Murray Petrie and Ricardo Velloso. 2008. "Fiscal Risks: Sources, Disclosure, and Management." Departmental Paper 09/01, Fiscal Affairs Department. Washington, DC: International Monetary Fund.

Cepiku, Denita, Alessandro, Hinna, Danila Scarozza and Andrea B. Savignon. 2017. "Performance Information Use in Public Administration: An Exploratory Study of Determinants and Effects." *Journal of Management and Governance* vol. 21(4): 936–991.

Chadha, Jagjit S., Hande Küçük and Adrian Pabst. 2021. "Commentary: Proposals for a New Fiscal Framework." *National Institute Economic Review* 256. Cambridge University Press: 1–15. doi: 10.1017/nie.2021.14

Chwieroth, Jeffrey. 2007. "Neoliberal Economists and Capital Account Liberalization in Emerging Markets." *International Organizational* vol. 61/2.

Codogno, L. 2012. "The International Crisis and EU Policy Responses." *Dipartimento Del Tesoro*, Shanghai. http://www.dt.mef.gov.it/modules/documenti_en/analisi_progammazione/eventi/121106_Shanghai_new_

Codogno, Lorenzo and Francesco Nucci. 2007. "Budgetary Safety Margins: An Assessment, Fiscal Policy: Current Issues and Challenges." Paper presented at the "9th Banca d'Italia Workshop on Public Finance SADIBA", Italy.

Codogo, Favero. 2003, Yield spread in EMU goverment bonds, Economic Policy18/(37)

Cohen-Setton, Jeremie and Natascha Vella. 2010. "Unnoticed Potential Output Revisions and Their Impact on the 'Stimulus/Austerity Debate'." *VOX CEPR Policy Portal.*

Collignon, Stefan. 2008. "The Lisbon Strategy, Macroeconomic Stability and the Dilemma of Governance with Governments; or why Europe Is Not Becoming the World's Most Dynamic Economy." *International Journal of Public Policy* vol. 3(1): 72–99.

Constâncio, Vitor. 2020. "The Return of Fiscal Policy and the Euro Area Fiscal Rule." *Comparative Economic Studies* vol. 62: 358–372.

Cutler, Tony, John Williams and Karel Williams. 2003. *Keynes, Beveridge and Beyond.* London: Routledge.

Dall'Erba, Sandy and Fang Fang. 2017. "Meta-Analysis of the Impact of European Union Structural Funds on Regional Growth." *Regional Studies* vol. 51(6): 822–832.

Dall'Erba, Sandy and Julie Gallo. 2007. "The Impact of EU Regional Support on Growth and Employment." *Czech Journal of Economics and Finance (Finance a uver)* vol. 57(7–8): 324–340.

Darvas, Zsolt, Phillipe Martin and Xavier Ragot. 2018. "European Fiscal Rules Require a Major Overhaul." *Policy Contribution* No. 18. Brussels: Bruegel.

Davidson, Michael. 2017. "Vaccination as a Cause of Autism-myths and Controversies." *Dialogues in Clinical Neuroscience* vol. 19(4): 403–407. doi: 10.31887/DCNS.2017.19.4/mdavidson

Debrun, Xavier, Jonathan D. Ostry, Tim Willems and Charles Wyplosz. 2019a. "Public Debt Sustainability." In *Sovereign Debt: A Guide for Economists and Practitioners*, edited by Ali Abbas, Pienkowski Alex and Rogoff Kenneth. Oxford: Oxford University Press.

Debrun, Xavier, Jonathan D. Ostry, Tim Willems and Charles Wyplosz. 2019b. "Public Debt Sustainability." *CEPR Discussion Papers* 14010, C.E.P.R. Discussion Papers. https://ssrn.com/abstract=3464539

De Grauwe, Paul. 2006. "On Monetary and Political Union." Paper prepared for the "CESifo Workshop on." *Enlarging the Euro Area.*

Dembiński, Paul H. 1992. *Gospodarka rynkowa dla każdego.* [A Market Economy for Everyone]. Warsaw: Editions Spotkania.

Dembinski, Paul. H. 2012. *Finanse po zawale. Od euforii finansowej do gospodarczego ładu* [Finance after a Heart Attack. From Financial Euphoria to Economic Governance]. Warsaw: Publisher EMKA.

De Simone, Elina, Giuseppe Lucio Gaeta and Salvatore Ercolano. 2012. "Exploring Convergence in some OECD Public Social Expenditure Trends." *MPRA Paper* 22496.

Dodson, Jago. 2006. "The 'Role' of the State: Government, Neoliberalism and Housing Assistance in Four Advanced Economies." *Housing, Theory and Society* vol. 23(4).

Dumciuviene Daiva, Alina Stundziene and Grazina Startiene. 2015. "Relationship Between Structural Funds and Economic Indicators of the European Union." *Inzinerine Ekonomika-Engineering Economics* vol. 26(5): 507–516.

Dumenil, G. and D. Levy. 2009. "The Neoliberal (counter-) Revolution." In *Neoliberalism: A Critical Reader*, edited by A. Saad-Filho and D. Johnston, 9–19. London and Ann Arbor: Pluto Press.

Eberhardt, Markus and Andrea Presbitero. 2015. "Public debt and growth: Heterogeneity and non-linearity." *Journal of International Economics* vol. 97(1): 45–58.

Eijffinger, Sylvester and de Jakob Haan. 2000. *European Monetary and Fiscal Policy.* Oxford University Press. https://econpapers.repec.org/scripts/showcites.pf?h=repec:oxp:obooks:9780198776161

Eisl, Andreas. 2020. "The Ambiguous Consensus on Fiscal Rules: How Ideational Ambiguity Has Facilitated Social Democratic Parties' Support of Structural Deficit Rules in the Eurozone." *MaxPo Discussion Paper* 20/4, Max Planck Sciences Po Center on Coping with Instability in Market Societies, Paris.

Erhard, Ludwig. 2012. *Dobrobyt dla wszystkich* [Prosperity for All]. Warsaw: PTE.

Esposito, Giovanni, Giuseppe L. Gaeta and Giorgio Trasciani. 2017. "Administrative Change in the EU: A Cross-Country Empirical Study on the Contextual Determinants of Npm Reform Rhetoric." *Annals of Public and Cooperative Economics* vol. 88(3): 323–344.

European Commission. 1995. *Council Regulation (EC) No. 2236/95 of September 18, 1995 laying down general rules for the granting of Community financial aid in the field of trans-European networks, OJ. WE L 228, 23/09/1995*. European Commission.

European Commission. 1997. *Council Regulation (EC) No 1466/97 of 7 July 1997 on the strengthening of the surveillance of budgetary positions and the supervision and coordination of economic policies, O.J. WE L 209, 2.08.1997*. European Commission.

European Commission. 1999. *Regulation (EC) No 1655/1999 of the European Parliament and of the Council of 19 July 1999 amending Regulation (EC) No 2236/95 laying down general rules for the granting of Community financial aid in the field of trans-European networks, OJ. WE L 197/1, 29.07.1999*. European Commission.

European Commission. 2001. *White Paper – European Transport Policy for 2010: Time to Decide*. European Commission (COM(2001)0370).

European Commission. 2002. "Public Finances in EMU 2002." *European Economy* No. 3.

European Commission. 2005a. "Public Finances in EMU 2002." *European Economy* No. 3.

European Commission. 2005c. *Council Regulation (EC) No. 1055/2005 of 27 June 2005 amending Regulation (EC) No. 1466/97 on the strengthening of the surveillance of budgetary positions as well as the supervision and coordination of economic policies, OJ. UE L 174, 7.07.2005*. European Commission.

European Commission. 2005d. "Specifications on the Implementation of the Stability and Growth Pact and Guidelines on the Format and Content of Stability and Convergence Programmes Specifications on the Implementation." https://ec.europa.eu/info/sites/default/files/code_of_conduct_en1.pdf, Brussels

European Commission. 2006. "Public Finances in EMU 2002." *European Economy* No. 3.

European Commission. 2007a. "Public Finances in EMU 2002." *European Economy* No. 3.

European Commission. 2007b. *Regulation (EC) No 680/2007 of the European Parliament and of the Council of 20 June 2007 laying down general rules for the granting of Community financial aid in the field of trans-European transport and energy networks*. European Commission.

European Commission. 2009. *Special Eurobarometer 295*. Brussels: European Commission. https://data.europa.eu/data/datasets/s673_68_2_ebs295?locale=en

European Commission, 2011, White Paper on Transport, Brussel.

European Commission. 2012a. "Assessment of the 2012 National Reform Programme and Convergence Programme For (Poland, and Other Countries)." *Commission Staff Working Document*. Accessed 15 July 2018. https://ec.europa.eu/info/sites/info/files/file_import/swd2012_latvia_en_0.pdf

European Commission. 2012b. *Cyclical Adjustment of Budget Balances*. European Commission. Accessed 10 June 2018. http://ec.europa.eu/economy_finance/db_indicators/gen_gov_data/documents/2012/ccab_spring_en.pdf

European Commission. 2012c. "Fiscal Sustainability Report." *European Economy* No. 8.

European Commission. 2012d. "The 2012 Ageing Report, Economic and Budgetary Projections for the 27 EU Member States (2010–2060)." *European Economy* No. 2.

European Commission. 2013. "Overview of CAP Reform 2014–2020." *Agricultural Policy Perspectives Brief* No. 5. http://ec.europa.eu/agriculture/policy-perspectives/policy-briefs/05_en.pdf

European Commission. 2014a. "Assessing Public Debt Sustainability in EU Member States: A Guide." *ECFIN Occasional Papers* No. 200.

European Commission. 2014b. "Community Committee for the Farm Accountancy Data Network (FADN) Definitions of Variables Used in FADN Standard Results." European Commission. http://fadn.pl/wp-content/uploads/2012/12/RICC-882-rev9.2-Definitions-of-Variables.pdf

European Commission. 2014c. "The EU Explained: Agriculture. A Partnership Between Europe and Farmers. The EU's Common Agricultural Policy (CAP): For Our Food, for Our Countryside, for Our Environment." http://ec.europa.eu/agriculture/cap-overview/2014_en.pdf.

European Commission. 2015a. Health Check of the Common Agricultural Policy. Brussels.

European Commission. 2015b. "Agriculture and Rural Development. History of the CAP." http://ec.europa.eu/agriculture/

European Commission. 2016. "Transport, Executive Summary, Work Package 5, Ex Post Evaluation of Cohesion Policy Programmes 2007–2013, Focusing on the European Regional Development Fund (ERDF) and the Cohesion Fund (CF)." Brussels.

European Commission. 2017a. *White Paper on the Future of Europe*. European Commission.

European Commission. 2017b. *White Paper on the Future of Europe*. European Commission, COM(2017)2025.

European Commission. 2018a. *Standard Eurobarometer 89: Spring 2018*. European Commission http://ec.europa.eu/commfrontoffice/publicopinion/index.cfm/Survey/getSurveyDetail/instruments/STANDARD/surveyKy/2180

European Commission. 2018c. "Final Report." https://ec.europa.eu/info/sites/default/files/2018_efb_annual_report_en.pdf

European Commission. 2019a. *Standard Eurobarometer 92*. European Commission. https://data.europa.eu/data/datasets/s2255_92_3_std92_eng?locale=en

European Commission. 2019b. "Vade Mecum on the Stability and Growth Pact." *Institutional Paper* 101. Brussels.

European Commission. 2020a. "Medium-Term Budgetary Frameworks. A Contribution to Definitions and Identification of Good Practices." www.euifis.eu/images/MTBF_PAPER.pdf

European Commission. 2020b. *Special Eurobarometer 468*. Brussels: European Commission. https://data.europa.eu/data/datasets/s2156_88_1_468_eng?locale=en

European Commission. 2021a. *Special Eurobarometer 469*. Brussels: European Commission. https://data.europa.eu/data/datasets/s2169_88_2_469_eng?locale=en

European Commission. 2021b. *Standard Eurobarometer*. Brussels: European Commission. https://europa.eu/eurobarometer/screen/home

European Court of Auditors. 2018. "Annual Report: EU Sustains Improvements in Financial Management for Third Year in a Row." Luxemburg: Curia Rationum European Court of Auditors.

European Court of Auditors. 2021a. *Special Report 16/2021: Common Agricultural Policy and Climate: Half of EU Climate Spending but Farm Emissions are Not Decreasing*, Luxemburg: Curia Rationum European Court of Auditors.

European Court of Auditors. 2021b. *The 2021–25 Strategy of the European Court of Auditors*. Luxemburg: Curia Rationum European Court of Auditors.

European Fiscal Board. 2019. *Assessment of EU Fiscal Rules with a Focus on the Six and Two-Pack Legislation.* Brussels. https://ec.europa.eu/info/sites/default/files/2019-09-10-assessment-of-eu-fiscal-rules_en.pdf

European Parliament. 2013a. *Regulation (EU) No 1315/2013 of the European Parliament and of the Council of 11 December 2013 on Union guidelines for the development of the trans-European transport network and repealing Decision No 661/2010 / EU.* European Parliament.

European Parliament. 2013b. *Regulation (EU) No 1316/2013 of the European Parliament and of the Council of 11 December 2013 establishing the Connecting Europe Facility, amending Regulation (EU) No 913/2010 and repealing Regulations (EC) No 680/2007 and (EC) No 67/2010.* European Parliament.

European Union Independent Fiscal Institutions. 2018. Working paper, Brussels.

Eyraud, Luc, Xavier Debrun, Andrew Hodge, Victor Lledó and Catherine Pattillo. 2018. *Second-Generation Fiscal Rules: Balancing Simplicity, Flexibility, and Enforceability*, IMF Staff Discussion Note SDN/18/04

Eyraud, Luc, Vitor Gaspar and Tigran Poghosyan. 2017. "Fiscal Politics in the Euro Area." *IMF Working Paper* No. 17/18. https://ssrn.com/abstract=2938319 or http://dx.doi.org/10.2139/ssrn.2938319

Farah, Andrea and Almudena Gómez-Ramos. 2014. "Competitiveness vs. Sustainability: An Assessment of Profitability as a Component of an Approach on 'Sustainable Competitiveness' in Extensive Farming Systems of Central Spain." *Sustainability* vol. 6(11).

Farole, Thomas, Andres Rodríguez-Pose and Michael Storper. 2011. "Cohesion Policy in the European Union: Growth, Geography, Institutions." *Journal of Common Market Studies* vol. 49(5): 1088–1111.

Ferge, Zsuzsa. 2000. "What Are the State Functions Neoliberalism Wants to Get Rid of?" In *Not for Sale: In Defense of Public Goods*, edited by A. Anton, M. Fisk and N. Holmstrom, 181–204. London: Westview Press.

Ferrara, Antonella Rita, Philip McCann, Guido Pellegrini, Dirk Stelder and Flavia Terribile. 2017. "Assessing the Impacts of Cohesion Policy on EU Regions: A Non-Parametric Analysis on Interventions Promoting Research and Innovation and Transport Accessibility." *Papers in Regional Science* vol. 96(4).

Ferucci, Gianluigi, Vitold, Herzberg, Ricardo, Soussa and Alfred, Taylor. 2004. "Understanding Capital Flows." *Financial Stability Review* vol. 16: 89–97.

Fetai, Besnik. 2017. "The Effects of Fiscal Policy During the Financial Crises in Transition and Emerging Countries: Does Fiscal Policy Matter?" *Economic Research-Ekonomska Istraživanja* vol. 30(1): 1522–1535. doi: 10.1080/1331677X.2017.1340181

Florén, Britta, Pegah Amani and Jennifer Davis. 2017. "Climate Database Facilitating Climate Smart Meal Planning for the Public Sector in Sweden." *International Journal on Food System Dynamics* vol. 8(1): 1–9.

Fourçans, Andre and Thiery Warin. 2007. "Stability and Growth Pact II: Incentives and Moral Hazard." *Journal of Economic Policy Reform* vol. 10(1): 51–62.

Franco, D. 2005. "The Stability Pact Pains: A Forward-Looking Assessment of the Reform Debate." *Discussion Paper*, vol. 101, Center for Economic Research, Tilburg University.

Franek, S. and M. Postuła. 2019. *Pomiar siły instrumentów fiskalnych oraz ich skuteczność w poprawie stabilności finansów publicznych w krajach Unii Europejskiej* [Measurement of the Strength of Fiscal Instruments and Their Effectiveness in Improving the Sustainability of Public Finances in the European Union Countries]. Warsaw: 334, NBP.

Franek, Sławomir and Marta Postuła. 2020. "Does Eurozone Membership Strengthen the Significance of Fiscal Instruments?" *Annals of Economics and Finance*, Society for AEF vol. 21(1): 131–151.

Friedrich, Heinemann, Marc Daniel Moessinger and Mustafa Yeter. 2018. "Do Fiscal Rules Constrain Fiscal Policy? A Meta-regression-analysis." *European Journal of Political Economy. Elsevier* vol. 51(C): 69–92.

Funtowicz, Silvo and Jerome Ravetz. 2006. "Values and Uncertainties." In *Handbook of Transdisciplinary Research*, edited by G. Hirsch Hadorn, H. Hoffmann-Riem, S. Biber-Klemm, W. Grossenbacher-Mansuy, D. Joye, C. Pohl, U. Wiesmann and E. Zemp, 361–368. Heidelberg (Germany): Springer.

Galar, M., A. Fernández, E. Barrenechea, H. Bustince and F. Herrera. 2012. "A Review on Ensembles for the Class Imbalance Problem: Bagging-, Boosting-, and Hybrid-Based Approaches." *Journal Systems, Man, and Cybernetics* vol. 42(4).

Galbraith, James. K. 2016. *Welcome to the Poisoned Chalice: The Destruction of Greece and the Future of Europe*. London: Yale University Press.

Gali, J., D. Lopez-Salido and J. Valles. 2005. "Understanding the Effects of Government Spending on Consumption." *NBER Working Paper*, nr 11578.

Gali, Jordi, David J. Lopez-Salido and Javier Valles. 2007. "Understanding the Effects of Government Spending on Consumption." *Journal of the European Economic Association* vol. 5(1): 227–270.

Galor, O., Ö. Özak and A. Sarid. 2020. "Linguistic Traits and Human Capital Formation." *AEA Papers and Proceedings* vol. 110: 309–313.

Giles, D., E. A. Lindsay, M. Tedds and G. Werkneh. 2002. "The Canadian Underground and Measured Economies." *Applied Economics* vol. 34(4).

Gellner, Ernest. 1983. *Nations and Nationalism*. Oxford: Blackwell.

Gerrish, Ed. 2017. "The Effect of the Child Support Performance and Incentive Act of 1998 on Rewarded and Unrewarded Performance Goals" *Journal of Policy Analysis and Management* vol. 36(1): 65–96.

Ghosh, Atish R., Marcos Chamon, Christopher Crowe, Jun I. Kim and Jonathan D. Ostry. 2009. "Coping with the Crisis: Policy Options for Emerging Market Countries." *IMF Staff Position Note* no SPN/09/08. www.imf.org/external/pubs/ft/spn/2009/spn0908.pdf

Glendinning Simon. 2016. "The European Hamlet." In *The Routledge Handbook of Philosophy and Europe*, edited by Meacham Darian and de Warren Nicolas, 155–167. London: Routledge.

Gopalakrishna, B. and D. S. Leelavathi. 2011. "Infrastructure and Human Development in India: An Inter-State Comparison." *Journal of Global Economy* vol. 7(4): 292–311.

Gorynia, Marian. 2017. "Rola państwa w zarządzaniu zasobami wspólnymi – uwagi dotyczące zasobów wodnych" [The Role of the State in Managing Common Resources – Comments on Water Resources]. In *Państwo a gospodarka, Książka jubileuszowa z okazji 30-lecia Olimpiady Wiedzy Ekonomicznej*, edited by Owsiak Stanisław, 135–148. Warsaw: PTE.

Government Offices of Sweden. 2017. "Swedish Government Offices Yearbook 2017." https://www.government.se/49c2fc/contentassets/13ca34fb7bd24f1c9c4dc0ac88093992/swedish-government-offices-yearbook-2017.pdf

Government Offices of Sweden. 2018. "Swedish Government Offices Yearbook 2018." https://www.government.se/information-material/2019/09/swedish-government-offices-yearbook-2018/

Granado, F. Javier Arze del, Jorge Martinez-Vazquez and Robert M. McNab. 2018. "Decentralized Governance, Expenditure Composition, and Preferences for Public Goods." *Public Finance Review* vol. 46(3): 359–388. doi: 10.1177/1091142116639127

Greenwood, Dan. 2011. "The Problem of Coordination in Politics: What Critics of Neoliberalism Might Draw from Its Advocates." *Polity* vol. 43(1): 36–57.

Greenwood, Justin, Roger Levy and Rachel Stewart. 1995. "The European Union Structural Fund Allocations: 'Lobbying to Win' or Recycling the Budget?" *European Urban and Regional Studies* vol 2(4): 317–338.

Grimm, Heike M. 2011. "The Lisbon Agenda and Entrepreneurship Policy: Governance Implications from a German Perspective." *Public Administration* vol. 89(4): 1526–1545.

Grossman, Gene M. and Elhanan Helpman. 1990. "Trade, Innovation, and Growth." *The American Economic Review* vol. 80(2).

Guerguil, Martine, Pierre Mandon and Rene Tapsoba. 2017. "Flexible Fiscal Rules and Counter-Cyclical Fiscal Policy." *IMF Working Paper* No. 16/8.

Günaydın, Ihsan and Levent Yahya Eser. 2009. "Maliye Politikasındaki Yeni Trend: Mali Kurallar." *Maliye Dergisi* vol. 156: 51–65.

Guzek Marian. 2015. *Capitalism on the Edge*. Translated by Łyś Waldemar. Poznań: Bonami.

Hallerberg, Mark, Rolf Strauch and Juergen Von Hagen. 2007. "The Design of Fiscal Rules and Forms of Governance in European Union Countries." *European Journal of Political Economy* vol. 23(2): 338–359.

Hallett, Hughes A. and John Lewis. 2005. "European Fiscal Discipline Before and After EMU, Permanent Weight Loss or Crash Diet?" *Vanderbilt University Department of Economics Working Papers* 0516.

Halper, Stefan. 2010. *The Beijing Consensus: How China's Authoritarian Model Will Dominate the Twenty First Century*. New York: Basic Books.

Hampe, P. 2010. "Zur Entstehungsgeschichte und zum Bedeutungswandel eines verqueren Begriffes." *Ifo Schnelldienst* vol. 90.

Harvey, David. 2007. *A Brief History of Neoliberalism*. Oxford: Oxford University Press.

Harvey, David. 2008a. "Neoliberalism as Creative Destruction." *The ANNALS of the American Academy of Political and Social Science* vol. 610(1).

Hashimzade, Nigar and Gareth D. Myles. 2010. "Growth and Public Infrastructure." *Macroeconomic Dynamics* vol. 14(S2): 258–274.

Hausner, Jerzy. 2013. "The Global Crisis: The Need for a New Economic Policy." *Warsaw Forum of Economic Sociology* vol. 8(4): 31–58.

Heilperin, Michael A. 1960. *Studies in Economic Nationalism*. Geneva: Ludwig von Mises Institute.

Heimberger, Philipp, Jakob Huber and Jakob Kapeller. 2020. "The Power of Economic Models: The Case of the EU's Fiscal Regulation Framework." *Socio-Economic Review* vol. 18(2): 337–366.

Heimberger, P., C. Gräbner, J. Kapeller, et al. 2020. "Structural change in times of increasing openness: assessing path dependency in European economic integration". *Journal of Evolutionary Economics* vol. 30: 1467–1495. https://doi.org/10.1007/s00191-019-00639-6.

Heitger, Bernhard. 2001. "The Scope of Government and Its Impact on Economic Growth in OECD Countries." *Kiel Working Paper* No. 1034.

Helm, Dieter and Colin Mayer. 2016. "Infrastructure: Why It Is Under Provided and Badly Managed." *Oxford Review of Economic Policy* vol. 32(3): 343–359.

Hernaus, Tomislav, Vesna B. Vuksic and Mojca I. Štemberger. 2016. "How to Go from Strategy to Results? Institutionalising BPM Governance Within Organisations." *Business Process Management Journal* vol. 22(1).

Hessami, Zohal. 2010. "The Size and Composition of Government Spending in Europe and Its Impact on Well-Being." *Kyklos* vol. 63(3): 346–382.

Hobsbawm, Eric J. 1992. *Nations and Nationalism since 1780: Programme, Myth, Reality*. New York: Cambridge University Press.

Holgado, Molina, María del Mar, Fernández Salinas, Antonio José, Martín Rodríguez and Antonio José. 2015. "A Synthetic Indicator to Measure the Economic and Social Cohesion of the Regions of Spain and Portugal." *Revista de Economía Mundial* vol. 39: 223–239. www.redalyc.org/articulo.oa?id=86639636009

Holscher, Jens, Nicole Nulsch and Florian Stephan Johannes. 2017. "State Aid in the New EU Member States." *Journal of Common Market Studies* vol. 55(4).

Horsman, Mathew and Andrew Marshall. 1994. *After the Nation-State: Citizens: Tribalism and the New World Disorder*. London: Harper Collins.

Hovik, Sissel and Gro S. Hanssen. 2015. "The Impact of Network Management and Complexity on Multi-Level Coordination." *Public Administration* vol. 93(2): 506–523.

Hubner, Danuta. 2021. "Focusing on the Future." https://danuta-huebner.pl/wp-content/uploads/2021/07/Focusing-on-the-future.pdf, Brussels.

Hudrliková, Lenka. 2013. "Composite Indicators as a Useful Tool for International Comparison: The Europe 2020 Example." *Prague Economic Papers* vol. 22(4): 459–479.

IMF. 2017. "Fiscal Rules – Anchoring Expectations for Sustainable Public Finances." www.imf.org/external/np/pp/eng/2009/121609.pdf

International Monetary Fund. 2021. "Strengthening the Credibility of Public Finances." *Fiscal Monitor*. Washington.

Jääskeläinen, A. and H. Laihonen. 2014. "A Strategy Framework for Performance Measurement in the Public Sector." *Public Money and Management* vol. 34(5).

Jabri, Sana, El-Koursi El-Miloudi, Thomas Bourdeaud'huy and Etienne Lemaire. 2010. "European Railway Traffic Management System Validation Using UML/Petri Nets Modelling Strategy." *European Transport Research Review* vol. 2(2): 113–128.

Jahan, Selim. 1998. *Consumption, Natural Resource Use and Environment: Impact for Human Development* (mimeo). New York: UNDP.

Jankovics, L. and Monika Sherwood. 2017. "Independent Fiscal Institutions in the EU Member States: The Early Years." *European Economy – Discussion Papers*, Directorate General Economic and Financial Affairs (DG ECFIN), European Commission.

Jansen, Dennis W., Qi Li, Zijun Wang and Jian Yang. 2008. "Fiscal Policy and Asset Markets: A Semiparametric Analysis." *Journal of Econometrics, Elsevier* vol. 147(1): 141–150.

Jones, Daniel Stedman. 2012. *Masters of the Universe: Hayek, Friedman, and the Birth of Neoliberal Politics*. Princeton, NJ: Princeton University Press.

Jorda, Oscar, Sanjay R. Singh and Alan M. Taylor. 2020. "Longer-Run Economic Consequences of Pandemics." *Federal Reserve Bank of San Francisco Working Paper*. doi: 10.24148/wp2020-09

Juncker, Jean-Claude, Donald Tusk, Jeroen Dijsselbloem, Mario Draghi and Martin Schulz. 2015. *Completing Economic and Monetary Union*. Brussels: European Commission.

Kaplanoglou, Georgia and Vasillis T. Rapanos. 2011. "The Greek Fiscal Crisis and the Role of Fiscal Governance." GreeSE, 48. *Hellenic Observatory*, London, UK.

Kegalj, Igor. 2013. "Environmental Aspects of the Adriatic Transport Corridor in the Context of European Integrations." *Naše More* vol. 60(3–4): 53–60.

Keliuotytė-Staniulėnienė, Greta. 2015. "Fiscal Sustainability and Its Impact on Financial Stability in Lithuania and Other New Member States of the European Union." *Ekonomika* vol. 94(2): 28–46. doi: 10.15388/Ekon.2015.2.8231G

King, Stephen. D. 2010. *Losing Control. The Emerging Threats to Western Prosperity*. London: Yale University Press.

Kleer, Jerzy. 2017. "Prawdopodobne scenariusze dla Europy." *Studia Ekonomiczne* vol. 1(92): 113–134.

Klein, D. B., R. Daza and V. Di Giovinazzo. 2013. "Ideological Profiles of the Economics Laureates: Franco Modigliani." *Economic Journal Watch* vol. 10(3): 472–493.

Kofman, Jonathan. 1990. "How to Define Economic Nationalism? A Critical Review of Some Old and New Standpoints." In *Economic Nationalism in East-Central Europe and South America*, edited by H. Szlajfer, 1918–1939. Genève: Librairie Droz.

Kołodko, Grzegorz W. 2008. *Wędrujący świat* [Wandering World]. Warsaw: Wydawnictwo Prószyński i S-ka.

Kołodko, Grzegorz W. 2010. *Świat na wyciągnięcie myśli* [The World at Your Fingertips]. Warsaw: Wydawnictwo Prószyński i S-ka.

Kołodko, Grzegorz W. 2010. *Globalization, Crisis and What Next?* Warsaw: Poltext.

Kołodko, Grzegorz W. 2013. *Dokąd zmierza świat. Ekonomia polityczna przyszłości* [Where the World is Going. Political Economy of the Future]. Warsaw: Wydawnictwo Prószyński i S-ka.

Kołodko, Grzegorz W. 2016. "How to Destroy a Country. The Economics and the Politics of the Greek Crisis." *Rivista di Politica Economica* vol. IV–VI: 37–61.

Kolodko, Grzegorz W. 2017. "Economics and Politics of the Currency Convergence: The Case of Poland." *Communist and Post-Communist Studies* vol. 50: 183–194.

Kołodko, Grzegorz W. and Andrzej K. Koźmiński. 2017. *Nowy pragmatyzm kontra nowy nacjonalizm* [New Pragmatism Versus New Nationalism]. Warsaw: Wydawnictwo Prószyński i S-ka.

Kopits, George. 2016. "The IMF and the Euro Area Crisis: The Fiscal Dimension." Independent Evaluation Office of the International Monetary Fund. *Background Paper* No. BP/16–02/07.

Kopits, George and Steven Symansky. 1998. "Fiscal Policy Rules." *IMF Occasional Paper* No. 162.

Krejdl, Ales. 2006. "Fiscal Sustainability – Definition, Indicators and Assessment of Czech Public Finance Stability." *Working Paper* No. 3. Czech National Bank. www.cnb.cz/en/research/research_publications/cnb_wp/download/cnbwp_2006_03.pdf

Krugman, Paul. 2009. "How Did Economists Get It So Wrong?" *The New York Times*. www.nytimes.com/2009/09/06/magazine/06Economic-t.html

Kuhn, Thomas S. 1996. *The Structure of Scientific Revolution*. Chicago: The Chicago University Press.

Kuitto, Kati. 2016. "From Social Security to Social Investment? Compensating and Social Investment Welfare Policies in a Life-Course Perspective." *Journal of European Social Policy* vol. 26(5): 442–459.

Kumar, A., B. Bello and H. Reichert. 2009. "Lineage-Specific Cell Death in Postembryonic Brain Development of Drosophila." *Development* vol. 136(20): 3433–3442.

Kutan, Ali and Taner Yigit. 2007. "European Integration, Productivity Growth and Real Convergence." *European Economic Review* vol. 51(6): 1370–1395.

Laihonen, Harri, Aki Jääskeläinen and Sanna Pekkola. 2014. "Measuring Performance of a Service System - from Organizations to Customer-perceived Performance." *Measuring Business Excellence* vol. 18(3). doi: 10.1108/MBE-08-2013-0045

Laman, Mammadzada, Karimov Tural and Umid Abuzarli. 2018. "Analyze of Waste Management at the European Union Level." *Quality – Access to Success* vol. 19: 282–285.

Larch, M. 2016. *Independent Fiscal Councils: The Neglected Siblings of Independent Central Banks*. Brussels: Directorate-General for Economic and Financial Affairs, European Commission.

Larch, Martin and Thomas Branedle. 2018. "Independent Fiscal Councils: Neglected Siblings of Independent Central Banks? An EU Perspective." *Journal of Common Market Studies* vol. 56(2): 267–283.

Laryea, Samuel and Roland B. Watermeyer. 2018. "Comparison of Two Infrastructure Project Implementation Models in a Developing Country, Proceedings of Institution of Civil Engineers." *Management, Procurement and Law* vol. 171(1): 1–58.

Legrain, Philippe. 2010. *Aftershock: Reshaping the World Economy After the Crisis*. London: Little Brown.

Levi-Faur D. 1997. "Friedrich List and the Political Economy of the Nation-State." *Review of International Political Economy* vol. 4(1).

Lévy, Bernard Henri. 2021. "Filozofowie powinni filozofować." *Res Humana* vol. 5(174).

Lewin, Kurt. (1851) 1964. *Field Theory in Social Science: Selected Theoretical Papers*. New York: Harper.

Liargovas, Panagiotis and Marios Psychalis. 2020. "Fiscal Reforms in the EMU: The Greek Response." *European Politics and Society*. doi: 10.1080/23745118.2020.1827776

Lin, Justin Yifu. 2012. "Structural Economics. A Framework for Rethinking Development and Policy." *World Bank Publications* No. 2232.

Lin, Justin Yifu. 2017. "New Structural Economics and Industrial Policies for Catching-Up Economies." In *Advances in the Theory and Practice of Smart Specialization*, edited by S. Radosevic, A. Curaj, R. Gheorghiu, L. Andreescu and I. Wade, 183–199. London: Academic Press.

Lledo, Victor, Yoon Sungwook, Fang Xiangming, Mbaye Samba and Kim Young. 2017. *Fiscal Rules at a Glance*. Washington, DC: International Monetary Fund.

Love, Peter E. D., Zahir Irani, Jim Smith, Michael Regan and Henry J. Liu. 2017. "Cost Performance of Public Infrastructure Projects: The Nemesis and Nirvana of Change-Orders." *Production Planning and Control* vol. 28(13).

Lupu, Dan, Mihai Bogdan Petrisor, Ana Bercu and Mihaela Tofan. 2018. "The Impact of Public Expenditures on Economic Growth: A Case Study of Central and Eastern European Countries." *Emerging Markets Finance and Trade* vol. 54(3): 552–570.

MacEwan, Arthur. 1999. *Neo-liberalism Or Democracy? Economic Strategy, Markets, and Alternatives for the 21st Century*. London: Zed Books.

Manoharan, Aroon, James Melitski and Daniel Bromberg. 2015. "State Strategic Information System Plans: An Assessment Integrating Strategy and Operations Through Performance Measurement." *International Journal of Public Sector Management* vol. 28(3).

Maślanka, Łukasz. 2021. „Wybory i prezydencja – perspektywy europejskiej polityki Francji." *Biuletyn PISM* vol. 147(2345). www.pism.pl/publikacje/wybory-i-prezydencja-perspektywy-europejskiej-polityki-francji

Maynou, Laia, Marc Saez, Andres Kyriacou and Jordi Bacaria. 2016. "The Impact of Structural and Cohesion Funds on Eurozone Convergence, 1990–2010." *Regional Studies* vol. 50(7): 1127–1139.

Mazlish, B. (1972). "The Tragic Farce of Marx, Hegel, and Engels: A Note." *History and Theory* vol. 11(3): 335–337. https://doi.org/10.2307/2504684

Mazzucato, Mariana. 2017. *The Entrepreneurial State. Debunking Public vs. Private Sector Myths*. London: Anthem Press.

McCarthy, C. 2018. "Taoiseach Leo Varadkar Vision for the Future of Europe." Debate in European Parliament, Strasbourg, January 17. www.iiea.com/eu27/taoiseach-leo-varadkars-vision-future-europe/

Mendez, Carlos. 2013. "The Post-2013 Reform of EU Cohesion Policy and the Place-Based Narrative." *Journal of European Public Policy* vol. 20(5).

Metcalf, Janet. 2017. "Learning from Errors." *Annual Review of Psychology* vol. 68: 464–489.

Milea Om, Nicoleta E. Pascu and Daniela Popa. 2015. "Agricultural Policy Objectives Under the Europe 2020 Strategy." *Quality – Access to Success* vol. 16: 31–34.

Mises, Ludwig. 1989. *Liberalizm w klasycznej tradycji* [Liberalism in the Classical Tradition]. Warsaw: Oświaty Kaganiec.

Mohl, Philipp and T. Hagen. 2010. "Do EU Structural Funds Promote Regional Growth? New Evidence from Various Panel Data Approaches." *Regional Science and Urban Economics* vol. 40(5): 353–365.

Molina, M. M. H., J. A. S. Fernández and J. A. R. Martín. 2015. "A Synthetic Indicator to Measure the Economic and Social Cohesion of the Regions of Spain and Portugal." *Revista De Economia Mundial* vol. 39.

Monbiot, George. 2016. "Neoliberalism – the Ideology at the Root of All Our Problems." *The Guardian,* April 15.

Morris, Richard and Ludger Schuknecht. 2007. "Structural Balances and Revenue Windfalls – The Role of Asset Prices Revisited." *EBC Working Paper* No. 737. *SSRN Electronic Journal.* 10.2139/ssrn.970621

Moullin, Max. 2017. "Improving and Evaluating Performance with the Public Sector Scorecard." *International Journal of Productivity and Performance Management* vol. 66(4).

Mourre, Gilles, George M. Isbasoiu. Paternoster Dario and Salto Matteo. 2013. "The Cyclically-Adjusted Budget Balance Used in the EU Fiscal Framework: An Update." *Economic Papers* No. 478.

Moździerz Anna. 2015. "Tax Policy and Income Inequality in the Visegrad Countries." *Naše gospodarstvo/Our Economy* vol. 61(6): 12–18. doi: 10.1515/ ngoe-2015-0022

Mundell, Robert A. 2000. "The International Financial Architecture. The Euro Zone and its Enlargement in Eastern Europe." *Distinguished Lectures Series* No. 1.

Muratbekova, Zhazira, Kuandyk Ainabek and Nazgul Davletbayeva. 2017. "Public Sector Audit as a Provider of High-Quality Information on Activity of the Governments." *Journal of Advanced Research in Law and Economics* vol. 8(5): 1579–1584.

Murova, Olga and Aman Khan. 2017. "Public Investments, Productivity and Economic Growth: A Cross-state Study of Selected Public Expenditures in the United States." *The International Journal of Productivity and Performance Management* vol. 66. doi: 10.1108/ IJPPM-12-2015-0190

Nakano, Takeshi. 2004. "Theorizing Economic Nationalism." *Nations and Nationalism* vol. 10(3).

Nath, Nirmla and Umesh Sharma. 2014. "Performance Management Systems in the Public Housing Sector: Dissemination to Diffusion." *Australian Accounting Review* vol. 24(1): 2–20.

Newman, Joshua and Anthony Perl. 2014. "Partners in Clime: Public-Private Partnerships and British Columbia's Capacity to Pursue Climate Policy Objectives." *Canadian Public Administration* vol. 57(2): 217–233.

Normansyah, I., M. C. Kamil and W. Idawati. 2015. "The Use of Institutional Theory in Understanding Implementation of Public Sector Accrual Based Accounting Standard (Case Study on Financial and Development Supervisory Board in Indonesia." *International Journal of Applied Business and Economic Research* vol. 13(7): 5237–5257.

Nucci, F. 2007. "Budgetary Safety Margins: An Assessment, Fiscal Policy: Current Issues and Challenges." *9th Banca d'Italia Workshop on Public Finance SADI*BA, Italy.

Osiatyński, Jerzy. 2014. "Czy trwałe wypełnianie kryteriów konwergencji z Maastricht musi zapewniać korzyści gospodarce?" (Is Meeting the Convergence Criteria from Maastricht Always Beneficial for the Economy?). *Ekonomista* vol. 2: 275–286.

Palley, Thomas. 2018. "Three Globalizations, Not Two: Rethinking the History and Economics of Trade and Globalization." *FMM Working Paper* No. 18.

Palová, Dana and Katarína Václavíková. 2018. "Comparison of Europe 2020 Implementation Process Among European Union Members States." *Journal of Applied Economic Sciences* vol. 12(8): 2376–2387.

Panizza, Ugo and Andrea Presbitero. 2014. "Public Debt and Economic Growth: Is There a Causal Effect?" *Journal of Macroeconomics* vol. 41(C): 21–41.

Parliament Sets Out its Vision for the Future of Europe. 2017. *Press Releases*. https://www.europarl.europa.eu/news/en/press-room/20170210IPR61812/parliament-sets-out-its-vision-for-the-future-of-europe

Patrizii, Vincenzo and Giuliano Resce. 2015. "Public Sector Contribution to Competitiveness." *Italian Economic Journal* vol 1(3): 401–443.

Pereira, Rui M. and Alfredo Marvao Pereira. 2017. "The Economic and Budgetary Impact of Climate Policy in Portugal: Carbon Taxation in a Dynamic General Equilibrium Model with Endogenous Public Sector Behavior." *Environmental and Resource Economics* vol. 67(2).

Persson, Torsten and Guido Tabellini. 2002. "Political Economics: Explaining Economic Policy." *Southern Economic Journal* vol. 86(3).

Pfeifer Michaela. 2012. "Comparing Unemployment Protection and Social Assistance in 14 European Countries. Four Worlds of Protection for People of Working Age." *International Journal of Social Welfare* vol. 21(1): 13–25.

Pickel, Andreas. 2003. "Explaining, and Explaining with, Economic Nationalism." *Nations and Nationalism* vol. 9(1).

Portes, Jonathan and Simon Wren-Lewis. 2015. "Issues in the Design of Fiscal Policy Rules." *The Manchester School* No. 83.

Postuła, Marta. 2015. "Impact of the Council Directive on Requirements for Budgetary Frameworks of the Member States on the Polish Public Finance System." *Central European Management Journal* vol. 23(1): 95–111. doi: 10.7206/mba.ce.2084-3356.136

Postuła, Marta. 2017. "Success Factors in the Fiscal Consolidation Process." Available at SSRN: https://ssrn.com/abstract=2963500 or doi: 10.2139/ssrn.2963500

Postuła, Marta, Jarosław Klepacki and Agnieszka Alińska. 2018. "The Impact of Standardised fiscal rules index on the Yield on Ten-Year Government Bonds in the Visegrád Group Countries in 2005–2016." *Central European Management Journal* vol. 26(3): 49–70. doi: 10.7206/jmba.ce.2450-7814.325 (Original work published 2018).

Postuła, Marta and Katarzyna Radecka-Moroz. 2020. "Fiscal Policy Instruments in Environmental Protection." *Environmental Impact Assessment Review* vol. 84: 106435. doi: 10.1016/j.eiar.2020.106435

Poterba, James.1994. "State Responses to Fiscal Crisis: The Effects of Budgetary Institutions and Politics." *Journal of Political Economy* vol. 102(4): 799–821.

Presbitero, Andrea and Ursula Wiriadinata. 2020. "The risks of high public debt despite a low interest rate environment." *VOX CEPR Policy Portal*. https://voxeu.org/article/risks-high-public-debt-despite-low-interest-rate-environment

Raczkowski, Konrad and Marta Postuła. 2022. "Managing the Increase in the EU Public Debt Risk amid the Corona Crisis." *Risks* vol. 1/2022.

Radecka-Moroz, Katarzyna. 2015. "Uzyskiwanie rezultatów przy realizacji budżetu UE – doświadczenia Europejskiego Trybunału Obrachunkowego" [Obtaining Results in the Implementation of the EU Budget – the Experience of the European Court of Auditors]. In *Zarządzanie finansami publicznymi a efektywność* [Public Finance Management and

Efficiency], edited by Lubińska Teresa, Będzieszak Marcin and Marska-Dzioba Natalia, 24–34. Warsaw: Difin.

Radło, Mariusz J. 2002. *Strategia Lizbońska. Konkluzje dla Polski* [The Lisbon Strategy. Conclusions for Poland]. Warsaw: Instytut Spraw Publicznych, Warszawa.

Radu, Liliana A., Corina Pirlogea and M. Dimitriu. 2011. "European Funds Absorption and Sustainable Development." *Quality – Access to Success* vol. 12: 619–624.

Radulescu, Magdalena, Aleksandra Fedajev, Crenguta Ileana Sinisi and Constanta Popescu. 2018. "Europe 2020 Implementation as Driver of Economic Performance and Competitiveness. Panel Analysis of CEE Countries." *Sustainability* vol. 10(2): 566.

Rajan, Raghuram G. 2010. *Fault Lines: How Hidden Fractures Still Threaten the World Economy*. Princeton, NJ: Princeton University Press.

Rambarran, Richard. 2015. "Crisis without End: Neoliberalism in a Globalized Environment Modeling the Historic Rise of Neoliberalism and its Systematic Role in Recent Economic Downturns." *MPRA Paper*. https://mpra.ub.uni-muenchen.de/67410/

Rankin, Janet. 2017. "Europe Should Have Its Own Economy and Finance Minister, Says EC." *The Guardian*. www.theguardian.com/business/2017/dec/06/europe-should-have-its-own-minister-of-economy-and-finance-says-ec

Ratajczak, Marek. 2017. "Spór o rolę Państwa w Gospodarce." *Ruch Prawniczy, Ekonomiczny i Socjologiczny* vol. 79(1): 5–23. doi: 10.14746/rpeis.2017.79.1.1

Rebelo, Sergio and Easterly William. 1993. "Fiscal Policy and Economic Growth, an Empirical Investigation." *Journal of Monetary Economics* vol. 32: 417–458.

Rediker, Douglas A. 2015. "State Capitalism by Stealth, the New 21st Century Economic Reality." www.piie.com/publications/opeds/oped.cfm?ResearchID=2781, 16.04.2015.

Reich, Robert B. 1992. *The Work of Nations: Preparing Ourselves for 21st Century Capitalism*. New York: Vintage Books.

Reinhart, Carmen M. and Kenneth S. Rogoff. 2009. "The Aftermath of Financial Crises." *American Economic Review* vol. 99(2): 466–472.

Reinhart, Carmen M. and Kenneth S. Rogoff. 2010. "Growth in a Time of Debt." *American Economic Review: Papers & Proceedings* 100: 573–578.

Reuter, Wolf Heinrich. 2015. "National Numerical Fiscal Rules: Not Complied With, But Still Effective?" *European Journal of Political Economy* vol. 39: 67–81.

Reuters. 2015. "Europe can Handle Future Crises without IMF – Bailout Fund Chief." August 28.

Rockström, Johan, Will Steffen, Kevin J. Noone, E. F. Lambin. T. M. Lenton, M. Scheffer et al. 2009. "A safe operating space for humanity." *Nature* vol. 461: 472–475 doi: 10.1038/461472a

Rodrik, Dani. 2004. "Industrial Policy for the Twenty-First Century." Chap. 5 in *One Economics, Many Recipes: Globalization, Institutions, and Economic*. Princeton, NJ: Princeton University Press.

Rodrik, Dani. 2011. *Jedna ekonomia, wiele recept. Globalizacja, instytucje, wzrost gospodarczy* [One Economy, Many Recipes. Globalization, Institutions, Economic Growth]. Warsaw: Wydawnictwo Krytyki politycznej, Warszawa.

Rodrik, D. S. 2020. "Why Does Globalization Fuel Populism?." *CEPR Discussion Paper* No. DP15002. Available at SSRN: https://ssrn.com/abstract=3650117

Rodrik, Dani. 2021. "Why Does Globalization Fuel Populism? Economics, Culture, and the Rise of Right-wing Populism." *Annual Review of Economics* vol. 13

Rogoff, Kenneth and Carmen Reinhart. 2009. "The Aftermath of Financial Crises." *NBER Working Paper* vol. 14587.

Roubini, Nouriel and Stephen Mihm. 2010. *Crisis Economics: A Crash Course in the Future of Finance*. New York: The Penguin Press.

Rutkauskas, Virgilijus. 2015. "Financial Stability, Fiscal Sustainability and Changes in Debt Structure After Economic Downturn." *Economika* 94(3): 70.

Sabani, Laura and Debora Digioacchino. 2009. "Education Policy and Inequality: A Political Economy Approach." *European Journal of Political Economy* vol. 25: 463–478.10.1016/j.ejpoleco.2009.06.002.

Sadowski, Zdzisław. 2011a. "Ekonomia w objęciach neoliberalizmu." *Ekonomista* No. 3.

Sadowski, Zdzisław. 2011b. *Przez ciekawe czasy* [Through Interesting Times]. Warsaw: Polish Economic Society.

Sauvant, Karl P. 2008. "The FDI Recession Has Begun." *Columbia FDI Perspectives* No. 1.

Schaechter, Andrea, Tidiane Kinda, Nina T. Budina and Anke Weber. 2012. "Fiscal Rules in Response to the Crisis-Toward the "Next-Generation" Rules, A New Dataset." *IMF Working Paper. Fiscal Affairs Department* No. WP/12/187.

Schick, Allan. 2010. "Post-Crisis Fiscal Rules: Stabilising Public Finance while Responding to Economic Aftershocks." OECD Journal on Budgeting vol. 10(2): 1–18.

Schilirò, Daniele. 2019. "Public debt and growth in Italy: Analysis and policy proposals." *International Journal of Business Management and Economic Research* vol. 10(5): 1–8.

Schiliro, Daniele. 2020. "COVID-19 Crisis and the Public Debt Issue: The Case of Italy." *International Journal of Business Management and Economic Research* vol. 11(4): 1851–1860.

Schmalz, Stefan and Matthias Ebenau. 2012. "After Neoliberalism? Brazil, India, and China in the Global Economic Crisis." *Globalization* 9(4).

Schoeller, Magnus G. and Olof Karlsson. 2021. "Championing the 'German Model'? Germany's Consistent Preferences on the Integration of Fiscal Constraints." *Journal of European Integration* vol. 43: 191–207. doi: 10.1080/07036337.2021.1877697

Schulz, Frank. 2018. "Germany Expects 20% Less from EU Structural Funds After 2020." *Euractiv*. www.euractiv.com/section/economy-jobs/news/germany-expects-20-less-from-eu-structural-funds-after-2020/

Šehović, D. 2015. "Analysis of Fiscal Rules in the European Monetary Union." *Journal of Central Banking Theory and Practice* vol. 4(1): 19–33. https://doi.org/10.1515/jcbtp-2015-0002

Sen, Amartya. 1999. *Development as Freedom*. New York: Alfred Knopf.

Sherwood, Monika. 2015. "Medium-Term Budgetary Frameworks in the EU Member States." *European Economy – Discussion Papers* 2015–021. Directorate General Economic and Financial Affairs (DG ECFIN). European Commission.

Słodowa-Hełpa, Małgorzata. 2020. "Economic Policy from the Perspective of Contemporary Challenges in Economic History – Hopes, Concerns and Dilemmas." *Studia Historiae Oeconomicae* 38: 4–36. doi: 10.2478/sho-2020-0001

Słodowa-Hełpa, M. 2021. *The Past in the Process of Searching for Recipes to Manage the Present and Creating the Future*. Rzeszów: Nierówności społeczne a wzrost gospodarczy.

Smith, Graham. 2003. *Deliberative Democracy and the Environment*. London: Routledge.

Speklé, Roland F. and Frank H. M. Verbeeten. 2014. "The Use of Performance Measurement Systems in the Public Sector: Effects on Performance." *Management Accounting Research* vol. 25(2): 131–146.

Stiglitz, Joseph E. 2003. "Globalization and growth in emerging markets and the New Economy." *Journal of Policy Modeling* vol. 25(5): 505–524. doi: 10.1016/S0161-8938(03)00043

Stiglitz, Joseph E. 2004. *Economics of the Public Sector*. New York: W.W. Norton & Company.

Stiglitz, Joseph E. 2010a. *Freefall: America, Free Markets, and the Sinking of the World Economy Paperback*. New York: W. W. Norton & Company.

Stiglitz, Joseph E. 2010b. *The Stiglitz Report: Reforming the International Monetary and Financial Systems in the Wake of the Global Crisis*. New York: The New Press.

Stiglitz, Joseph E., Jean-Paul Fitoussi and Martine Durand. 2018. *For Good Measure: Advancing Research on Well-being Metrics Beyond GDP*. Paris: OECD Publishing.

Stockhammer, Engelberd, Eckhart Hein and Lucas Grafl. 2011. "Globalization and the Effects of Changes in Functional Income Distribution on Aggregate Demand in Germany." *International Review of Applied Economics* vol. 25(1): 1–23

Streeck, Wolfgang. 2013. "The Politics of Public Debt. Neoliberalism, Capitalist Development, and the Restructuring of the State." *German Economic Review* vol. 15(1): 143–165.

Szalavetz, Andrea. 2015. "A Dynamic Capabilities Perspective of High-Growth Firms: Organizational Aspects." *International Journal of Management and Economics* vol. 48(1).

Szpringer, W. 2015. "Regulation of the Financial Market Infrastructure from the Perspective of Economic Analysis of Law – the Example of Central Counterparties." *Polish Yearbook of Law & Economics* vol. 6: 201.

Tamborini, Roberto and Matteo Tomaselli. 2020. "When Does Public Debt Impair Economic Growth? A Literature Review in Search of a Theory." *DEM Working Papers* No. 7, Department of Economics and Management.

Tanzi, Vito. 2005. "The Economic Role of the State in the 21st Century." *Cato Journal* vol. 25.

Tapsoba, Rene. 2012. "Do National Numerical Fiscal Rules Really Shape Fiscal Behaviours in Developing Countries? A Treatment Effect Evaluation." *Economic Modelling* vol. 29(4): 1356–1369. doi: 10.1016/j.econmod.2012.03.003

Thaler, Richard H. and Cass R. Sunstein. 2008. *Nudge: Improving Decisions About Health, Wealth and Happiness*. London: Penguin Books.

Thaler, Richard H., Cass R. Sunstein and John P. Balz. 2012. "Choice Architecture." *The Behavioral Foundations of Public Policy*, vol. 25. https://ssrn.com/abstract=2536504 or http://dx.doi.org/10.2139/ssrn.2536504

Thorsen, Dag Einar and Lie Amund. 2006. "What Is Neoliberalism?" In *Neoliberalism – Ideas and Political Reality*, edited by Dag Harald Claes et al., 33–48. Oslo: Universitetsforlaget.

Thurow, L. C. 2000. "Globalization: The Product of a Knowledge-Based Economy." *The ANNALS of the American Academy of Political and Social Science* vol. 570(1).

Tomasino, A. P., J. Fedorowicz and C. B. Williams. 2017. "Public Sector Shared Services Move Out of the Back-Office: The Role of Public Policy and Mission Criticality." *Data Base for Advances in Information Systems* vol. 48(3).

Tomaskovic-Devey, Donald, Ken-Hou Lin and Nathan Meyers. 2015. "Did Financialization Reduce Economic Growth?" *Socio-Economic Review* vol. 13(3): 525–548.

Tomkiewicz, Jacek. 2014. "Can We Count on a Fundamental Shift in Economic Policy So That It Is Aimed at Increasing Social Cohesion?" *Social Inequalities and Economic Growth* No. 39.

Torbat, Akbat E. 2008. "Global Financial Meltdown and the Demise of Neoliberalism." *Global Research*. www.globalresearch.ca/index.php?context=va&aid=10549

Torsten, P. and G. Tabellini. 2002. *Political Economics: Explaining Economic Policy*. 10.2307/1061733.

Trentmann, Frank. 2009. "Crossing Divides Consumption and Globalization in History." *Journal of Consumer Culture* vol. 9(2). doi: 10.1177/1469540509104374

Truger, Achim and Will Henner. 2013. "The German 'Debt Brake': A Shining Example for European Fiscal Policy?" *Revue de l'OFCE* No. 127, 153–188. doi: 10.3917/reof.127.0153

Truszczyński, Jan. 2021. "Konferencja w sprawie przyszłości Europy: czy owa oferta dla aktywnych obywateli." *Res Humana* vol. 3(172).

van Middelaar, Luuk. 2019. *Alarums and Excursions: Improvising Politics on the European Stage*. Translated and edited by Liz Waters. New Castle: Agenda Publishing.

van Ravensway, James and Roger E. Hamlin. 2015. "Strategic Planning in US Municipalities." *Transylvanian Review of Administrative Sciences* vol. 15(SI): 55–70. Available at SSRN: https://ssrn.com/abstract=3410552

Venugopal, Rajesh. 2015. "Neoliberalism as Concept." *Economy and Society* vol. 44(2): 145–167.

Viscusi, Gianluigi and Carlo Batini. 2016. "Information Production and Social Value for Public Policy: A Conceptual Modeling Perspective." *Policy and Internet* vol. 8(3): 334–353.

Voigt, Stefan and Lorenz Blume. 2011. "Does Organizational Design of Supreme Audit Institutions Matter? A Cross-country Assessment." *European Journal of Political Economy* vol. 27: 215–229. doi: 10.1016/j.ejpoleco.2010.07.001

Von Hagen, Juergen and Guntram Wolf. 2006. "What Do Deficits Tell Us About Debt? Empirical Evidence on Creative Accounting with Fiscal Rules in the EU." *Journal of Banking & Finance* vol. 30(12): 3259–3279.

von Mises, Ludwig. (1927) 2005. *Liberalism: Classical Tradition*. Translated by Ralph Raico. Edited by Bettina Bien Greaves. Indianapolis: Liberty Fund.

Wagner, Helmut. 2013. "Is the European Monetary Union Sustainable? The Role of Real Convergence." In *Who Will Provide the Next Financial Model? Asia's Financial Muscle and Europe's Financial Maturity*, edited by Kaji Sahoko and Ogawa Eiji, 180–219. Osaka: Springer.

Wamser, Georg, Nam Chang Woon and Alina Schoenberg. 2013. "The Lisbon Agenda and Innovation-Oriented Cohesion Policy: A New Challenge for Economic Integration Among the EU Regions." *Journal of Economic Integration* vol. 28(1): 37–58.

Weerakkody, V., A. Omar, R. El-Haddadeh and M. Al-Busaidy. 2016. "Digitally-Enabled Service Transformation in the Public Sector: The Lure of Institutional Pressure and Strategic Response Towards Change." *Government Information Quarterly* vol. 33(4).

West, Damian and Deborah Blackman. 2015. "Performance Management in the Public Sector." *Australian Journal of Public Administration* vol. 74(1): 73–81.

Wickens, Michel M. and Merih Uctum. 2000. "Debt and Deficit Ceilings, and Sustainability of Fiscal Policies: An Intertemporal Analysis." *Oxford Bulletin of Economics and Statistics* vol. 62(2): 197–222.

Wildman, John, Peter McMeekin, Eleonore Grieve and Andrew Briggs. 2016. "Economic Evaluation of Integrated New Technologies for Health and Social Care: Suggestions for Policy Makers, Users and Evaluators." *Social Science and Medicine* vol. 169(C): 141–148.

Wilkin, Jerzy. 2012. *Teoria Wyboru Publicznego. Główne Nurty i Zastosowania* [Theory of Public Choice. Main Trends and Applications]. Warsaw: Scholar Publishing House.

Wilkin, Jerzy. 2013. *Jakość rządzenia w Polsce. Jak ją badać, monitorować i poprawiać?* [The Quality of Governance in Poland. How to Examine, Monitor and Improve it?]. Warsaw: Wydawnictwo Naukowe Scholar.

Wilkin, Jerzy. 2016. *Instytucjonalne i kulturowe podstawy gospodarowania* [Institutional and Cultural Foundations of Management]. Warsaw: Scholar.

Woźniak, M. G. 2012. "Teoretyczne i praktyczne kwestie budowy spójności społeczno-ekonomicznej dla gospodarki innowacyjnej [Theoretical and Practical Issues of Building Socio-Economic Cohesion for an Innovative Economy]." In *Gospodarka Polski 1990–2011. Transformacja. Modernizacja, t. 3: Droga do spójności społeczno-ekonomicznej* [Polish Economy 1990–2011. Transformation. Modernization, Vol. 3: The Path to Socio-Economic Cohesion], edited by M. G. Woźniak. Warsaw: PWN.

Wynen, Jan, Koen Verhoest and Sara Demuzere. 2016. "Quality Management in Public-Sector Organizations: Evidence from Six EU Countries." *International Journal of Public Administration* vol. 39(2): 122–134.

Wyplosz, Charles. 2012. "Fiscal Rules: Theoretical Issues and Historical Experiences." In *Fiscal Policy after the Financial Crisis*, edited by Alesina Alberto and Giavazzi Francesco, 495–525. Chicago: University of Chicago Press.

Wyplosz, Charles. 2019. "Fiscal Discipline: From Theory to Practice." In *European Fiscal Board Workshop 2019: Independent Fiscal Institutions in the EU Fiscal Framework*, 8–33. European Commission. https://ec.europa.eu/info/sites/default/files/2019_04_30_efb_workshop.pdf

Wysokinska, Zofia Maria. 2008. "Catching-Up Strategy: New Member States of the European Union in the European Internal Market for High-Tech and Environmental Products in the Context of the Renewed Lisbon Strategy." *Global Economy Journal* vol. 8(3): 1–28.

Xerri, Matthew J., Silvia A. Nelson, Yvonne Brunetto and S. R. M. Reid. 2015. "NPM and Change Management in Asset Management Organisations." *Journal of Organizational Change Management* vol. 28(4): 641–655.

Yared, Pierre. 2019. "Rising Government Debt: Causes and Solutions for a Decades-Old Trend." *Journal of Economic Perspectives* vol. 33(2): 115–140.

Young, Raymond and Jamie Grant. 2015. "Is Strategy Implemented by Projects? Disturbing Evidence in the State of NSW." *International Journal of Project Management* vol. 33(1).

Zachorowska-Mazurkiewicz, Anna and Ewa Okoń-Horodyńska. 2011. *Współczesne wymiary nierówności w procesie globalizacji* [Contemporary Dimensions of Inequality in the Process of Globalization]. Kraków: Wydawnictwo Uniwersytetu Jagiellońskiego.

Zaheer, A. N. and A. Rashid. 2017. "Analyzing the Role of Public Sector Marketing in Improving Social Effectiveness: A Case Study from Anhui Province, China." *International Review on Public and Nonprofit Marketing* vol. 14(1).

Zakaria, Fareed. 2009. *The Post-American World*. New York: W.W. Norton & Company.

Zdražil, P. and Grazina Kozuń-Cieślak. 2017. "The Role of Cross-border Cooperation Initiatives in Respect of Regional Development: Case Study of Euroregion Neisse." *Scientific papers of the University of Pardubice. Series D, Faculty of Economics and Administration* vol. 24(40): 244–254.

Żmuda, M. 2011. "Europe 2020 Strategy as a Plan of Socio-economic Growth of the European Union. Scientific." *Works of the University of Economics in Wrocław. Economics* vol. 211: 200–210.

Index

Note: Page numbers in *italics* indicate figures and page numbers in **bold** indicate tables on the corresponding page.

For Product Safety Concerns and Information please contact our EU representative GPSR@taylorandfrancis.com Taylor & Francis Verlag GmbH, Kaufingerstraße 24, 80331 München, Germany